The Definitive Guide to Conversational AI with Dialogflow and Google Cloud

Build Advanced Enterprise Chatbots, Voice, and Telephony Agents on Google Cloud

Lee Boonstra

Apress®

The Definitive Guide to Conversational AI with Dialogflow and Google Cloud

Lee Boonstra
AMSTERDAM, Noord-Holland, The Netherlands

ISBN-13 (pbk): 978-1-4842-7013-4
https://doi.org/10.1007/978-1-4842-7014-1

ISBN-13 (electronic): 978-1-4842-7014-1

Managing Director, Apress Media LLC: Welmoed Spahr
Acquisitions Editor: Celestin Suresh John
Development Editor: Matthew Moodie
Coordinating Editor: Aditee Mirashi

Cover designed by eStudioCalamar

Cover image designed by Freepik (www.freepik.com)

Distributed to the book trade worldwide by Springer Science+Business Media New York, 1 New York Plaza, Suite 4600, New York, NY 10004-1562, USA. Phone 1-800-SPRINGER, fax (201) 348-4505, e-mail orders-ny@springer-sbm.com, or visit www.springeronline.com. Apress Media, LLC is a California LLC and the sole member (owner) is Springer Science + Business Media Finance Inc (SSBM Finance Inc). SSBM Finance Inc is a **Delaware** corporation.

For information on translations, please e-mail booktranslations@springernature.com; for reprint, paperback, or audio rights, please e-mail bookpermissions@springernature.com.

Apress titles may be purchased in bulk for academic, corporate, or promotional use. eBook versions and licenses are also available for most titles. For more information, reference our Print and eBook Bulk Sales web page at http://www.apress.com/bulk-sales.

Any source code or other supplementary material referenced by the author in this book is available to readers on GitHub via the book's product page, located at www.apress.com/978-1-4842-7013-4. For more detailed information, please visit http://www.apress.com/source-code.

Printed on acid-free paper

To my wife Michele and my daughter Rebel. I love you to the moon and back.

Table of Contents

About the Author

 **Lee Boonstra** has been at Google since 2017. She is a Senior Developer Advocate and Conversational AI expert and has helped many businesses develop AI-powered chatbots and voice assistants at an enterprise scale. They are building smart AI platforms on the Google Cloud using Dialogflow for intent detection and natural language processing, speech recognition technology, and contact center technology.

Lee has worn different hats in the past 17 years. She began her career as an engineer developing websites and apps for famous brands and large enterprises such as ING Bank, KLM, and Heineken. She worked for Sencha Inc. as a lead technical trainer and curriculum creator before moving to Google as a developer advocate.

A developer advocate's role is to bridge the Google engineering team and the developer community. Her job is to give feedback to both parties, equally, in both ways. Developer relations at Google falls under engineering, and it includes writing public open source code, writing technical documentation, public speaking, and creating (video) content.

Besides writing and her work at Google, she is an active member of the DDMA Voice Committee in the Netherlands. This task force aims to increase the belief in the "voice channel" by showing brands and publishers its opportunities for marketing, sales, and service and, therefore, to give it a permanent place in the digital transformation.

With so many roles, there is one title that she is the proudest of: being the mother of her newborn, Rebel.

You can find Lee online via the Twitter handle @ladysign and at
`https://www.leeboonstra.dev`.

About the Technical Reviewers

 **Akash Parmar** is the Contact Center AI Solutions Lead for Europe, the Middle East, and Africa at Google. He enables large enterprises to transform their customer contacts across voice and digital channels into personalized conversations using Speech-to-Text (STT), Text-to-Speech (TTS), and Natural Language Understanding (NLU) AI technologies. He is passionate about enabling innovation and experimentation using AI and turning contact centers from a cost center into a value-generating center.

Before joining Google, he was an Enterprise Architect at Marks and Spencer in London where he replaced legacy IVR solutions across all stores and contact centers with a natural language platform built using Google Dialogflow which automated millions of contacts, reduced calls to stores, and improved self-service.

Throughout his career, spanning over 20 years, he has designed, built, and implemented contact center solutions for enterprise organizations like Argos Sainsbury's, Vodafone, Centrica, Royal Dutch Shell, Thomson Reuters, and Accenture.

He is a public speaker in global industry events like Google Next. He firmly believes that accelerated by COVID-19, the customer experience industry is going through the most rapid transformation in its history and will play a pivotal role in the future of large enterprises where customer expectations in the digital world will be the same as in the physical world.

You can reach him on LinkedIn or email him at `akash.parmar@gmail.com`.

Antonio Gulli has a passion for establishing and managing global technological talent for innovation and execution. His core expertise is in cloud computing, deep learning, and search engines. Currently, he serves as Engineering Director for the Office of the CTO, Google Cloud. Previously, he served as Google Warsaw Site leader, doubling the size of the engineering site.

So far, Antonio has been lucky enough to gain professional experience in four countries in Europe and has managed teams in six countries in EMEA and the United States: in Amsterdam, as Vice President for Elsevier, a leading scientific publisher; in London, as Engineering Site Lead for Microsoft working on Bing Search; in Italy and the United Kingdom, as CTO Europe and UK for Ask.com; and in several co-funded startups including one of the first web search companies in Europe.

Antonio has co-invented a number of technologies for search, smart energy, and AI, with 20+ patents issued/applied, and he has published several books about coding and machine learning, also translated into Japanese, Russian, Korean, and Chinese. Antonio speaks Spanish, English, and Italian, and he is currently learning Polish and French. Antonio is a proud father of two boys, Lorenzo (20 years) and Leonardo (15 years), and a little queen, Aurora (10 years).

For more information, you can visit `https://uk.linkedin.com/in/searchguy`.

Acknowledgments

This book would not have been possible without the help of some amazing people. Therefore, I would like to thank

- Celestin Suresh John (Acquisitions Editor), Matthew Moodie (Development Editor), and Aditee Mirashi (Coordinating Editor) from Apress, without your help this book couldn't go into production. Thank you so much for your hard work.

There are a lot of folks within Google that helped me in the background while writing this book. I'm very grateful for your support, help, and ideas.

- In particular, I would like to thank Contact Center AI Specialist, Akash Parmar, and Engineering Director, Antonio Gulli. Thank you for reading this book and doing the technical reviews! Very much appreciated!

- Thank you for your support and ideas for this book: Dialogflow Product Manager, Shantanu Misra; Conversational AI Incubator Manager (and co-founder API.ai), Pavel Sirotin; Developer Advocacy Manager, Dave Elliot; Customer Engineer, Wouter Roosenburg; Product Marketing Manager, Surbhi Agarwal; Head of Product AI, Antony Passemard; and VP of Engineering, Andrew Moore.

- Also a big thank you to the internal Contact Center AI and Dialogflow Champions community!

Lastly, I would like to express my gratitude to

- Lucienne de Boer, Customer Experience Product Owner at KLM Royal Dutch Airlines, for sharing the Dialogflow use case and enterprise learnings

- Pieter Goderis, Global Lead NLP at ING Bank, for sharing the Dialogflow use case and enterprise learnings

- Carla Verwijmeren, Voice Consultant at Smartvoices, for proofreading the book chapters

Introduction

To some people, writing a book can feel a lot like the process of childbirth. To others, their written book can feel like it's their baby. I wrote this book while I was six months pregnant from my firstborn, baby Rebel. Because of COVID-19, the Netherlands just went in lockdown, and I had to cancel all my Google work trips. With so much extra time, and since I can't sit still, I had to share my Conversational AI knowledge with the world and put it on paper. And yes, it was a process, but I put a lot of love into it! So this book release is my announcement!

—Lee Boonstra (Senior Developer Advocate, Conversational AI @ Google)

Who This Book Is For

This book is written for everyone (practitioners) interested in building chatbots for the Web, social media, voice assistants, or contact centers, using Google's Conversational AI/Cloud technology. Whether you are a UX designer/linguist, a web/conversational bot engineer, chatbot architect, back-end developer, a project manager, or a business decision-maker, that is, CTO or Chief Innovation Officer, this book is for you.

Some topics target engineers. I will share some code and explain what it does. Most of my code examples are written in JavaScript for Node.js. When you rather program in a different language, my examples will be apparent to understand (and rewrite) to a language of choice.

In the sections, I have added advanced tips and tricks, like answers to questions that I have heard while working with various (enterprise) Dialogflow customers.

I promise, even if you have been using Dialogflow before, you will likely still learn new things!

What You'll Learn

While reading this book, readers will learn the following:

- What's Dialogflow, Dialogflow Essentials, Dialogflow CX, and how machine learning is used

- How to create Dialogflow projects for individuals and enterprise usage

- Dialogflow Essentials concepts like intents, entities, custom entities, system entities, composites, and how to track context

- How to build bots quickly using prebuilt agents, small talk modules, and FAQ knowledge bases

- How Dialogflow can give an out-of-the-box agent review

- How to deploy text conversational UIs for web and social media channels

- How to build voice agents for voice assistants and phone gateways/ contact centers

- How to build multilingual chatbots

- How to orchestrate many (sub-)chatbots to build a bigger conversational platform

- How to use chatbot analytics, and how to test the quality of your Dialogflow agent

- How Dialogflow CX fits in, what's different in Dialogflow CX, and new Dialogflow CX concepts

These topics are targeted more at developers and engineers and contain more advanced use cases:

- Learn how to create fulfillment to connect to a web service in various ways

- Learn how to run back-end code from a local/development machine

- Learn how to secure your chatbots

- Learn how to integrate your chatbots in a website or native mobile (Flutter) app by creating your own custom integrations

- Learn how to create an omnichannel bot platform architecture

- Learn how to create rich responses in custom integrations

- Learn how to stream your voice UIs in IoT voice applications

- Learn using your own data warehouse for advanced chatbot analytics

---

Note Trying out the more advanced examples might require pay as you use Google Cloud resources. When you are new to Google Cloud, you can create a free Google Cloud account, which comes with 300 dollars of credits. These credits should be more than enough for playing around with these examples. Many of the Google Cloud products have a free usage tier (https://cloud.google.com/free).

Downloading the Code

The example code from each chapter is available as a zip file at the book's website, www.leeboonstra.dev, and www.apress.com/ISBN. It will point to a source code repository for Apress books on GitHub, where my code can be continuously updated.

CHAPTER 1

Introduction to Conversational AI

A chatbot is a user interface designed to simulate conversation with human users online. The word is a combination of the word **chat** (a conversation) and **robot**.

Conversational user interfaces like chatbots or voice-activated conversational UIs (like Siri, Google Assistant, or Alexa, but also robots in phone conversations) are trendy nowadays. Ten years ago, everyone wanted to build mobile apps; now it's the time everyone made or is working on conversational user interfaces.

What's so unique about chatbots, and why are they popular now? The first chatbots actually already appeared with the launch of personal computers. Let's dive into some history and go way back to 1950.

The History of Text Chatbots

Alan Turing, a British computer scientist, developed the Turing Test to figure out if **machines can think**. The Turing Test is a conversational test (or imitation game) to measure the machine's intelligence level in dialogues. The test involves having the machine compete with a human as a conversation partner. Human judges would interact with both using a computer keyboard and screen. If 30% of the judges can't reliably distinguish the machine from the human, the machine was considered to pass the test.

One of the first chatbots that was capable of attempting the Turing Test was chatbot **ELIZA**. A **Natural Language Processing** (NLP) computer program was created from 1964 to 1966 by Joseph Weizenbaum at the Massachusetts Institute of Technology (MIT). Under the hood, ELIZA itself examined the text for keywords, applied values to said

© Lee Boonstra 2021

L. Boonstra, *The Definitive Guide to Conversational AI with Dialogflow and Google Cloud*, https://doi.org/10.1007/978-1-4842-7014-1_1

keywords, and transformed the input into an output. ELIZA contained a script called **DOCTOR**, which provided a parody of a psychotherapist's responses in a Rogerian psychiatric interview, mostly rephrasing what the user said.

Chatbot **PARRY** was written in 1972 by psychiatrist Kenneth Colby at Stanford University. While ELIZA was a Rogerian therapist simulation, PARRY attempted to simulate a person with paranoid schizophrenia. It's described as *ELIZA with attitude*. The program implemented a rough model of a person's behavior with schizophrenia based on concepts, perceptions, and beliefs. It also demonstrated a conversational strategy and therefore was more advanced than ELIZA.

ELIZA and PARRY rely on simple tricks to appear like a human. Chatbot **ALICE** (which stands for Artificial Linguistic Internet Computer Entity) was written in the late 1990s by Richard Wallace. ELIZA inspired ALICE, but it differentiates itself by using a hardcoded database including conversation utterances. For example, it would check the phrase and its keywords for matching this database when you would type to ALICE.

Rather than using a static database, another chatbot called **Jabberwacky**, created in 1997 by British programmer Rollo Carpenter, keeps track of everything people have said to it and tries to reuse those statements matching them to the user's input. Neither of these chatbots has long-term memory, so they respond only to the last sentence written.

Although chatbots have been under development since the existence of computers, they did not become as mainstream as recently. It has everything to do with **Machine Learning** and **Natural Language Understanding**.

With old-school chatbots, you had to phrase your sentences carefully. Every grammar or spelling mistake, or if you would just say things differently, would result in a chatbot that didn't know what to answer. The fact is there are many different ways to say something. A chatbot that has been programmed with conditional if-else statements needs to be maintained and is still error-prone.

A chatbot built with Machine Learning, to be precise, a chatbot that can understand text (Natural Language Understanding), could understand and retrieve a particular answer for your question. No matter if you spell it wrong or say things differently.

Over the last few years, due to the serious efforts by companies like Google, Apple, Microsoft, Amazon, Facebook, and IBM, and their investments in AI, machine learning, voice conversations, cloud computing, and developer tools, conversational AIs are here to stay!

Today, chatbots are virtual assistants such as the Google Assistant and are accessible via many organizations' apps, websites, and instant messaging platforms.

You likely carry your virtual assistant with you since they are implemented in Android devices (Google Assistant) and iPhones/iPads (Siri). Or you have a voice-activated speaker such as Google Home, Google Nest Mini, Google Nest Hub, or Amazon Echo (Alexa) installed in your home. Smart conversational UIs like Google Assistant, Siri, or Alexa are also powered by machine learning.

Chatbots are not only popular in the consumer market. Also, in the business world, they are hot. So-called enterprise assistants are company chatbots that are modeled after customer service representatives or business processes. They can be deployed internally on channels such as web applications, Slack, or Skype. They can help, for example, IT departments or helpdesks to file tickets, look up information from various FAQ databases, replacements for customer care, order products, or share knowledge across employees. Also, chatbots in contact centers (whether through web chat or voice chat via the phone) could trim enormous business costs. Robots can pick up the phone, answer the most common questions, and reduce call and waiting times.

Chatbots can be deployed for the public on channels such as Facebook, WhatsApp, websites, apps, or SMS. There are brand engagement chatbots and customer care chatbots that can offer advice or answer the most frequently asked questions, such as the **KLM Royal Dutch Airlines** virtual assistant. It contains answers to frequently asked questions. Especially during the Corona time, lots of COVID-19-related questions came in. The KLM Royal Dutch Airlines virtual assistant is a public-facing text-based chatbot available through WhatsApp.

There are sales department bots who can help by answering most frequently asked questions or dealing with repetitive work/calls; therefore, a bot solution is very scalable. It makes a lot of sense for specific industries. For example, for a healthcare insurance company, the last months of the year will be hectic since that's the month that individuals can change their healthcare provider. For a retailer or travel agency, the holiday months will be hectic.

An example of a customer care chatbot is chatbot **Marie** from the **ING bank**, who can help you through Facebook Messenger when you have problems with your bank card (conversational banking). This chatbot started as an experiment for ING to test how far they could push the technology. Right now, chatbots are in all of their internal systems (web chat, apps, and call).

Why Do Some Chatbots Fail?

Sounds all like puppies and ice cream? Because of the long history of chatbots, customers often don't have a high impression of chatbots. There are a lot of chatbots that fail.

There are ten main drivers why chatbots fail to deliver delightful user experiences:

- Most chatbots are built on decision-tree logic, the old-school way. Bots with linguistic and Natural Language Processing/Machine Learning capabilities are not very common.

- Also, because of this old-school way of building bots, they usually can't hold contextual information for longer than a few chat bubbles and will end up losing track of what the user was saying before they posed the most recent question.

- Besides remembering contexts within a session, often chatbots weren't built to keep memory of multiple sessions. For example, you log in to the chatbot the next day. Your previous session is gone.

- For some bots, it's not clear what tasks it can do. Bots need to clarify that you are talking with a virtual agent, not a human. And ideally, they should explain up front what type of questions they can answer; you can steer the conversation.

- There are a lot of bots that are solving unrelated use cases. This happens when chatbot creators ignore analytics and won't look into the insights of other channels for the most frequently asked questions.

- There are chatbots that are not personal.

- Creating a chatbot in a silo (that doesn't connect to other systems) can be pretty harmful to both businesses and customers. Your customers will see you as a "one-company"; they won't understand that a chatbot can't get access to your background information while the company should have it.

- A bot just like a human advisor improves over time by learning from feedback and getting the right training. These provisions are often forgotten by creators, and hence the bot can become less relevant over time.

- Bots that do one thing very well are more helpful than bots that do many things poorly.

- Very few chatbots have an escalation workflow in place to let a human take over the conversation when the bot is unable to help. Once there is a hand-over, the user shouldn't repeat the discussion they had with the chatbot. Instead, a transcript should be presented to the employee.

If I can add one additional driver to this list, I would say that poor user experience (UX) design per chatbot channel could be painful for a user. Your virtual agent should be available on the channels where your customers are. If this is a website, you can show tables, links, and videos. Still, when the conversation is voice only, for example, in a contact center, you obviously can't copy your website text with hyperlinks, tables, and images to the voice assistant's output.

Machine Learning Simply Explained

Think about it. How did you learn your first language? I bet your parents or teachers did not hand you a dictionary and told you to read this book from A to Z. By the time that you reach the last page, and you are a master in, let's say, the English language. No! We learned through examples.

This is a car, and it drives on the highway; it has four wheels and a steering wheel. That over there, that's a bicycle. It has two wheels, and you peddle. By the time you have seen many cars and many bikes, you would distinguish one from another. And in case you were wrong, for example, you thought you saw a car, but it was actually a truck, you were told that you were wrong and that a truck is even bigger than a car or a truck has more wheels.

For computers, it works quite similarly. Data scientists program a model, and then we pass in a massive amount of data until, at some point, a computer starts to recognize patterns. For example, you will upload lots of car and bike photos, where every photo is labeled. When the computer is wrong, we teach it what the label should be, or we might need to upload more data. Just where humans become smarter when aging, with machine learning a computer becomes more intelligent over time by seeing more relevant data.

Machine Learning is a term that falls under **Artificial Intelligence** (AI). AI is the process of building smarter computers. It's a concept that has existed since the beginning of computers. Programmers create conditional *if* and *else* statements in code to tell a computer what happens under specific criteria, or else it should fall back. As a developer myself, I know how hard programming can be. We developers always write bugs. *Yeah, you do too.* There are always new requirements which let your conditions break. You still need a developer to maintain the code.

Machine Learning is the process of making a computer learn by itself. Since with Machine Learning, the computer becomes smarter by seeing more examples. It's actually a more effective way of making machines smarter than programming a smart machine.

Computer programs that use Machine Learning can be better at making predictions than humans but are only as good as the data that was given to them. This is because computers can remember and process massive amounts of data in a short time. That is why Machine Learning has been used in all industries—in healthcare to predict cancer, in retail to predict recommendations, in finance to detect fraud, and at every company that uses Natural Language Understanding (NLU) chatbots.

Natural Language Processing

Like Machine Learning, **Natural Language Processing (NLP)** is a subset of AI. It deals with the relationship between natural language, what we as humans speak, and AI. It's the branch of AI that enables computers to understand, interpret, and manipulate human language. NLP can make sense of unstructured data, like a spoken language, instead of structured data like SQL table rows and so on. NLP focuses on how we can program computers to process large amounts of natural language data, such as a chatbot conversation, in such a way that it becomes efficient and productive by automating it. NLP algorithms are typically based on Machine Learning algorithms. Instead of hand-coding large sets of rules, NLP can rely on Machine Learning to automatically learn by analyzing a set of examples.

NLP often refers to tools such as **speech recognition** for understanding spoken voice or audio files and **Natural Language Understanding (NLU)** for recognizing large amounts of written text, for example, to get entity or sentiment analysis—in the case of chatbots, to classify and match intents. Another subset of NLP is **Natural Language Generation (NLG)**. NLG is a software process to transform structured data into natural languages, such as generating reports or chatbot conversations.

Chatbots and Artificial Intelligence

The chatbot or smart assistant of the modern world is all about AI.

Let's look at the Google Nest Mini, the smart speaker of Google, which is actually nothing more than a speaker with a microphone connected to the Internet to get access to the Google Assistant, the AI of Google.

You talk to it. Somehow, the Google Assistant can listen to your spoken text and transform it to written text. That's a Machine Learning model called **Speech-to-Text** (STT). The Google Assistant can understand what was said. So it understands the written text. That's a Machine Learning model called **Natural Language Understanding**. The Google Assistant matches your text to a particular scripted flow, which we call **Intent Matching** or **Intent Classification**. Based on training examples, we can match the real intention of the user. Finally, when it finds an answer, it speaks it out for you through a text synthesizer. That's a **Text-to-Speech** Machine Learning model (TTS), a synthesizer that uses WaveNet models with voices that sound humanlike.

Machine Learning and Google

Google has invested heavily in Artificial Intelligence (AI) and Machine Learning. Google is a data company and has a mission—*to organize the world's information and make it universally accessible.*

Google uses Machine Learning algorithms in every Google product. Think about the spam filter in Gmail (classifying spam vs. non-spam), video recommendations on YouTube, Google Translate to translate text in other languages, relevance in Google search results, the Google Assistant, and so on. It's so commonly used. We take it for granted. This also means that every Google engineer gets trained in Machine Learning.

Google uses Machine Learning on absolutely massive data, and that requires robust infrastructure. For example, it is finding roads from satellite imagery, predicting click-through rate for the ad's auction, and so on. Yes, you could train a Machine Learning model on your laptop. Then, handling massive amounts of data would require you to keep your computer up and running for weeks or months. It requires lots of data storage, and it requires lots of computing power. That is why Google has lots of data centers all over the world, large buildings full of racks with computers, which can process data in parallel. You don't need to wait for weeks or months; the more machines you add, the faster the training time. With cloud technology, this could be done in minutes.

Google is also known for the framework **TensorFlow**. It's a famous Machine Learning (Python) framework for creating ML models, used by many data scientists and data engineers. It's one of the most popular open source projects on GitHub. It's created by Jeff Dean, who works for Google. And even though the framework is open source, and developers and companies all over the world make contributions, Google has a large dedicated team working on improving the codebase.

About Google Cloud

Google Cloud (formerly known as Google Cloud Platform/GCP) is Google's public cloud provider for computing resources for deploying, building, and operating applications—to deliver storage, compute, and services from data centers all over the world on fast and secure Google infrastructure. It's Google, but it doesn't mean that your data is Google's. Google Cloud is the commercial pay-per-use enterprise offering of Google. As written in the signed Google Cloud terms and conditions, you are the data owner. Google could process your data but can't and won't use it for themselves.

When you are building a chatbot, typically this doesn't mean that you only use a conversational AI tool Dialogflow. Just like building a website, you will likely need more resources. Think about a place to host your chatbot, store your data in a data warehouse or database, and you might want to use additional Machine Learning models to detect the contents of a PDF or the sentiment of a text.

By the time of writing, Google Cloud has over 200 products. There are products for computing, storage, networking, data analytics, and Machine Learning for developers, for example, Machine Learning APIs for recognizing images (Vision AI), videos (Video AI), texts (Natural Language API), languages (Translate API), and audio (Speech-to-

Text/Text-to-Speech API). Finally, there are Machine Learning tools for data scientists to train your models and identity and security tools. It's like Lego. By stacking all these resources on top of each other, you will build a product.

Open Source

Google believes in transparency, by making software and building developer communities. Google has over 280k of commits on the open source development platform GitHub, with project contributions that are over 15k since 2016. These include popular Google open source projects such as Android, Chromium, V8 JavaScript Engine, WebKit, Angular, TensorFlow, Kubernetes, Istio, and Go language. I'm sure you probably recognize a few. Besides these products that were born at Google, Google also contributes to other popular open source projects and standards. Think about HTML5, Linux Kernel, Python language, MySQL, GCC (GNU Compiler Collection), Spinnaker, and so on. Google wrote lots of industry research white papers, which inspire communities and other big software products, for example, MapReduce which was later used to create Hadoop.

Many of these great open source Google products started at Google in the late 1990s/ early 2000s. While many individuals or companies were thinking of building a simple web page, Google already had to maintain the most extensive and busiest website in the world (the Google search engine), which also needed to be scalable. The products that Google engineers created for solving high maintainability/scalable problems later became the groundwork for open source software. For example, the internal Borg container orchestration system became Kubernetes in the open source world.

And what works in the open source world, Google brought that back to the enterprise world by running these products in Google Cloud.

About Dialogflow

Now, let's talk more about AI for conversational. In September 2016, Google acquired the company called API.ai. **API.ai** (previously known as the company **Speaktoit**) released an end-to-end development suite for building conversational interfaces for websites, mobile applications, popular messaging/social media platforms, IoT, voice devices, and contact centers. In October 2017, the platform got a new name: **Dialogflow**. Dialogflow is making use of Artificial Intelligence subsets: Natural Language Understanding, speech recognition, and Named Entity Recognition (NER, for extracting values out of text) to recognize the intent, entities, and context of what a user says, allowing your conversational UI to provide highly efficient and accurate responses.

Companies of all sizes are using Dialogflow. Use cases are

- Internal business-to-employee chatbots

- Public-facing chatbots for connecting businesses to customers like customer service or sales departments

- Chatbots which control IoT devices (home entertainment, auto, self-service kiosks, etc.)

- Robots in contact centers for inbound and outbound calls

Customers of Dialogflow include Giorgio Armani, Mercedes, Comcast, The Wall Street Journal, KLM Royal Dutch Airlines, EasyJet, ING Bank, Marks & Spencer, Ahold, and so on.

At the moment of writing (June 2021), Dialogflow has over 1.7 million users. The reason why Dialogflow is so popular in the chatbot community is because

- Dialogflow is powered by state-of-the-art Machine Learning. Google is a recognized world leader in Artificial Intelligence, and Dialogflow benefits from Google's assets and capabilities in ML, NLU, and search. Apart from the built-in Machine Learning models, it's also possible to train your agents yourself to make your conversational UI smarter over time.

- With Dialogflow, you can separate your conversation from code. Since Dialogflow provides a Cloud web UI, you can separate your dialogues and entities from application/agent code. This makes your conversational UI more scalable; you don't need a developer to make or deploy changes.

- With Dialogflow, you can build chatbots faster than coding chatbots through a set of (Python) scripts. Besides the web UI, you can also build faster conversational UIs by enabling the prebuilt agents (templates) and Small Talk intents (to give your agent more personality), all with one single mouse click.

- Advanced fulfillment options and multichannel integrations. Dialogflow has over 32 channel integrations and SDKs. Therefore, you can easily integrate your agent with your on-premise environments as well as cloud environments to consume data from services. With the built-in multichannel integrations, you can quickly deploy your agent to the various built-in channels (social media channels like Twitter, Facebook Messenger, Skype, or Slack; voice-activated assistants such as the Google Assistant; phone or SMS services. Or you can deploy it to your website or apps by making use of the SDK through gRPC, REST, or client-side libraries for Java, Node.js, Python, Go, PHP, Ruby, or C#).

- Since Dialogflow is available through Google Cloud, it has the Google Cloud Terms of Services, SLA, and support packages. Being part of Google Cloud means excellent reliability, low latency, easy integration with over 200 Google Cloud services, such as data analytics services and tools (like BigQuery, Dataprep, or Pub/Sub); Machine Learning APIs (like sentiment detection, translation, speech-to-text transcription, text-to-speech synthesizer, data loss prevention for masking sensitive data, Vision AI like OCR detection on images) or cloud environments such as Cloud Functions, Kubernetes, Compute VMs, Cloud Run, or App Engine. Google Cloud services can be controlled with a powerful identity access management, error/debugging, logging, and monitoring.

- Powerful analytics. Use data analytics to monitor bot health and also better understand its interactions with users. Chatbase, a Google Cloud service that helps builders analyze and optimize bots more quickly, is complementary to Dialogflow. Using them in combination helps builders create world-class bots and then continually track and optimize them using Chatbase. All Dialogflow users get an automated set of basic Chatbase analytics directly from their console.

- Speech/voice integration besides text interfaces. Dialogflow also has speech recognition and Text to Speech integrated—handy for IoT devices or out-of-the-box integration with IVR telephony partners.

- Multilingual bot support. Over 20 languages are supported in Dialogflow.

Dialogflow Essentials and Dialogflow CX

The original Dialogflow tool recently had a name change; it's now called **Dialogflow Essentials** (Dialogflow ES) to make room for a new Google Cloud Conversational AI tool: Dialogflow Customer Experience (**Dialogflow CX**).

Dialogflow CX will be an alternative development suite for building conversational UIs and will exist next Dialogflow ES. Google will continue to support Dialogflow ES, as we have a huge user base. To understand why Google created another bot builder, let's first understand how Dialogflow ES works at a high level.

How Dialogflow Essentials Works

An intent in Dialogflow ES categorizes a user's intention. For each Dialogflow ES agent, you can define many intents, where your combined intents can handle a complete conversation. Each intent can contain parameters and responses.

Matching an intent is also known as **intent classification** or **intent matching**. (The next chapter will go into details about these concepts.) Once an intent is matched, it can return a response, gather parameters (entity extraction), or trigger webhook code (fulfillment), for example, to fetch data from a database. Dialogflow ES can keep track of a context, and just like a human, While turn-taking, Dialogflow ES can remember the context in a second and third turn. This is how it can keep track of previous user utterances. This is the main concept in Dialogflow ES.

How the Industry Is Changing Its Complexity

Large enterprises have been using Dialogflow ES over the past years. Here's an observation I see at Google. At the beginning (2016), most conversational AIs were simple chatbots (voice assistant bots, FAQ bots, etc.), for web or voice bots, like the Google Assistant. It typically uses one or two turn-taking turns. For example, "Hey Google, what's currently playing on ABC?"—"*The Bachelor* started at 8 p.m., an episode you have never seen before!"

As we all know, building conversational UIs is an ongoing process. When you capture the right chatbot insights, you will see what your customers are asking for. When you continue to build conversations on top of an existing agent, that bot becomes more complex over the years.

So conversation **complexity** is one observation. The other perception I made is that **businesses want to be where their customers are**. And thus, their chatbots will need to connect to more channels to create omnichannel experiences. Instead of building a single chatbot, companies now want to develop complete conversational platforms fed by a data lake and automate processes with RPA. Think of complex use cases such as replacing your customer care or HR department with robots. Having overloaded call centers and employees burned out by undervalued monotonous tasks, automation through chatbots and virtual (voice) agents can trim huge business costs. Through conversational AI in contact centers, businesses can reduce call time and on-hold time and offer 24/7 availability while improving our processes by capturing analytics.

Where Dialogflow CX Fits In

Dialogflow Essentials has been praised for its simplicity. You can build a chatbot or voice bot quickly. These are chat and voice applications, often, where a short utterance matches one intent, with a few turn-taking turns, for example, a retail chat or voice app where you can say: "Put milk on my shopping list."

Now imagine you are building a voice robot for the telephony helpdesk of a grocery store. This time, customers are not speaking a few sentences; instead, they speak with whole stories: "So, yesterday, right at opening time, I bought milk at So-And-So Store together with my 4-month-old baby, and when I came home, and I wanted to put the milk in the refrigerator, I noticed that the date is past the expiration date. I opened the carton and noticed the odd smell, but the taste was fine." Suddenly it becomes much more tricky to match the intent. For a human, it can become challenging to understand the intention; for an AI, this is difficult too! Because are we talking about buying *milk*, *bad products*, or *requesting a refund*?

The conversation in a contact center is **long-running** (you will stop the chat session once you hang up the phone); the dialogue is large and can have many turn-taking turns, where we need to remember the context—branched off in hundreds of possible outcomes. And look, I am not even mentioning the technical complexity of dealing with multiple speakers, interruptions, background noises, and so on.

Creating a virtual (voice) agent for a contact center or creating an automated bot platform is far more complicated where it reaches the borders of Dialogflow Essentials. Sure, when you have a large team of developers, they can tailor-make a solution on top of Dialogflow ES, as enterprises have been doing so in the past. But that means that you have to write a lot of supporting code rather than focusing on designing conversations. Here's where Dialogflow CX comes in handy.

Dialogflow CX Explained

Dialogflow CX empowers your team to accelerate creating enterprise-level conversational experiences through visual bot builders, reusable intents, and the ability to address multi-turn conversations.

It allows you to quickly create agents with

- Large and complex flows. Think of giant agent implementations with hundreds or thousands of intents.

- More than three turn-taking turns (keeping context) and conversations that branch off from each other in various outcomes.

- Repeatable dialogue parts in the flow (think of a login feature, saying yes/no to questions, etc.).

- Understanding the intent and context of long utterances.

- Working with teams collaborating on large implementations.

- Native Contact Center features such as DTMF, one-click telephony partner integration, barge-in, live agent hand-off.

- Agents where additional languages and regionalization (e.g., GDPR) are important.

- Flows with various outcomes and repeatable parts, for example, filing taxes. Usually, this requires you to fill out lots of forms, where questions jump to each other. If you would build a chatbot for this use case, Dialogflow CX would be great for this, because of the reusable flows, intents, and branching of answers.

> **Note**   Dialogflow CX has advanced their NLU. Even though Dialogflow ES
> is popular because of the outstanding NLU results, we saw a notable quality
> improvement by basing our NLU on the **BERT** language model. BERT stands for
> Bidirectional Encoder Representations from Transformers. It's a deep learning
> Transformer-based Machine Learning technique for Natural Language Processing
> pretraining, and it's developed by Google. It allows a system to automatically
> discover the representations needed for feature detection or classification from
> raw data. BERT is also used in Google search to understand user searches.

Dialogflow introduces new concepts such as **Pages** and **Flows** for creating reusable flows and branching, and on top of that, it comes with a visual flow builder to quickly preview and understand the flow of dialogues. Although this book is heavy on Dialogflow Essentials materials, in the Appendix of the book, Pages and Flows will be explained in more detail, should you want to make a start with Dialogflow CX. Together with the materials explained in all the chapters of this book, you will be able to use both products.

Dialogflow Essentials vs. Dialogflow CX

Dialogflow CX is a separate product that will coexist with Dialogflow Essentials. When you are an enterprise customer building a large and complex chatbot platform or contact center customer experience when data regionalization is crucial for you (because of GDPR) or your conversation requires lots of turn-taking turns and dialogue branches, Dialogflow CX could be the tool for you to use. Alternatively, when you want to choose a more simplistic tool, for less complex visual agents, or when you do want to build complex visual agents and you don't mind to get your hands dirty by writing some supporting (back-end) code, let's use Dialogflow Essentials.

About Contact Center AI

Contact Center AI (CCAI) is a Google Cloud solution for enabling virtual agents with humanlike interactions (and voices) in contact centers. Where Dialogflow Essentials and Dialogflow CX are Google Cloud products, CCAI is a solution built by telephony providers together with Google Cloud engineers. Therefore, the CCAI go-to-market is through telephony partners.

These partners include Genesys, Avaya, Mitel, Cisco, Twilio, and many more. They can enable CCAI on existing contact center hardware.

Companies that are successfully using CCAI are Verizon, GoDaddy, and Marks & Spencer.

Note   Why is it interesting to have robots pick up the phone?

As an example, think of a health insurance company. The majority of calls that come in via the contact center are people who ask if certain costs are covered. For example, "Are dentist costs part of my package?" The health insurance company has an enormous amount of inbound calls, for example, in the Netherlands, especially around the end of the year, since that's the only timeframe to legally switch from health insurance providers.

It's so busy on the helpdesk line that many people will be put on hold. Instead of dealing with huge waiting lines and hold times, wouldn't it be great if a voice bot picks up the phone and answers the most common questions for you? It frees up the live agents who are working in the contact center to answer more complex or personal questions.

A similar situation we have seen in 2020. Google have helped many businesses such as the travel and tourism industry impacted by COVID-19. Contact centers of tour operators and airlines couldn't handle the call load, as all trips and flights got cancelled. People were put on hold for hours or got disconnected and asked to call back on a later time. By enabling CCAI in contact centers, answering most common questions, businesses were able to free up their lines, save costs, and help their customers better.

CCAI Architecture

The cornerstone in a CCAI architecture built by the telephony providers is Dialogflow CX. Dialogflow provides automated interaction with the user and contains automatic speech recognition (ASR) and Text to Speech with humanlike phone models.

It gives customers 24/7 access to immediate conversational self-service.

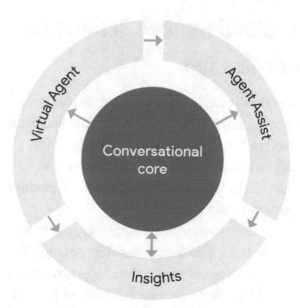

Figure 1-1. *Architecture overview of Contact Center AI by Google Cloud*

As seen in Figure 1-1, the Contact Center AI product includes additional Google Cloud components: **Agent Assist** and **Contact Center AI Insights**.

Agent Assist empowers human agents with continuous support during their calls by identifying intent and providing real-time, step-by-step assistance.

Now imagine you have a virtual agent picking up the phone; however, it does not know what to answer to the customer (e.g., because it wasn't trained with training phrases on that topic). CCAI can connect you to a live agent through agent hand-over, but in the background still listen in to provide suggestions (or fill in forms) on the screen to the live agent to speed up the call time.

Contact Center AI Insights uses Natural Language Processing to identify call drivers and sentiment that helps contact center managers learn about customer interactions to improve call outcomes. It enables Contact Center management teams to hear what customers are saying. Based on that, they can make data-driven business decisions and increase operational efficiency.

The CCAI architecture is built on top of existing telephony hardware provided by the telephony partners.

About Google Cloud Speech Technology

Cloud Speech-to-Text API

The **Speech-to-Text API** (STT) is a Google Cloud **automatic speech recognition (ASR) API** which enables the recognition and translation of spoken language into text through an API (via REST or gRPC calls and client-side libraries).

Google has over 20 years of experience in speech technology. The first patent dated from 2003, back then Google launched over 40 voice languages for the Google search engine, to search by using your voice.

In 2012, Google started to use deep neural networks, which was also the start of the speech models used for the Google Assistant. Besides the Google Assistant and Search, Google uses speech recognition in various other Google products: Dialogflow, the caption feature in Google Meet, Android Speech, YouTube TV subtitles, and Video AI, just to name a few.

The STT API started in 2017 and is part of Google Cloud. With the support of over 73 languages in more than 125 variants, it can transcribe speech, and it can auto detect a language. It also adds punctuation and speaker diarization (separating different speakers), and by the time of writing it can even run on-premise. STT is one of Google's most popular Cloud products. You would think that Speech-to-Text is most used in voice bot scenarios, but in fact customers are using STT for all kinds of things, like generating subtitles in videos or live meetings, phone call monitoring, retrieving transcripts from audio files, or building voice commands in applications.

ASR through the Cloud Speech-to-Text API from Google Cloud is a key piece in the Contact Center AI solution, where it will take a caller's spoken voice and convert it into text, so it can detect the intention with Dialogflow or collect analytics for CCAI Insights.

Note   The Cloud Speech-to-Text API is part of the Google Cloud terms and conditions. This means Google cannot and will not use your voice data to train the Speech models for someone else's usage. Therefore, you don't have to worry that competitors using the same STT API will get access to your business data.

Browsers like Chrome or operating systems like Android might have built-in Speech recognizers as well; however, businesses prefer to choose the Cloud Speech-to-Text solution because of the enterprise terms and conditions or additional STT features such as running the Speech models on-premise in your own data center. On top of that, it has been trained with different datasets.

Cloud Text-to-Speech API

Google Cloud's **Text-to-Speech** (TTS) generates speech from text. It's like a Speech synthesizer. By the time of writing, there are over 90 different voices to choose from.

Google Cloud's TTS allows developers to create natural-sounding, synthetic human speech as playable audio; it's like a voice synthesizer. You can use the audio data files you create using TTS to power your applications or augment media like videos or audio recordings.

TTS converts text or Speech Synthesis Markup Language (SSML) input into audio data like MP3 or LINEAR16 (the encoding used in WAV files).

WaveNet

In the past, we had standard Machine Learning models for generating voices. They sounded very robotic. Mainly because of the Google Assistant, we've created more advanced models: WaveNet models.

It synthesizes speech with more humanlike emphasis and inflection on syllables, phonemes, and words. When a virtual agent's voice sounds like a robot, users will treat the virtual agent as a robot and, therefore, ask dumb questions in a "computer" style, like "video game releases PS5" instead of "What are the latest video games which came out on PlayStation 5 this month?".

With WaveNet Machine Learning TTS models, Google can capture a person's voice in a short time rather than having an actor for weeks or months in a studio and generate new "voices" from it by learning the sound waves.

Custom Voice

With the Google Cloud Text-to-Speech API, and built-in speech synthesis in Dialogflow, there are many generated voices to choose from. However, at Google Cloud, we heard many requests from enterprise users who want to use their own custom unique voices in their conversations.

For example, to use their brand actor's voice on Google Assistant or contact centers. That process is usually also costly because you would need to rent an actor and have them in the studio for weeks to record every phrase.

With Machine Learning, Google can now generate custom voices. It's possible to record your own voice (or from an actor), for 30min, by reading a certain voice script. It will generate the voice for you.

The technology Google is using under the hood is called **Tacotron 2**. It makes use of sequence-to-sequence learning (Seq2Seq). This makes it possible to convert training models from one domain to sequences in another domain. (For example, through Seq2Seq, Dialogflow has multilinual support to so many different languages, because it's easy to roll out to new languages.)

Note in Figure 1-2, Google uses a sequence-to-sequence model optimized for TTS to map a sequence of letters to a series of features that encode the audio. These features, an 80-dimensional audio spectrogram with frames computed every 12.5 milliseconds, capture the pronunciation of words and various subtleties of human speech, including volume, speed, and intonation. Finally, these features are converted to a 24 kHz waveform using a WaveNet-like architecture.

It's almost impossible to differentiate the original voice actors' voice compared to the generated voice.

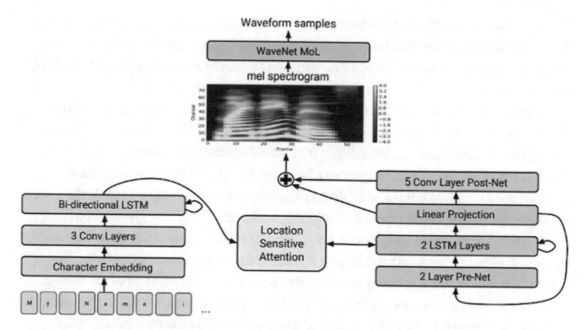

Figure 1-2. *A detailed look at Tacotron 2's model architecture. The lower half of the image describes the sequence-to-sequence model that maps a sequence of letters to a spectrogram*

Other Google Conversational AI Products

Google is betting heavily on Conversational AI technology. Chatbots and Conversational AI are the top priority for Google as well as for Google Cloud.

Where the previous section explained the Conversational AI products in Google Cloud, here are other Conversational AI products, researches, and tools at Google you might have heard of.

Google Assistant

The Google Assistant is the AI of Google, just as Siri is the AI for Apple, and Alexa the AI for Amazon.

Google Assistant initially debuted in May 2016 as part of Google's messaging app Allo and its voice-activated speaker Google Home. After a period of exclusivity on Google Pixel smartphones, it began to be deployed on other Android devices in February 2017, including third-party smartphones and Wear OS (formerly known as Android Wear), and was released as a stand-alone app on the iOS operating system in May 2017.

As of summer 2020, the Google Assistant is available on more than 1 billion devices and is available in more than 80 countries; it now helps more than 500 million people every month to get things done across smart speakers and smart displays, phones, TVs, cars, and more.

When you have used the Google Assistant before, you know that you can ask the Google Assistant anything. This could be a question, such as "Hey Google, who is the king of the Netherlands?" (It will tell you it's Willem-Alexander.) Follow up questions. "Who is his wife?" (It knows the context of Willem-Alexander; his wife is Maxima.) You can integrate it with IoT, home automation if you have Assistant-supported devices such as smart light bulbs, thermostats, Android TVs, and so on ("Hey Google, turn on the TV," "Turn up the heat," "Play Song 2 on Spotify," etc.). You can also ask questions that are particular to your brand, let's say buying a product from a particular store (e.g., "Buy Tony Hawk Pro Skater 2."); then you will make use of the app ecosystem of the Google Assistant. In the previous example, buying a video game is not a native Google Assistant task, as it depends on a store, location, and in-stock. This could only work from the context of a third-party "app" (within the Google Assistant ecosystem, these are called Actions).

It means that you will have to deploy your actions to the Google Assistant—similar to how Android, iOS, Windows, or MacOS work with opening applications. But instead of tapping/clicking an app icon, you can invoke your actions by asking the Google Assistant to open or talk to your brand: "Hey Google, talk to Lee Boonstra's video game store." At that moment, you will hear a voice change. It switches from the native Google Assistant experience to the voice and dialogues of your app.

Actions on Google

In December 2016, Google launched **Actions on Google**, a developer platform for the Google Assistant. Actions on Google allows third-party developers to build actions (apps) for Google Assistant that provide extended functionality on top of the native Google Assistant. There are over one million Actions in the Actions directory which is like an app store for Actions on Google, except that you don't download Actions. You just invoke them by talking to it. You can do this by using the wake word, such as "Hey Google, talk to my <appname>."

> **Tip**   Fun fact, 90% of the Actions are built with Dialogflow because of Google's direct integration. With Dialogflow, it's really easy to bring your conversation to the Google Assistant; it's just a flip of a switch. See Chapter 7 of this book.

Actions Builder

The Actions on Google platform comes with an SDK, visual components, extensive documentation, and an additional tool for building Actions: **Actions Builder**.

With both Dialogflow and Actions Builder, you can build conversations for the Google Assistant. The main reason for choosing Dialogflow Essentials over Actions Builder is because Dialogflow ES is part of Google Cloud and comes with enterprise terms and conditions, SLAs, and support. When you want to build multichannel virtual agents (bots that support Google Assistant and/or social media chatbots), then Dialogflow Essentials is the tool you want to pick. Dialogflow ES has direct integration with the Actions on Google framework. Dialogflow is a mature tool, largely used by the community.

Actions Builder works best for simple use cases that let users get things done quickly. It has consumer terms and conditions.

AdLingo

AdLingo is part of Area 120 by Google (incubator program) and allows brands to acquire customers by turning ads into AI-powered personalized conversations at scale. How? AdLingo ads enable brands to embed their virtual agent in a display ad to reach potential customers at scale and where they are looking for information. In other words, with the help of AdLingo, you can turn your Dialogflow agent into an ad. Instead of having your customers visit your website, you can have a much larger reach by displaying the conversational ad on other (external) websites!

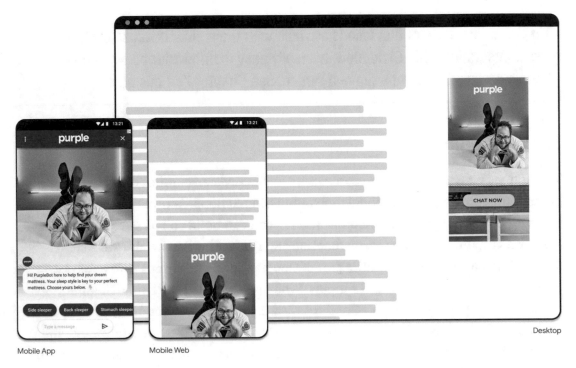

Figure 1-3. *With AdLingo, you can turn your display ads into chatbots, to start conversations with potential customers without them visiting your website first*

Chatbase

Chatbase is a cross-platform plug-and-play service that helps chatbot developers accelerate finding product-market fit by providing key bot metrics and workflows for fixing bots. It unlocks insights from data to create the right AI-powered conversational experiences for customer service. You can use Chatbase through their portal, but you can also use it through Dialogflow, as it's partly integrated.

Duplex

You might have seen the **Duplex** video during Google IO 2018 (voice robots making appointments with hairdressers). The video went viral. It has over 4M views and over 29K likes by the time of writing. It's a project by Google which allows certain users to make a restaurant reservation by phone. However, instead of the user speaking directly to the restaurant employee, Google Duplex, with the help of Google Assistant, speaks for the user. It does this with an AI-based but human-sounding voice.

Meena & LaMDA

Meena is a 2.6 billion parameter end-to-end trained neural conversational model. It's created by Google to handle a wide variety of conversational topics better to develop a chatbot that is not specialized but can still chat about virtually anything a user wants. Besides being a fascinating research problem, such a conversational agent could lead to many interesting applications, such as further humanizing computer interactions, improving foreign language practice, and making relatable, interactive movie and video game characters.

However, current open-domain chatbots have a critical flaw—they often don't make sense. They sometimes say things inconsistent with what has been said so far or lack common sense and basic knowledge about the world. Moreover, chatbots often give responses that are not specific to the current context. For example, "I don't know" is a sensible response to any question, but it's not specific.

Meena can conduct conversations that are more sensible and specific than existing state-of-the-art chatbots.

The Meena model is trained on 341GB of text, filtered from public domain social media conversations. Compared to an existing state-of-the-art generative model, Meena has 1.7x greater model capacity and was trained on 8.5x more data.

At the time of writing, besides sensibleness, Google focuses on other attributes such as personality and tackling fact-checking, safety, and bias in models, which is very much needed before making Meena available to the public.

Meena sets the base for **LaMDA** (Language Model for Dialogue Applications), which was introduced at Google I/O in May 2021. LaMDA is open domain, which means it is designed to converse on any topic. It was trained on dialogue to mimic a more natural way of conversing by looking at individual words and whole sentences and paragraphs, working out their relationships, and grasping the bigger picture to try and predict what will be said next and what its response should be. That way, it can respond in a way that actually makes sense in terms of the whole conversation, not just the last phrase uttered.

Summary

This chapter gave you all the background information on chatbots and the history of chatbots, Google Cloud, AI, Machine Learning, Natural Language Processing, Dialogflow Essentials, Dialogflow CX, Speech-to-Text, Text-to-Speech, and Contact Center AI.

In the last section, we talked about other Google conversational AI projects and tools. That includes the Google Assistant, Actions on Google (Google's virtual assistant and development platform), AdLingo (turning ads into virtual agents), Chatbase (insights), Duplex (remember robots calling hairdressers), and Meena (sensible conversational model).

Now that you know some background information, it's time to start building our own Dialogflow agents!

Further Reading

- More about Google Cloud

  `https://cloud.google.com`

- A cheatsheet with all Google Cloud products and descriptions

  `http://4words.dev/`

- Open Source at Google

  `https://opensource.google/`

- More about Dialogflow

  `https://cloud.google.com/dialogflow`

- More on TensorFlow

  `https://www.tensorflow.org/`

- More on BERT

  `https://github.com/google-research/bert`

- More on Contact Center AI

  `https://cloud.google.com/solutions/contact-center`

- Learn more about DeepMind's WaveNet

  `https://deepmind.com/blog/article/wavenet-generative-model-raw-audio`

- Learn more about Tacotron2

  `https://ai.googleblog.com/2017/12/tacotron-2-generating-human-like-speech.html`

- More on Chatbase

  https://chatbase.com/

- More on Meena

  https://ai.googleblog.com/2020/01/towards-conversational-agent-that-can.html

- More information on LaMDA

  https://blog.google/technology/ai/lamda/

- More on Actions on Google

  https://developers.google.com/assistant

- More on Actions Builder

  https://developers.google.com/assistant/conversational

- Duplex video which went viral

  https://www.youtube.com/watch?v=D5VN56jQMWM

- More on Tacotron2

  https://google.github.io/tacotron/publications/tacotron2/index.html

CHAPTER 2

Getting Started with Dialogflow Essentials

Dialogflow Essentials is the tool you can use to build conversational UIs. It comes as a trial and a pay-as-you-go edition. In this chapter, you will learn how to set up your first Dialogflow agent with Dialogflow Essentials.

This includes: the location of your agent and its data storage, logging, monitoring, user roles, and quotas. It discusses in-depth information on all the possible settings. At the end of the chapter, developers can learn how to set up Dialogflow for API access.

Dialogflow Essentials Editions

Dialogflow Essentials pay-as-you-go edition is the enterprise tier of Dialogflow and is part of Google Cloud. The pay-as-you-go edition is targeted at organizations that need enterprise-grade service. Dialogflow Essentials pay as you go has coverage against the most important global compliance & regulation standards (e.g. GDPR), and provides an SLA, support packages, and Google Cloud Terms of Services. On top of this, it has a higher quota limit and voice interaction and is fully integrated with Google Cloud, making it easy to consume other Cloud services to build a full advanced solution. (Think of additional machine learning APIs such as Translation, masking sensitive user data (GDPR) with the DLP API, sentiment detection with the NLP API, Cloud Functions fulfillment, BigQuery data warehouse for analytics, etc.)

The no-charge Dialogflow trial is not part of Google Cloud.

L. Boonstra, *The Definitive Guide to Conversational AI with Dialogflow and Google Cloud*,
https://doi.org/10.1007/978-1-4842-7014-1_2

Just like other free Google tools, Dialogflow free version is part of the no-charge Google consumer terms. This means, like in the case of Gmail, that your data can be used to improve products, machine learning model training, or advertising.

Where is the Dialogflow data processed? You can choose this while creating a project. Part of Google Cloud also means the best latency. When you are connected to Google Cloud, you will use the Google Cloud cables under the ocean. Therefore, your connection will be much faster and will be secure.

Figure 2-1. *Dialogflow location dropdown*

As seen in Figure 2-1, by default, the PII data (like chat history, analytics, and logs) are stored in the global Dialogflow servers. Before you create a new Dialogflow agent, you can choose a location for your Dialogflow project. At the time of writing this, you can choose between the US, Asia (Japan), Australia (Sydney), and the UK (London), and you can find this setting in the dropdown next to the Dialogflow logo. After selecting the region, you will switch to a new Dialogflow environment where you can create a new agent.

Note   The regions Australia, Asia, and the UK don't offer all the same features as for the USA (Global). For example, region Asia is missing beta features such as the FAQ knowledge base, and it doesn't come with prebuilt agents, small talk, and out-of-the-box integrations. The last one seems essential, but you can build integrations manually as described in Chapter 10.

Besides, you can turn the storage of data off in the Dialogflow settings screen; see Figure 2-2. Click the cogwheel icon right under the Dialogflow logo. Once the data is turned off, no PII data will be stored. Especially for European countries that deal with the GDPR, this might be interesting.

Note   Since Brexit happened, the United Kingdom is not part of the European Union anymore. This means according to the General Data Protection Regulation (GDPR) compliance that storing logs and history data into the UK region isn't compliant. The best solution is to create your agent in the global region (to get access to all the features), but turn off all logs in Dialogflow. Instead, you can store the chat history in Google Cloud BigQuery where you can choose Europe as a region. This approach is explained in Chapter 13.

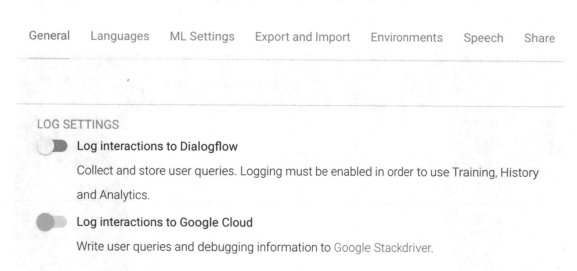

General   Languages   ML Settings   Export and Import   Environments   Speech   Share

LOG SETTINGS

Log interactions to Dialogflow

Collect and store user queries. Logging must be enabled in order to use Training, History and Analytics.

Log interactions to Google Cloud

Write user queries and debugging information to Google Stackdriver.

Figure 2-2. *Log Settings in the settings panel*

However, I do advise that you still capture the analytics of your chatbot. You could easily do this by building an additional layer that pushes incoming messages from the Dialogflow SDK directly to Google Cloud BigQuery. BigQuery is part of Google Cloud, and Europe can be chosen for data storage. Other Google Cloud resources allow you to store data in a data center of a particular country. (For example, Google Cloud Storage can store the data in a data center in the Netherlands).

Creating a Dialogflow Trial Agent

Dialogflow is a Software as a Service (SaaS) solution; it runs in your browser.

Let's create an example agent.

Open `https://dialogflow.cloud.google.com/`.

Sign in with a Google identity. For consumers, this can be a Gmail address, and for organizations this can be a Google Cloud Identity or Google Workspace entity tied to your own domain.

If you have used Dialogflow before, you will automatically log in to an active Dialogflow project.

If it's your first time logging in to Dialogflow, it might be that you see a pop-up (see Figure 2-3). You will need to agree to the Dialogflow trial terms and conditions, with additional Firebase terms and conditions. The last one will be used when using the no-charge cloud services, such as the inline fulfillment editor, which under the hood uses a no-charge Firebase cloud function.

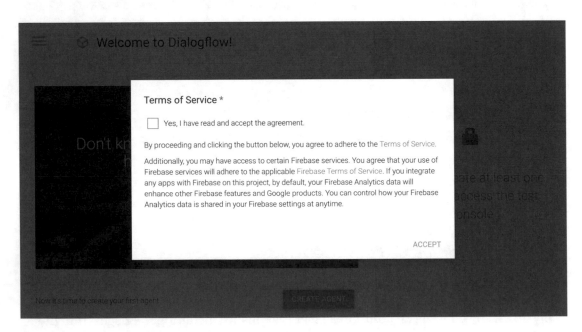

Figure 2-3. *First-time users can accept the consumer terms of service*

In case you are planning to build voice bots in your browser or with Google Assistant, make sure you have enabled **Web & App Activity**. You can access this settings page from `http://myaccount.google.com/activitycontrols` (see Figure 2-4).

Figure 2-4. *Web & App Activity in your Google profile*

Next, click the **Create Agent** button.

To create another new project, click the dropdown (under the Dialogflow logo, see Figure 2-5). It will show you a list of active Dialogflow projects, wherein at the bottom, there will be the menu option: **Create Agent**.

Figure 2-5. *You can select Dialogflow agents with the dropdown*

In the create agent screen (see Figure 2-6), you will need to

- Set a Dialogflow *project name*

- Set a *default language* (additional languages can be added in later steps)

- Set a *default time zone* (when conversations are mapped to date/time objects, it will use the default time zone)

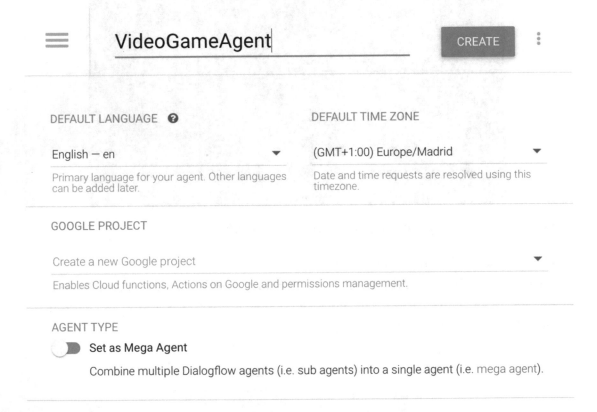

Figure 2-6. *Creating a new agent in Dialogflow Essentials*

Optionally, you could point to an existing Google Cloud project. When you leave it empty, Dialogflow will create an underlying project in Google Cloud for you.

Do not enable the Mega Agent switch. We will discuss this feature in Chapter 9 to orchestrate multiple sub-chatbots. For now, leave it off.

Click **Create**, and Dialogflow will create a new Dialogflow standard (no charge) project for you.

Creating Dialogflow Agents for Enterprises

When you are working for an enterprise, and you want to create a secure Dialogflow agent committed to compliance, you can create a Dialogflow project, as before. Still, you will have to upgrade the project to a (paid) enterprise tier. Afterward, you will have to enable the Dialogflow API in your Google Cloud project.

First, navigate to `http://console.cloud.google.com`. Sign in with a Google identity. For consumers, this can be a Gmail address, and for organizations this can be a Google Cloud Identity or Google Workspace entity tied to your own domain.

First-time Google Cloud users will need to accept the Google Cloud terms and conditions page while setting the country of origin (see Figure 2-7).

Figure 2-7. *Accept the Google Cloud terms and conditions*

When it's your first time using Google Cloud, you will need to provide a billing account. Google Cloud is pay per use, and even while it comes with free credits (which are more than enough for building chatbots), you will have to specify a payment method, such as a credit card. This will protect Google Cloud from robots abusing free accounts. In the left menu, you can select **Billing ➤ Create account**. You will specify a billing account name, organization name, and a country (the currency will be tied to it). On the next screen, you can enter your payment address and payment method details.

Once you are logged in to the Google Cloud console and have a valid billing account, you will need to create a project. Click the **Select a project** button in the blue top bar, next to the Google Cloud logo. (See Figure 2-8.)

Figure 2-8. *Google Cloud project selector in the Google Cloud console*

In the pop-up, click **New Project** as shown in Figure 2-9.

Figure 2-9. *Create a new Google Cloud project in the Google Cloud console*

In the create project screen, you will need to

- Set a *project name*.

- Select a *Billing Account*. This billing account will be used to invoice this project.

Click **Create**.

Next step, let's open in another browser tab the Dialogflow console:

`http://console.dialogflow.com`

The steps will be similar to the previous section. However, now you can import your newly created Google Cloud project in the create agent screen.

Click **Create**.

The last steps are to upgrade your Dialogflow plan from a trial tier to an enterprise tier. In the menu, click the **Upgrade** button (see Figure 2-10).

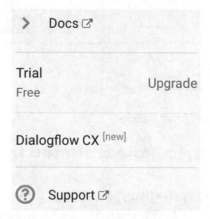

Figure 2-10. *Upgrade to Dialogflow pay as you go*

You will see a pop-up like Figure 2-11, and you can select a plan. There are two plans to choose from, *Trail* and *Essentials*. The primary difference between both plans is that the *Essentials* plan offers enterprise-ready features, such as Google Cloud terms and conditions, and SLA, support, and higher quotas.

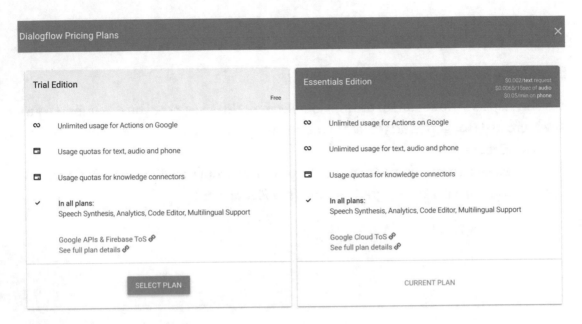

Figure 2-11. *Select a Dialogflow edition*

By selecting the Essentials plan, you agree with the Google Cloud (enterprise) terms and conditions.

After you have set the enterprise plan, you will see that the enterprise plan is active for your project in the menu (notice Figure 2-12), and you can change it at any time.

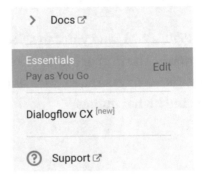

Figure 2-12. *Notice the selected plan in your Dialogflow menu*

Quotas

Besides the Cloud terms and conditions, SLA, and support, another reason for many customers to make use of the Enterprise tier is the higher call quota. Each time you interact with Dialogflow, a user utterance will be seen as a single API/Dialogflow agent call. The trial Dialogflow version has a maximum of API calls. The trial version can get a maximum of 180 text chatbot calls per minute, whereas the enterprise tiers can have 600 requests per minute. Google Cloud has documentation on all the quotas, and often the quota can be increased. To request a higher quota, click **Apply for a higher quota** in the quota edit form to submit a **Dialogflow Quota Increase Request** (`https://console.cloud.google.com/apis/api/dialogflow.googleapis.com/quotas`).

User Roles and Monitoring

Since you are using Google Cloud, enterprises can create and view custom audit reports, logging, and debugging through **Cloud Logging**.

Enterprise admins can invite and enroll chatbot users from the Google Cloud console by using Cloud IAM. It's possible to set user and group privileges or set security and control policies. They can also use directory sync (like **Active Directory Sync**) to import and enroll company users. This can be done via webhooks with Cloud Directory Sync and the Directory API.

Suppose you have integrations with other Google Cloud resources, like Cloud Functions or additional machine learning APIs, and you don't want to grant full project access to an application. In that case, you must assign the Dialogflow API roles (**Admin**, **Client**, or **Reader**) in the Google Cloud IAM console. You can find this configuration when you select **IAM & Admin** in the Google Cloud console and look for the service account used by Dialogflow. (See the Settings panel in Dialogflow for the name.)

Note   Developers should avoid working on the same agent at the same time. A single Dialogflow agent for multiple users can cause conflicts when saving and training the agent simultaneously.

The Dialogflow Console provides the **Owner/Admin** role to the user who created the agent. If you want to change the Owner/Admin, add multiple Owners/Admins for one agent, or remove Owners/Admins for an agent, you will need the Google Cloud console for IAM & Admin as well.

Using VPC Service Controls

VPC Service Controls can help you mitigate the risk of data exfiltration from Dialogflow. You can create a service perimeter, which is an organization-level method that protects the resources and data that you specify in your project. You can protect agent data and intent detection request and responses. When you create a service perimeter, include Dialogflow (`dialogflow.googleapis.com`) as a protected service.

Using Developer Features

When developers want to use Dialogflow by using the SDKs, you will need to enable the Dialogflow API from the cloud console. It's possible to enable this via the Google Cloud console by clicking this link: `https://console.cloud.google.com/flows/enableapi?apiid=dialogflow.googleapis.com`—or by using the Google Cloud command-line tools (gcloud), they can answer the following command:

```
gcloud services enable dialogflow.googleapis.com
```

There are multiple authentication options, but it is recommended that you use service accounts for authentication and access control. A service account provides credentials for applications, as opposed to end users. Projects own service accounts, and you can create many service accounts for a project. For more information, see Service accounts.

Configuring Your Dialogflow Project

Click the cogwheel icon right under the Dialogflow logo to enter the settings page.

On this page, you can add additional languages, tweak the ML settings, share the project with others, or create multiple environments.

Let's have a look through all these settings.

General

As you can see in Figure 2-13, in the general tab, the following settings are available:

- **Description**: Description of the agent.

- **Default Time Zone**: Default time zone for the agent.

- **Google Project**

  - **Project ID**: Google Cloud project linked to the agent

  - **Service Account**: Service account used by Dialogflow for system integration

  - **Trial or Pay as you Go**

- **Beta Features**: Toggle to enable beta features for the agent.

- **Log Settings**

  - **Log interactions to Dialogflow**: You will be able to use the History and Training features in Dialogflow.

  - **Log interactions to Google Cloud**: This option is only available if **Log interactions to Dialogflow** is enabled. Disabling Dialogflow's logging will also disable this setting. It will make use of logging features in Google Cloud (previously known as Stackdriver).

- **Delete Agent**: Completely deletes the agent and cannot be undone. If the agent is shared with other users, those users must be removed from the agent before you can delete it.

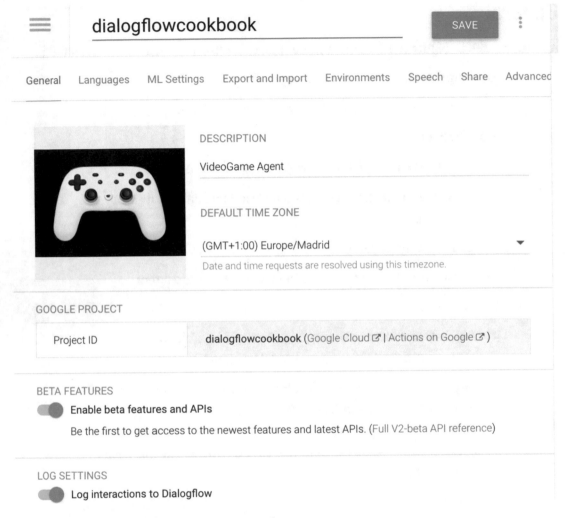

Figure 2-13. Dialogflow settings panel

Languages

The languages tab is where you can add additional languages to your agent. As seen in Figure 2-14, Dialogflow Essentials supports 21 agent languages; you can pick multiple from the pop-up.

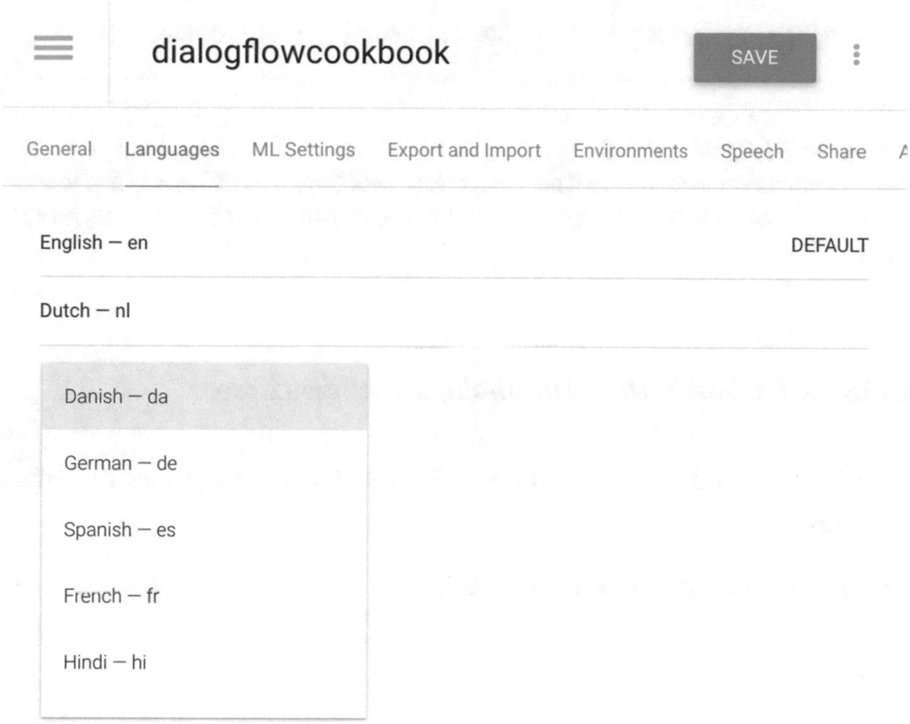

Figure 2-14. *Select Dialogflow languages*

ML Settings

The Dialogflow Essentials main concept is **Intent Classification**. (Chapter 3 will go into details on how this works.) Training phrases will be labeled with an intent name by a conversational designer. Once a chatbot is in production, the underlying Dialogflow machine learning model can match a user utterance with the defined intent based on the training phrases the model was trained on. Sometimes, various intents contain similar training phrases. One intent might be more relevant than the other intent. Especially when your agent grows, and more intents will be added to your agent, it can happen that the wrong intents got matched. The generic solution to this problem would be to change the **ML Classification Threshold**. The threshold value is like a confidence score. If the returned value is less than the threshold value, then a fallback intent will be triggered, or if there are no fallback intents defined, no intent will be triggered.

You can find the ML Classification Threshold in the settings section under the **ML Settings** tab; see Figure 2-15.

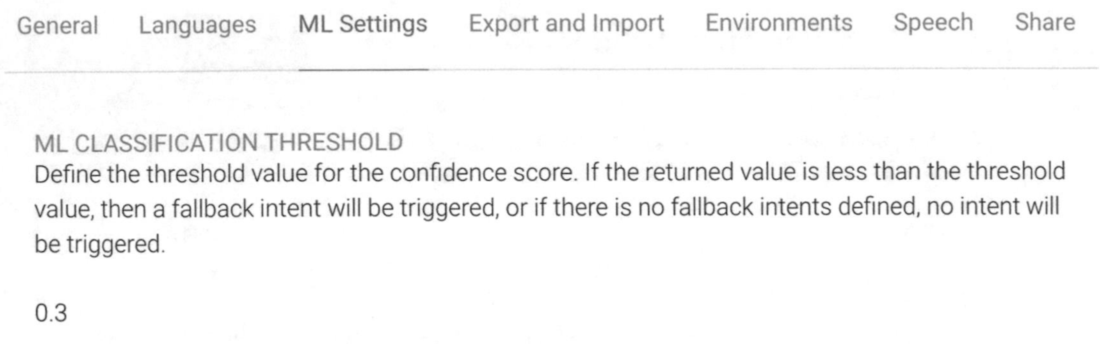

General   Languages   ML Settings   Export and Import   Environments   Speech   Share

ML CLASSIFICATION THRESHOLD
Define the threshold value for the confidence score. If the returned value is less than the threshold value, then a fallback intent will be triggered, or if there is no fallback intents defined, no intent will be triggered.

0.3

Figure 2-15. *ML Classification Threshold, a confidence score*

You can find the confidence level in your RAW API response; notice the following line in Figure 2-16:

```
"intentDetectionConfidence": 0.7057321,
```

Diagnostic info

Raw API response

```
18      "intent": {
19        "name": "projects/dialogflowcookbook/agent/intents/763feda0-f905-40ce-adfe-
    df58e684ce7d",
20        "displayName": "Get_Url"
21      },
22      "intentDetectionConfidence": 0.44944352,
23      "languageCode": "en",
24      "sentimentAnalysisResult": {
25        "queryTextSentiment": {}
26      }
27    },
```

CLOSE   COPY RAW RESPONSE

Figure 2-16. *When you click the Diagnostic Info button in the simulator, you can see the RAW API response, with the intentDetectionConfidence*

Sometimes, you don't want to fix the ML confidence level on the agent level but the intent level. Maybe because certain intents are exceptional, it's possible to change the priority per intent. You can give the intent a higher or lower priority. It's even possible to ignore specific intents, maybe because you are still working on it.

The way how you can do this is by selecting the intent from the intent screen.

At the top of your intent screen, you can click the blue dot. This will show a little pop-up; look into Figure 2-17 to find this feature.

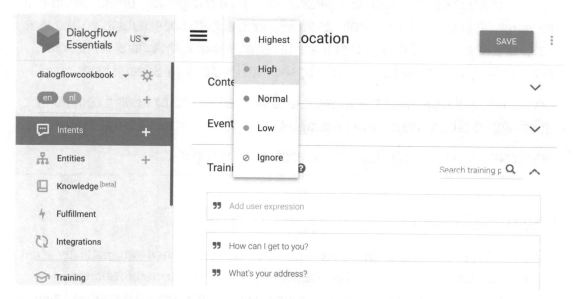

Figure 2-17. *Each intent can have individual priorities to improve the intent detection*

Automatic Spell Correction

If this is enabled and user input has a spelling or grammar mistake, an intent will be matched as though it was written correctly (based on its training phrases and used entities). The detect intent response will contain the corrected user input. This also applies to matches involving both system and custom entities. For example, "I want to buy purchase an Swtch." It will figure out the right intent and write down the correct parameter, which will be "Switch."

Spell correction is available for all languages supported by Dialogflow.

Note   If the misspelled and corrected user input matches different intents, the intent matching the misspelled user input is selected.

Spell correction can't correct ASR (automatic speech recognition) errors, so we don't recommend enabling it for agents using ASR inputs. Auto Speech Adaptation might help; see Chapter 7. But neither of these features works with Actions on Google since Actions on Google uses its own Speech-to-Text/Text-to-Speech layer.

Corrected input can match the wrong intent. You can fix this by adding commonly mismatched phrases to negative examples.

Spell correction increases the agent's response time slightly.

Automatic Training

By default, the underlying machine learning model will be updated automatically when intents or entities have been added or edited. You can disable or enable automatic agent training. A use case for this is, for example, when you want to test how well your machine learning model performs. In Chapter 13, machine learning model health will be discussed.

Agent Validation

By default, Dialogflow will run an agent review of your agent each time you make changes to your agent. As seen in Figure 2-18, you can disable or enable agent validation in the settings section; see Chapter 5 for more information.

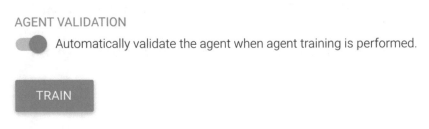

Figure 2-18. Enable agent validation

Export and Import

Note Figure 2-19; in this tab, you can import and export agents. **Export** means you will create a backup of the agent. It will return a zip file, which contains JSON files of all the intents and entities.

With **Restore from Zip**, you can replace the current agent version with a new one. All the intents and entities in the older version will be deleted. There is also **Import from Zip**, which uploads new intents and entities without deleting the current ones. Intents and entities with the same name will be replaced with the more recent version.

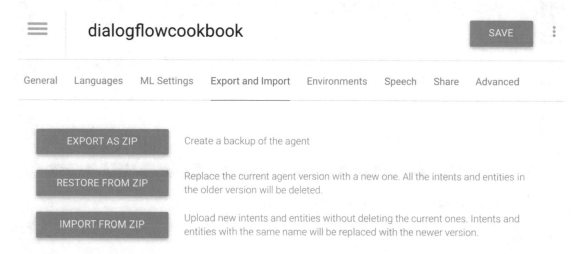

Figure 2-19. *Export and Import*

Environments

As seen in Figure 2-20, to access the environment settings, click the **Environments** tab. You can create multiple versions of your agent and publish them to separate environments. When you edit an agent, you are editing the draft agent. At any point, you can save the draft agent as an agent version, which is an immutable snapshot of your agent.

When you save the draft agent, it is published to the default environment. When you create agent versions, you can publish them to custom environments. You can create a variety of custom environments such as testing, development, production, and so on. And via the options menu, it's also possible to revert to previous versions.

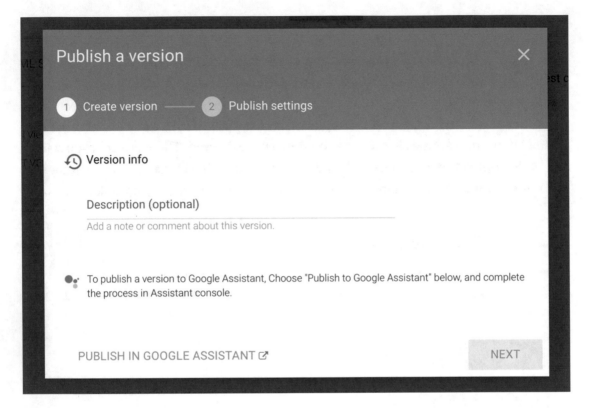

Figure 2-20. *Publish a version to an environment*

Speech

To access the speech settings, click the **Speech** tab.

These contain the speech recognition settings (**Speech to Text**) and speech synthesis (**Text to Speech**) settings.

Improve Speech Recognition Quality

In this section, you can find settings for the speech recognition model. It's making use of the Google Cloud Speech-to-Text model under the hood. There are two toggle switches available.

Enable Enhanced Speech Models and Data Logging

By enabling speech models and data logging, you agree to the terms and conditions of the data logging agreement (which amends the agreement governing the customer's use of Google Cloud services). Enabling data logging will improve your Speech-to-Text.

Enable Auto Speech Adaptation

To bias your Speech to Text model, to make sure it understands how you trained your agent, you can enable Auto Speech Adaptation. See Chapter 7, "Improving Speech to Text Quality" section, for more information.

Text to Speech

In this section, you can find the settings for the **Text to Speech** synthesizer to tweak the voices and audio output.

Enable Automatic Text to Speech

Automatically convert default text responses to speech in all conversations. You will get both the text version and the audio string. You can test this in the simulator (see Figure 2-21); after enabling this setting, you will see a little widget with an audio player.

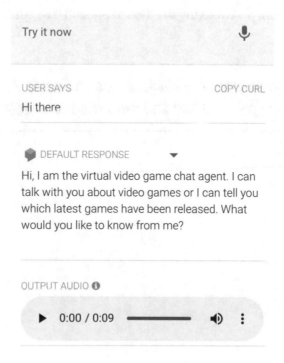

Figure 2-21. *Text to Speech in the simulator*

Voice Configuration

Note Figure 2-22; configure your agent's synthesized voice in the V2 API and Telephony integration with the following settings:

- **Agent Language**: Choose the default language for voice synthesis.

- **Voice**: Choose a voice synthesis model.

- **Speaking Rate**: Adjust the voice speaking rate.

- **Pitch**: Adjust the voice pitch.

- **Volume Gain**: Adjust the audio volume gain.

- **Audio Effects Profile**: Select audio effects profiles you want to be applied to the synthesized voice. Speech audio is optimized for the devices associated with the selected profiles (e.g., headphones, large speakers, phone calls).

For more information on tweaking the Text to Speech, see Chapter 7, the SSML section.

Note   All of these settings won't include Actions on Google. As the Google Assistant uses, it's on Speech to Text and Text to Speech models.

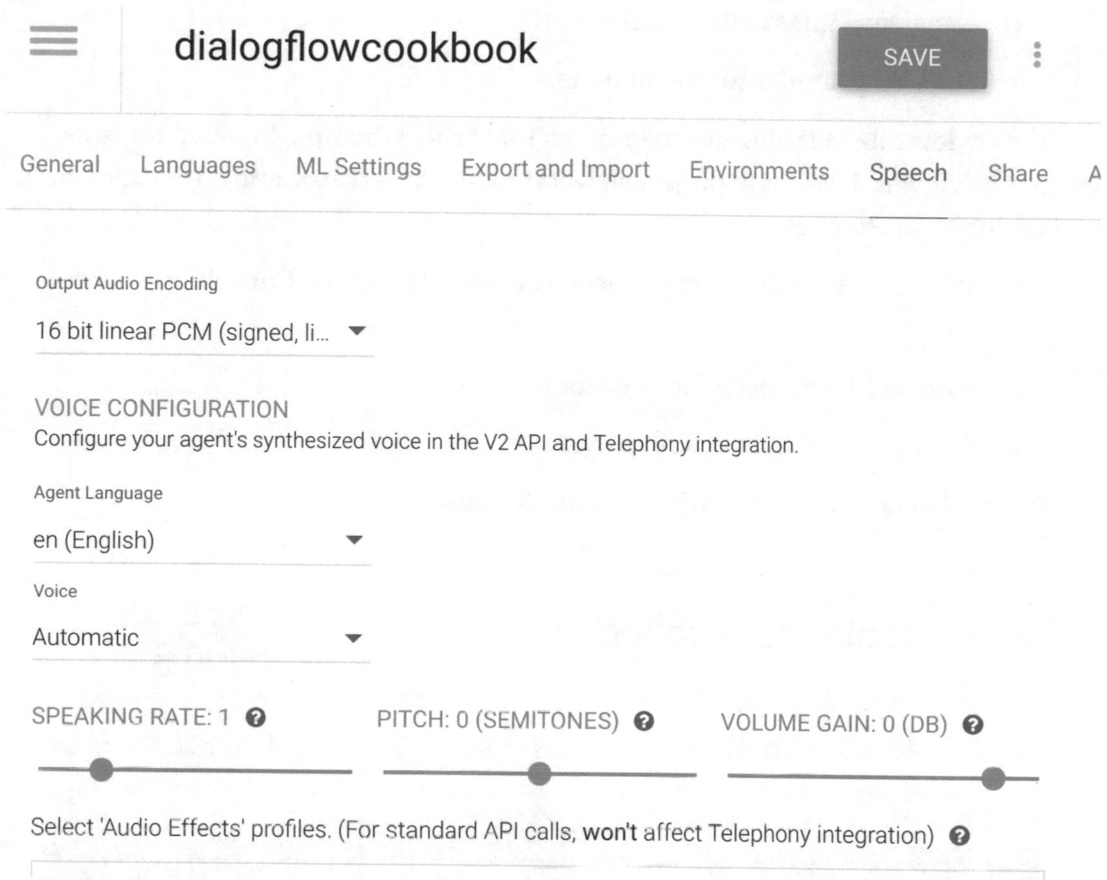

≡   dialogflowcookbook   SAVE   ⋮

General   Languages   ML Settings   Export and Import   Environments   **Speech**   Share   A

Output Audio Encoding

16 bit linear PCM (signed, li... ▼

VOICE CONFIGURATION
Configure your agent's synthesized voice in the V2 API and Telephony integration.

Agent Language

en (English)   ▼

Voice

Automatic   ▼

SPEAKING RATE: 1 ❷   PITCH: 0 (SEMITONES) ❷   VOLUME GAIN: 0 (DB) ❷

Select 'Audio Effects' profiles. (For standard API calls, **won't** affect Telephony integration) ❷

Figure 2-22. Voice configuration

Share

Note Figure 2-23; the **Share** tab allows you to share your Dialogflow agent with others. You can add an email address, and you will specify the role of this user, either **Reviewer** or **Developer**.

The developer role in Dialogflow maps to an IAM role in the Google Cloud Console: **Project ➤ Editor**. It grants to project editors that need edit access to all Google Cloud and Dialogflow resources:

- Edit access to all Cloud project resources using Cloud Console or APIs

- Edit access to Dialogflow Console to edit agents

- Can detect intent using an API

- See IAM primitive role definitions

The **review** role in Dialogflow maps to an IAM role in the Google Cloud Console: **Project ➤ Viewer**. It grants to project viewers that need read access to all Google Cloud and Dialogflow resources:

- Read access to all Cloud project resources using Cloud Console or APIs

- Read access to Dialogflow Console

- Cannot detect intent using an API

Press **Add** and don't forget to hit the **Save** button.

Figure 2-23. *Share settings. Don't forget to hit Save!*

Advanced

At the time of writing, in the **Advanced** tab (Figure 2-24), there is only one setting to control: **Sentiment Analysis**. You can enable sentiment analysis for supported languages. Enabling sentiment analysis will return a score and a magnitude with your intent detections.

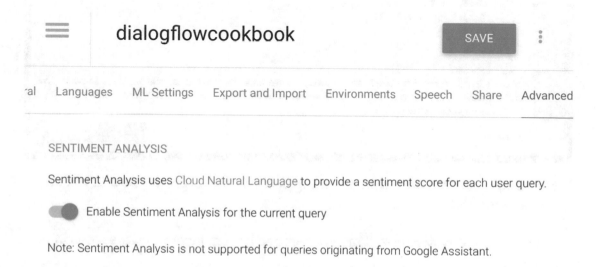

Figure 2-24. *Enable sentiment analysis*

The **score** of a sentiment detection indicates the overall emotion of the user utterance. The **magnitude** of a sentiment detection indicates how much emotional content is present within the user utterance, and this value is often proportional to the length of the user's utterance.

You can test it in the simulator (Figure 2-25). Try typing "Thank you for helping me." It returns a positive query score between 0 and +1. Next, type "That didn't work at all." in the simulator. You will now see a negative score between –1 and 0 show up.

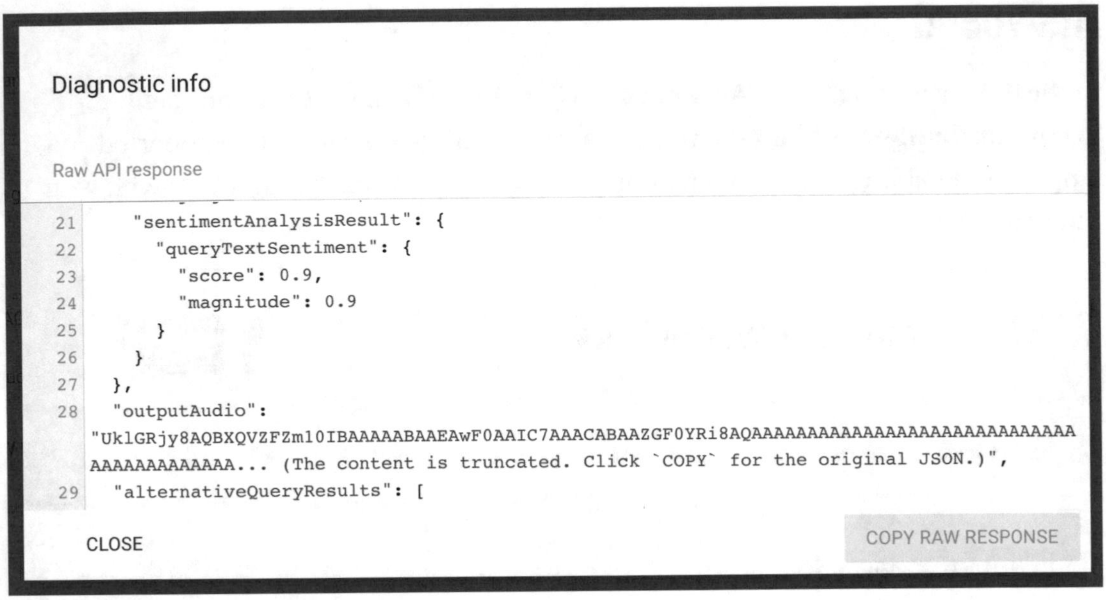

Diagnostic info

Raw API response

```
21        "sentimentAnalysisResult": {
22          "queryTextSentiment": {
23            "score": 0.9,
24            "magnitude": 0.9
25          }
26        }
27      },
28      "outputAudio":
     "UklGRjy8AQBXQVZFZm10IBAAAAABAAEAwF0AAIC7AAACABAAZGF0YRi8AQAAAAAAAAAAAAAAAAAAAAAAAAAAAAA
     AAAAAAAAAAAA... (The content is truncated. Click `COPY` for the original JSON.)",
29      "alternativeQueryResults": [
```

CLOSE   COPY RAW RESPONSE

Figure 2-25. *When a user says something positive, the API response will yield a positive sentiment*

For more information on sentiment, check out the sentiment analysis section in Chapter 13.

Note   Each Google Cloud project can have only one Dialogflow agent. In case your Dialogflow agent needs a test and development version, you can make use of the **versions** feature in Dialogflow. Or you could create more Google Cloud projects, one for the test agent and one for the development agent.

Configuring Your Dialogflow for Developers

You are a developer, and you want to have developer access.

Select **IAM & Admin ➤ Service Accounts**. You will see a service account email addresses, like Figure 2-26.

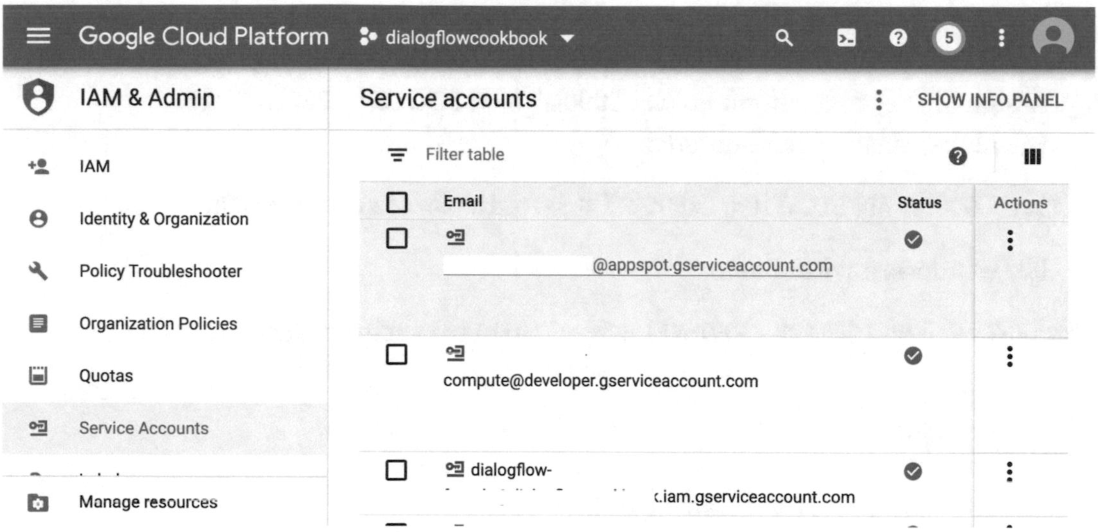

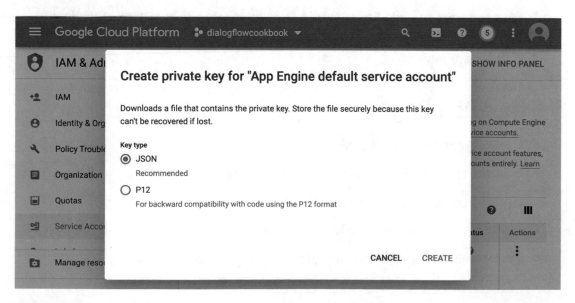

Figure 2-26. *Service accounts in the Google Cloud Console*

If you have not already, download a service account key for this service account, and set the GOOGLE_APPLICATION_CREDENTIALS environment variable to its path. You can download the service account JSON key by clicking the options button in the **actions** column and selecting **Create key**. In the pop-up, you can choose **JSON** and **Create**. (See Figure 2-27.)

Figure 2-27. *Create a private key from a service account*

It will download the JSON file to your disk, and you will need to assign this to an environment variable called `GOOGLE_APPLICATION_CREDENTIALS`.

Assign the key to environment var `GOOGLE_APPLICATION_CREDENTIALS`.

For Linux/MacOS environments:

```
export GOOGLE_APPLICATION_CREDENTIALS=/path/to/service_account.json
```

For Windows environments:

```
set GOOGLE_APPLICATION_CREDENTIALS=c:\path\to\service_account.json
```

Summary

This chapter addresses the following tasks:

- You want to start with Dialogflow and set up a Dialogflow trial agent.

- You are working for an enterprise, and you want to create a secure virtual agent committed to compliances; you can create a Dialogflow Essentials pay-as-you-go agent.

- You have created a Dialogflow project, and now you want to configure it.

- You are a developer, and you want to have developer access.

In case you want to build this example, the source code for this book is available on GitHub via the book's product page, located at `www.apress.com/ISBN`. Look for the _dialogflow-agent folder.

Further Reading

- Compare Dialogflow editions

    `https://cloud.google.com/dialogflow/docs/editions`

- Firebase terms and conditions

    `https://firebase.google.com/terms/`

- Dialogflow Enterprise/Google Cloud terms and conditions

    `https://cloud.google.com/terms/`

- Dialogflow tiers and pricing

  `https://cloud.google.com/dialogflow/pricing#es-agent`

- Dialogflow tiers and quotas

  `https://cloud.google.com/dialogflow/quotas`

- The blog post about storing Dialogflow data in BigQuery

  `https://cloud.google.com/blog/products/ai-machine-learning/simple-blueprint-for-building-ai-powered-customer-service-on-gcp`

- Directory Sync in Google Cloud

  `https://tools.google.com/dlpage/dirsync/`

- Google Cloud IAM

  `https://cloud.google.com/resource-manager/docs/access-control-org`

- Dialogflow access control

  `https://cloud.google.com/dialogflow/es/docs/access-control`

- Request a higher quota

  `https://console.cloud.google.com/apis/api/dialogflow.googleapis.com/quotas`

- VPC service controls

  `https://cloud.google.com/vpc-service-controls/docs/service-perimeters`

- Service accounts

  `https://cloud.google.com/docs/authentication#service_accounts`

- Authenticating as a service account

  `https://cloud.google.com/docs/authentication/production`

- Data logging

  `https://cloud.google.com/dialogflow/es/docs/data-logging`

## CHAPTER 3

Dialogflow Essentials Concepts

Developers or UX designers can train a Dialogflow Essentials agent (Machine Learning model) through the Dialogflow Web console. It's based on intents. An intent categorizes an end user's intention for one conversation turn. Your Dialogflow agent will contain many intents. Each intent contains training phrases, contexts, and responses.

This chapter will go into the details of training a Dialogflow Essentials agent. It will cover how intents work and how you can create intents. It discusses entities and working with contexts. At the end of the chapter, you will test your agent in the Dialogflow simulator.

Intents in Depth

As an example, Figure 3-1 shows the intent page for buying a video game console.

© Lee Boonstra 2021
L. Boonstra, *The Definitive Guide to Conversational AI with Dialogflow and Google Cloud*,
https://doi.org/10.1007/978-1-4842-7014-1_3

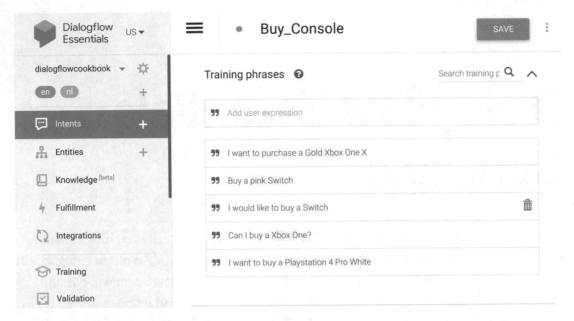

Figure 3-1. *Create an intent with training phrases*

Dialogflow can interpret human conversation's meaning when an agent has been trained with a given labeled dataset of training phrases.

When a user communicates with the chatbot through written text or spoken voice (user utterances), Dialogflow will do intent classification. Because of the NLP engine (which gets continuous improvements over time), it doesn't matter if the user utterance is written differently or contains spelling/grammar mistakes. It will understand what has been asked and match it by checking all the intents added to the Dialogflow agent. Once there's an intent match, it will return the intent fulfillment/response.

Dialogflow does not self-learn in the way that a goal-driven AI such as AlphaZero* does. Google does not disclose all implementation details (secret sauce) of the underlying technologies such as the NLP or Speech to Text engines, simply because they may change rapidly and fall out of date with the documentation.

Read more about AlphaZero, `https://en.wikipedia.org/wiki/AlphaZero`

Setting Up Intents

An **intent** is a messaging object that describes an action. When you visualize a conversation as a part of a tree diagram (Figure 3-2), all the tree branches are (follow-up) intents.

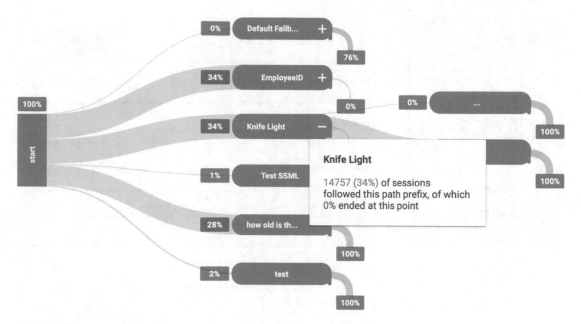

Figure 3-2. *Visualize a conversation as a tree diagram. Each node is an intent*

Let's log in to the Dialogflow Essentials console. Open in your browser:
`https://dialogflow.cloud.google.com/`.

You can create new intents when you click the *Intents* menu item and then the
Create New Intent button. This will open the intents screen (Figure 3-3). You will need
to specify an intent name, training phrases, and responses.

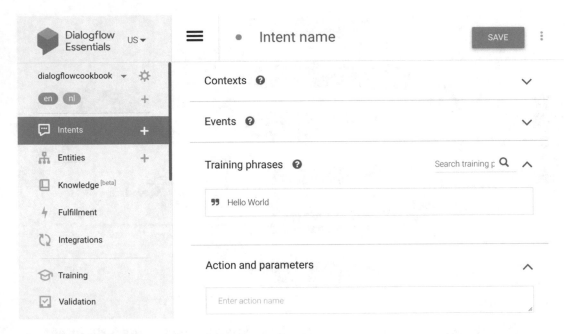

Figure 3-3. *Creating a new intent*

Tip   Dialogflow Essentials doesn't have a folder system for intents. Thus, you will need to be creative with the way you name intents. I've seen companies giving intents numerical ids in ranges, which likely map to fulfillments in databases. I've also seen companies naming intents to group them better:

UseCase.MainCategory.SubCategory like: `webshop.console.order` and `webshop.videogame.cancelorder`.

In the end, you should decide for yourself what works best. If it's a small agent, a structure like this probably doesn't matter, but be aware that your agent eventually will scale.

Let's build a cool chatbot that can help by providing video game information such as upcoming game releases. It should also be possible to have a conversation with the chatbot about video games. If you would have a conversation in real life with a friend about this topic, what would it look like? Probably something like this:

Me: What video games are you currently playing?

Friend: Oh, on the Nintendo Switch, I play Animal Crossing, and on the PlayStation, I am currently playing the latest Star Wars game. How about you?

Me: I'm playing Call of Duty.

Me: What's your favorite video game?

Friend: My favorite games are Heavy Rain and Beyond to Souls. I enjoyed the Uncharted series too.

Me: Heavy Rain? Isn't that this boring, quick-time adventure?

Friend: I love single-player games the most. My favorite games are games with a story. The stories of those games are great.

Me: Oh. For which system did it come out?

Friend: PlayStation 3 and 4.

Me: I like multiplayer games more. What's your favorite multiplayer game?

Friend: I sometimes play Call of Duty. But I am not that great at it. I think I enjoy Heart Stone on the iPad more.

When we analyze this conversation, you can clearly see that there are three conversation topics:

- Collect user's info on current playing game

- Collect user's favorite overall game

- Collect user's favorite multiplayer game

When we would take this conversation and train it in Dialogflow, those three training topics are the intents.

An **intent** categorizes a user's intention. For each Dialogflow agent, you, as a UX designer (agent modeler) or developer, may define many intents, where your combined intents can handle a complete conversation. By defining intents, an underlying machine learning model will be trained.

When an end user writes or says something in a chatbot, referred to as a **user expression** or **utterance**, Dialogflow matches the expression to your Dialogflow agent's best intent based on the training phrases and the built-in NLP, the under the hood Dialogflow machine learning model was trained on. Matching an intent is also known as **intent classification** or **intent matching**. The matched intent can return a response, gather parameters (**entity extraction**), or trigger webhook code (**fulfillment**) (e.g., to fetch data from a database).

An intent in Dialogflow contains the following:

- **Context**: Using contexts, you can control a conversation's flow when turn-taking, for example, based on our example conversation. At some point, the friend (or chatbot) will mention his favorite video game. A follow-up question has been asked: "On what system did it come out?" It refers to the favorite video game that was mentioned before. We will discuss setting contexts later in this chapter.

- **Training phrases**: See Figure 3-4. This is the dataset you are using to train each individual intent. When a user says something, it will be matched against these training phrases. It doesn't matter if the user utterance is spelled differently or told differently. When set up correctly, the Dialogflow Natural Language Understanding (NLU) will likely understand what's meant and can figure out which intent has the match.

Tip   When you provide training phrases, a good practice is to have at least 15 to 20 different examples, depending on your intent's complexity. Do not make these phrases too similar.

Suppose we would create the *Collect user's info on current playing game* intent in Dialogflow. The training phrases could be

- *What video games are you currently playing?*

- *Which game are you playing now?*

- *Which games are you playing lately?*

- *Are you playing any video games lately? Which ones?*

- *What are you playing right now?*

- *What's your latest game purchase?*

- *What's the most recent game you played?*

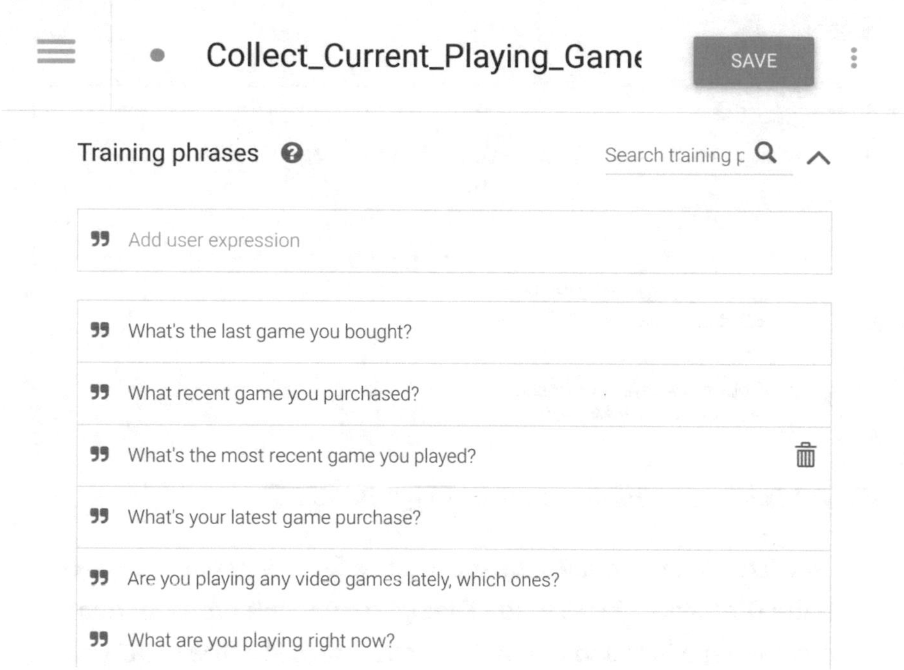

Figure 3-4. *Training phrases of an intent*

- **Events:** *(See Figure 3-5.)* Intents are typically triggered when a user expression matches an intent training phrase. However, you can also trigger intents using events, a mechanism to trigger code after a certain feature or action, for example, a **platform event** such as the **Google Assistant Welcome** event, which will be triggered when the Google Assistant action is launched, or a **custom welcome event** when your web chatbot starts the Dialogflow agent on a page load.

Tip   Some Dialogflow Essentials users use custom events to make intents reusable. Dialogflow Essentials doesn't come with a feature to reuse intents. If you think of a conversation as a tree diagram, then there will be tree branches (like login flows or yes/no flows) which come back on certain moments of a conversation. You could manually support this when working with events. In fulfillment code implementations, you would fire custom events by setting the followupEventInput field of the WebhookResponse. You can optionally set the followupEventInput. parameters field to provide parameters to the intent. Dialogflow intents can be configured to listen to these events before returning a response.

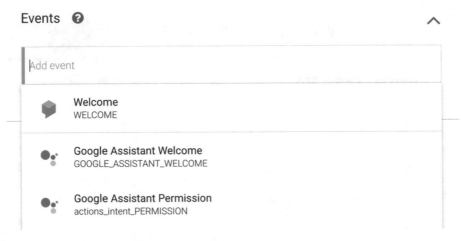

Figure 3-5. *An intent can have an event to get invoked*

- **Action**: This feature makes the most sense for developers who work with the Dialogflow SDK. In the Dialogflow console, you can define an action name for each intent. Dialogflow provides the action name to your implementation that integrates the Dialogflow agent through the SDK when an intent is matched.

  For example, if we create a new intent to fetch game releases of a particular month, the video game results aren't hardcoded in the Dialogflow interface. Instead, developers would call a web service with a database that will filter and return video game results. In Dialogflow, I could set the action name to *fetch_videogames*, which could (depending on your fulfillment implementation) trigger a function in your codebase.

- **Parameters**: When an intent is matched at runtime, Dialogflow provides the extracted values from the user expression as *parameters*, which could be sent to a fulfillment code/back-end code. We will discuss the parameters more in the next section.

- **Responses**: You define text, speech, or visual responses to return to the end user. These may provide the end user with answers, ask the end user for more information, or terminate the conversation.

In our example, the chatbot's response could be: *Oh, on the Nintendo Switch, I play Animal Crossing, and on the PlayStation, I am currently playing the latest Star Wars game.*

It's possible to specify multiple different responses. Dialogflow will alternate through the response selection, so your answer could be unique each time. An alternative response would be: *I bought the Death Stranding game recently, but I haven't started it yet.*

Responses can also have a **custom payload**. Some platforms support a custom payload response to handle nonstandard, advanced responses. These custom payloads are supplied in a JSON format defined in the platform's documentation. You would use this to create rich cards, for example. Depending on the integrations you have enabled for Dialogflow, you will see different response tabs for entering custom payloads.

And responses have an **end of the conversation switch**. You can specify if the response is the end of the conversation. It will stop the conversation. For example, on specific platforms, like the Google Assistant, it will close the action (app).

- **Fulfillment switches**: When the answer for this conversation isn't hardcoded in Dialogflow, but it comes out of a different system, you should mark *enable webhook call for this intent*. When an intent is matched at runtime, the Dialogflow agent continues collecting parameters from the user until the user has provided data for each of the required parameters. This process is called slot filling. By default, Dialogflow does not send a fulfillment webhook request until it has collected all required data from the user. Dialogflow sends a fulfillment webhook request for each conversational turn during slot filling if a webhook for slot filling is enabled.

  In the fulfillment screen, you can set up the webhook. We will discuss fulfillment in detail in Chapter 10.

When you start a new Dialogflow project, you will always get two predefined intents: a *welcome intent*, which will be triggered when you start the conversation, and a global *fallback intent* that will be activated when Dialogflow cannot find an intent match at all.

A Dialogflow agent can handle 2k different intents. If you need more intents, you might want to look into the mega-agent feature; see Chapter 9. Each intent can have 2k maximum training phrases per language, or 100k in total per Dialogflow agent per language.

Entities in Depth

An **entity** is a (variable) messaging object to take action on. It's like a parameter that collects a value for a particular key.

In Dialogflow, you can create **custom entities**, or you can make use of **system entities**. Custom entities can be created in the Dialogflow agent. Dialogflow recognizes system entities such as names of the month, currencies, and country names out of the box.

Creating Custom Entities

To create custom entities, in the menu bar, click *Entities* ➤ *Create Entity*. (See Figure 3-6.)

On this screen, you can give your entity a name and a list of possible values. The first value of an entry will be used for sending to a back end; all the other value options (the synonyms) will be used to recognize the entry. You can use the tab key to create more synonyms.

After creating the custom entity, don't forget to press the *Save* button.

Our chatbot doesn't contain that much advanced logic yet. After completing the previous recipe, your chatbot only can have a simple conversation with you. Imagine that you would also be able to request the latest release dates for a particular game console, like:

"Which games were released for **PlayStation 5** this month?"

PlayStation 5 is a variable part. I could ask PlayStation 5, Xbox Series X, Nintendo Switch, or Windows to return me different results. PlayStation 5 is a custom entity. In fact, if I would connect this conversation to a web service, it would send a parameter to filter the responses on to a back-end system, for example:

platform = PS5

For Dialogflow to understand that PlayStation 5 is an entity, we would need to create an entity "platform" containing all the possible options.

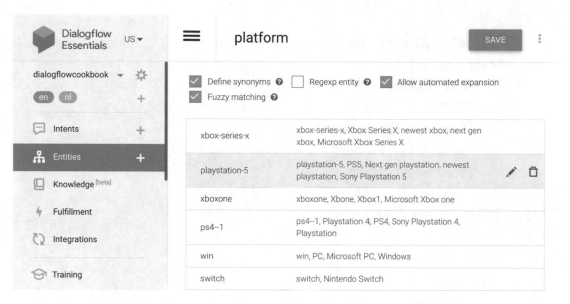

Figure 3-6. *Creating custom entities*

There is an easier way to enter all the entity entries. When you click the three bullets next to the save button (the options button), it allows you to switch to Raw mode. Here, you can enter the entries in JSON or CSV format. Listing 3-1 shows a code example in JSON.

Listing 3-1. Example entities in JSON format

```
JSON:
[
    {
        "value": "xbox-series-x",
        "synonyms": [
            "xbox-series-x",
            "Xbox Series X",
            "newest xbox",
            "next gen xbox",
            "Microsoft Xbox Series X"
        ]
    },
```

```
    {
        "value": "playstation-5",
        "synonyms": [
            "playstation-5",
            "PS5",
            "Next gen PlayStation",
            "newest PlayStation",
            "Sony Playstation 5"
        ]
    },
    {
        "value": "xboxone",
        "synonyms": [
            "xboxone",
            "Xbone",
            "Xbox1",
            "Microsoft Xbox One"
        ]
    },
    {
        "value": "ps4--1",
        "synonyms": [
            "ps4--1",
            "Playstation 4",
            "PS4",
            "Sony Playstation 4"
        ]
    },
    {
        "value": "win",
        "synonyms": [
            "win",
            "PC",
            "Microsoft PC",
            "Windows"
```

```
        ]
    },
    {
        "value": "switch",
        "synonyms": [
            "switch",
            "Nintendo Switch"
        ]
    },
    {
        "value": "new-nintendo-3ds",
        "synonyms": [
            "new-nintendo-3ds",
            "N3DS",
            "3DS",
            "Nintendo 3DS",
            "New Nintendo 3DS"
        ]
    }
]
```

Listing 3-2 shows a code example in CSV format.

Listing 3-2. Example entities in CSV format

```
"xbox-series-x","xbox-series-x","Xbox Series X","newest xbox","next
gen xbox","Microsoft Xbox Series X"
"playstation-5","playstation-5","PS5","Next gen playstation","newest
playstation","Sony Playstation 5"
"xboxone","xboxone","Xbone","Xbox1","Microsoft Xbox one"
"ps4--1","ps4--1","Playstation 4","PS4","Sony Playstation 4"
"win","win","PC","Microsoft PC","Windows"
"switch","switch","Nintendo Switch"
"new-nintendo-3ds","new-nintendo-3ds","N3DS","3DS","Nintendo 3DS","New
Nintendo 3DS"
```

It's also possible to import or export entities from the Entities screen. Click the option (three bullets) button next to the Create Entity button. Click **Upload Entity** and select to upload a JSON or CSV file which contains the entities. For uploading files, it needs to conform to the following rules:

- Each entry corresponds to a new line.

- The reference value and synonyms should be separated by commas.

- Each reference value and synonym should be enclosed in double quotes.

- The reference value should be at the beginning of the line.

- Include the reference value twice if you want it to be matched by the entity.

Programmatically, it's possible to add entities too. This makes sense if you have an extensive list of entities that needs to be automatically imported from a database.

The Dialogflow API method **projects.agent.entityTypes.batchUpdate** could do this.

A Dialogflow agent can handle 250 different custom entities. If you need more entities, you might want to look into the mega-agent feature; see Chapter 8. Each entity can have 30K different entries, 200 synonyms per entity entry. A Dialogflow agent has a maximum of 1M entity values and synonyms.

Advanced Custom Entities

By default, entity matching requires an exact match for one of the entity entries. In case your customers misspell the entity, for example, they type PayStation 4 instead of PlayStation 4, it's clear that a typo was made. **Fuzzy matching** allows you to identify non-exact matches of your entity. Just select the *Fuzzy Matching checkbox*, and save the entity type.

With the **allow automated expansion** checkbox, you enable Dialogflow to extract other parameters than what's been specified in the custom entity. If we use the same *video-game-platform* entity, you can see that we don't define an entity entry for "GBA / Gameboy Advanced." With automated expansion enabled, it takes the exact user input, and it will be used as the *video-game-platform* parameter.

It's also possible to create lists and composite entities. A **list entity** can be compared with the select box (select dropdown) in HTML. You can pick one or multiple from a list of values. For example, I could create an entity FirstPersonShooter Games, with the values:

- *Call of Duty*

- *PUBG*

- *Fortnite*

- *Battlefront*

- *Doom*

As can be seen in Figure 3-7, let's say I would tell the chatbot: "My favorite games are Call of Duty, Fortnite, and PUBG." The parameter that got the extracted values (which will be sent to the back end) will look like an array:

```
fps_games = ["Call of Duty", "Fortnite","PUBG"]
```

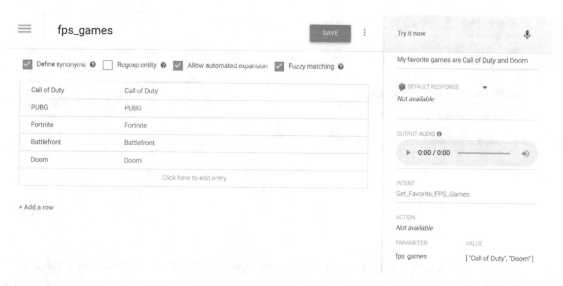

Figure 3-7. *Creating list custom entities. Note the value in the simulator; it's an array of values!*

A **composite entity** is a more advanced object; the composite entity can be composed using other entities. Let's say I have an entity called **@product**, which is composed of other custom entities:

@platform @product_edition @product_color

As can be seen in Figure 3-8, let's say I would ask the chatbot: "I would like to buy a PlayStation 4 Pro Black edition." The parameter that got the extracted values (which will be sent to the back end) will now look like a JSON object:

```
product = {
    platform: "Playstation 4",
    product_color: "Black",
    product_edition: "Pro"
}
```

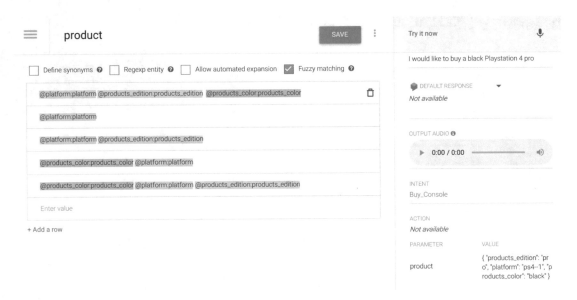

Figure 3-8. *Creating composite entities, note the value in the simulator, which is an object!*

To create composite entities, you will have to disable the synonyms checkbox, and then you can start referring to other entities by using the @ notation.

The last more advanced feature is regular expressions in entities.

Some entities need to match patterns rather than specific terms—for example, national identification numbers, IDs, product numbers, license plates, and so on. With **regexp entities**, you can provide regular expressions for matching.

It uses Google's RE2 engine, a software library for regular expressions via a finite-state machine. A **finite-state machine** (**FSM**) is a mathematical model of computation. It is an abstract machine that can be in exactly one of a finite number of *states* at any given time. Therefore, it works a bit differently compared to other regular expression engines. You can find a link to the syntax in the See also section.

You will have to **enable the regex** checkbox; it will automatically disable synonyms, and you can start writing regular expressions as entry values (see Figure 3-9), such as

`(MS|Nintendo|Sony)\d{8}` would catch: **MS12345678**

- Fixed word, Sony, Nintendo, or MS

- Digits

- Repeat the last, eight times

Figure 3-9. Creating regex entities

The source code for this book is available on GitHub via the book's product page, located at `www.apress.com/978-1-4842-7013-4`.

The entities that I have been using for these examples are

- @fps_games

- @platform

- @product

- @products_color

- @products_edition

- @producttype

Creating Intents with Entities in Training Phrases

Typically, when you want to create new intents, and those intents need to extract your predefined custom entities, you would make sure that the entities have been created first.

Then, in your intent training phrases, you can start feeding it examples. Dialogflow will automatically annotate the variable objects based on what's declared in your entities.

When Dialogflow starts marking certain words in the training phrases (Figure 3-10), you will know that the extraction worked. Else, you can select words from the training phrases and start marking them yourself by pointing them to the correct entities from the pop-up box.

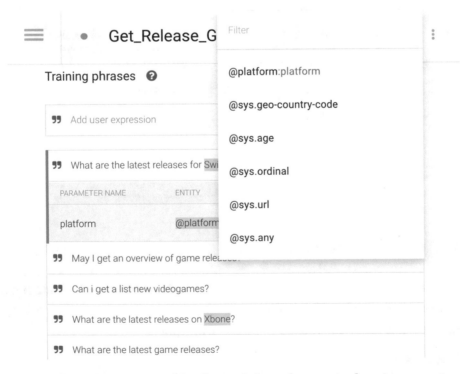

Figure 3-10. *Hover over a word in the training phrase, and assign a custom or system entity to it*

Marked entities should be assigned to parameters. This is what you will receive on a back-end system when you would enable fulfillment. In the Dialogflow simulator, you can click the Diagnostic Info button once you fire a text query.

This will show you a RAW API JSON response as seen in Listing 3-3.

Listing 3-3. RAW API JSON response, note the parameters section

```
{
  "responseId": "5c1ccce4-6445-42fc-be98-fa37f726d633-0f0e27e1",
  "queryResult": {
    "queryText": "What are the latest releases for Switch?",
    "parameters": {
      "platform": [
        "switch"
      ]
    },
    "allRequiredParamsPresent": true,
    "fulfillmentMessages": [
      {
        "text": {
          "text": [
            ""
          ]
        }
      }
    ],
    "intent": {
      "name": "projects/dialogflowcookbook/agent/intents/188fe06c-e630-
      494a-8fff-961d0d73866e",
      "displayName": "Get_Release_Games"
    },
    "intentDetectionConfidence": 1,
    "languageCode": "en"
  }
}
```

Assigning parameters usually happens automatically, after the annotation of the entity in the training phrase, but if it didn't work, you could tweak the following. See Table 3-1 which describes all the entity settings.

Table 3-1. *Entity settings*

Setting Name	Description
action name	You can specify an action name, which will be shown in the (queryResult) API response.
is required checkbox	If the entity is required for the conversation to be finished, this box will need to be checked.
parameter name	The parameter key shows how it will be shown in the API response.
entity name	The entity that it was mapped to. This could be a system entity.
value	The extraction value for the entity from the user utterance.
is list checkbox	If this is a list entity, you will need to enable this checkbox to get an array as a parameter.
prompt	When the required checkbox is checked, you can enter a follow-up question to ask for the missing required parameter.

Keeping Context

A **context** represents additional information included with user input or with an intent returned by the Dialogflow API.

There are two ways how you can set the context, with follow-up questions or by setting manually input and output.

Dialogflow can remember the context. For example, let's think of this flow:

"Let's talk more about favorite games."

> "What is your favorite game?"

"It's Call of Duty Modern Warfare."

> "Oh, I played that one. Are you stuck in the game? Need any help?"

"Do you know a good walkthrough for level 4 of this game?"

> "Here's a youtube video walkthrough of Call of Duty Modern Warfare level 4."

In the previous scenario, "talking about favorite games," the context is steered through follow-up questions. The conversation takes various turns; these are automated as a follow-up response to questions (from Dialogflow or your fulfillment code). It will continue the conversation.

Like a human, Dialogflow can remember that in the second and third turn-taking turns, "the game" refers to *Call of Duty Modern Warfare*. It can keep track of previous user utterances. In other words, contexts are helpful for differentiating user input, which may be vague. Contexts can also be set through additional details from your application, such as user setting and preferences, previous user input where the user is in your application, geographic location, and so on.

It's also possible to set contexts for other conversation intents without steering the conversation. You can park parameters in contexts for a later moment. This is where manually setting input and output is for. Think of this scenario:

"The very first game I played is Doom."

> "Ah, yeah, I played that game as well."

… (In the meantime, maybe other types of questions have been asked.)

"The very first video game console that I bought was the Dreamcast."

> "Is that where you played Doom on?"

It's possible to have max. Five input contexts per intent and a maximum of thirty output contexts per intent since multiple output contexts can be applied to an intent. When an intent is matched, any output contexts used to the intent become active.

Setting Up Follow-Up Intents

To set up follow-up intents is pretty straightforward. You will start by creating a **new intent**. You will need to make sure that your response will end with **another question** to keep the conversation going. Click **Save**.

Go back to the intents overview page.

Hover with your mouse over the previously created (new) intent. (See Figure 3-11.)

A hyperlink, **Add follow-up Intent**, will show up.

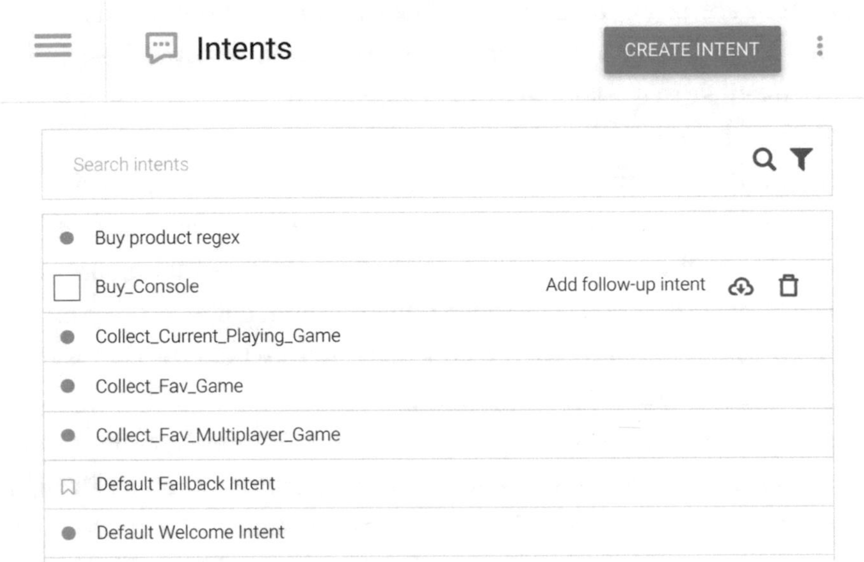

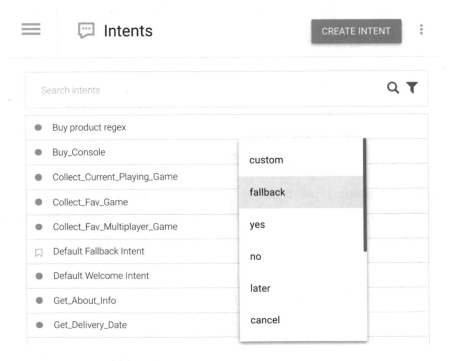

Figure 3-11. *Setting up the following intents*

When you click the **add follow-up intent** link, a pop-up will appear (Figure 3-12) with all the follow-up intent options.

Figure 3-12. *Using predefined follow-up intents*

Click **custom**.

You will see that a new child intent was created, nested under your first intent. (See Figure 3-13.)

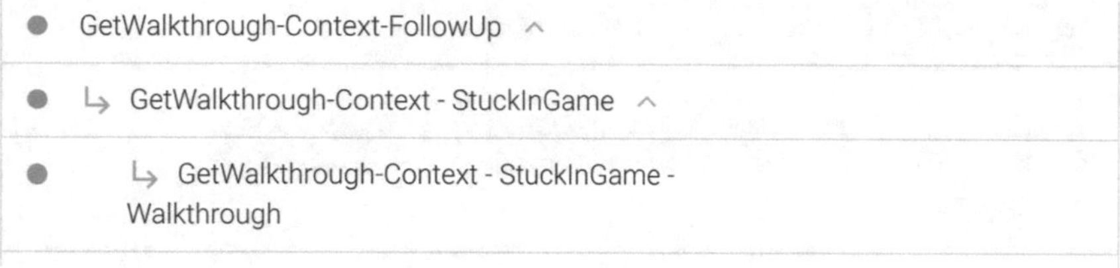

●	GetWalkthrough-Context-FollowUp ∧
●	↳ GetWalkthrough-Context - StuckInGame ∧
●	↳ GetWalkthrough-Context - StuckInGame - Walkthrough

Figure 3-13. *Nesting of follow-up intents*

You can click the child's intent and continue by providing training phrases and responses (and nest even deeper by using the same procedure).

When opening these child intents, you will notice that the input and output contexts are automatically set with predefined names and default lifespan count numbers. (See Figure 3-14.)

The input context in the parent is always empty. The child intents use the input context to provide the previous (parent) intent. The output context can be the last intent if the conversation has no output contexts (see Figure 3-14).

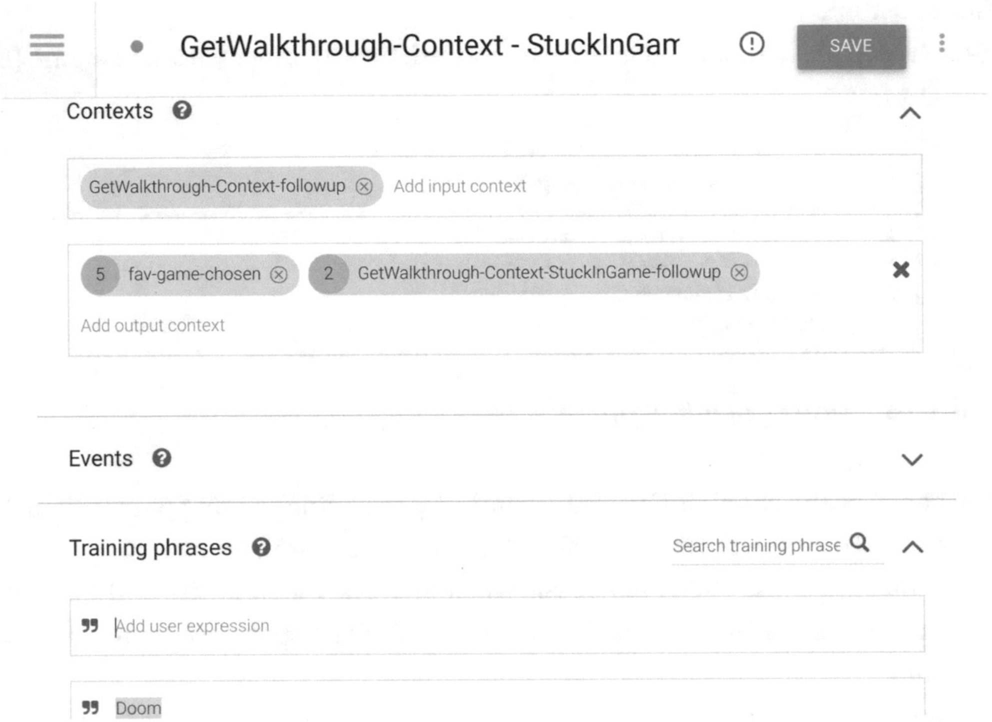

Figure 3-14. *Predefined context in follow-up intents*

There are different types of predefined follow-up questions to choose from. The advance of using a predefined follow-up is that it comes with training phrases, out of the box with all the supported Dialogflow languages. Table 3-2 shows an overview of the various follow-up intents.

Table 3-2. *Predefined follow-up intents*

Follow-Up	Description
custom	Write in your custom expressions.
fallback	Fallback if no other expression is triggered.
yes	Common expressions to capture an affirmative response.
no	Common expressions to capture a negative response.
later	Common expressions to do something later.
cancel	Common expressions to cancel an action or exit.
more	Common expressions to get more information or manage lists.

Manually Setting Input and Output in "Normal" Intents

Instead of using follow-up intents, you can also specify input and output yourself in "normal" intents.

Create a new intent if this intent needs to keep a user parameter in the context for later usage. You can specify a name in the **output**.

When you create another new intent, which needs to do something with the stored context, you will need to specify the same content name as before, but now in the **input**.

Input contexts in an intent have a primary function: they restrict this intent from being triggered when the context is not active.

Note   If you apply more than one input context per intent, they work with the AND logic. This means both contexts should be active if you want this intent to be triggered.

Lifespan

Contexts aren't forever active in a chat session; they exist in certain **lifespan** criteria:

- Contexts expire when an intent is matched, and the context was retrieved.

- After the number of DetectIntent requests specified by the lifespan_count parameter.

- After 20 minutes and no intents are matched for a **DetectIntent** request.

The default lifespan is five conversational turns for normal intents where manually input and output are set. The default lifespan for follow-up intents is two conversational turns. You can override the defaults by selecting the lifespan number (Figure 3-15) and typing a new lifespan count number.

Figure 3-15. *The lifespan number*

When you quit the chat session, your context will be lost. If you want to save this somehow for your user's next visit, you will need back-end fulfillment code, which gets and sets the context through the SDK and stores this, for example, in a database. This typically works when working with user logins.

Note   There are some best practices for naming contexts:

- Use alphanumeric names (like mycontext1).

- Use - or _ instead of spaces (my_context1/my-context1).

- Names are not case sensitive (myContext123 and mycontext123 are considered equivalent).

- All context names are lowercase when using the API (mycontext123).

Keeping Context with the SDK

In a real-world application, you will fetch the context parameters through the SDK in fulfillment code.

In fact, if we look into the previous scenario, it's possible that a user would start the video game console intent first. So the first game played hasn't been set in the context yet. When you work with the SDK in fulfillment code, then you could check if the context for first-game-chosen has been set, and if so, your response answer will be different.

If you want to fetch the context via the SDK, you can get this from a Sessions type **detectIntent** call. It will contain a field, `queryResult.outputContexts`, which will provide a list of all active contexts.

Sometimes, you might want to set the context on runtime from your fulfillment code instead of designing context in the intents from the Dialogflow Console. For example, maybe you want to capture a device location while the user interacts with your (live) agent. You would just make a detectIntent request call and specify queryParams.context as an object.

Listing 3-4 shows how the JSON for a detectIntent request would look like.

Listing 3-4. An example of a detectIntent POST request

```
POST https://dialogflow.googleapis.com/v2/{session=projects/*/agent/
sessions/*}:detectIntent

{
  "queryInput": {
    "text": {
      "languageCode": "en-US",
      "text": "I would like to add pizza to my shopping cart."
    }
  },
  "queryParams": {
    "contexts": [
      {
        "name": "projects/project-id/agent/sessions/session-id/contexts/
        product-chosen",
        "lifespanCount": 5,
        "parameters": {
          "product": "Pizza",
          "device-location" "@52.3377871,4.8698096,17z"
        }
      }
    ]
  }
}
```

However, it is possible to point to context parameters in the Dialogflow Console as hardcoded response texts. The notation is like this: **#context-name.$parameter-name**. If the parameter is given in the last answer (instead of the context), you can refer to it with the dollar notation: **$parameter-name**.

For example, here's a youtube video walkthrough of **#fav-game-chosen.$fav-game** level: **$level**.

Testing in the Simulator

You can have a conversation with your Dialogflow agent by speaking or typing messages in the Dialogflow simulator any time (Figure 3-16). This is a useful tool to test that your agent behaves as expected.

The Dialogflow simulator can be found on the right side of the screen.

At the top, you can start writing your user utterances, or you can speak it in. It has built-in browser microphone integration. To use this, first-time users will need to allow the microphone permissions pop-up when Dialogflow is loaded.

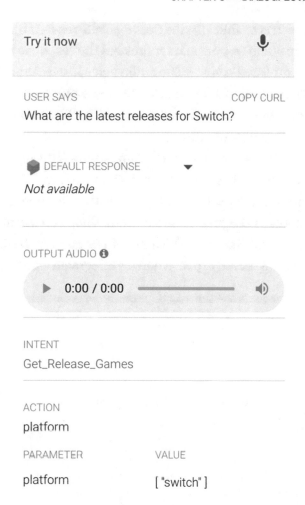

Figure 3-16. *Testing in the simulator*

The user says section returns the results of the built-in Dialogflow Speech to Text model captured when using the microphone function. Else, it repeats the written text query.

Once an intent was matched, the default response block will show the response from Dialogflow or returned from the fulfillment.

There is an integrations dropdown; should you have Google Assistant or any other integration enabled, you will see the output from those channels. (This might differ, depending on how you entered this in the intent response.)

When Text to Speech is enabled (in the **Settings ➤ Speech** tab), certain languages can have an automatic audio response; it synthesizes the response text. You can press the play button to hear the audio voice. The audio voice is tweakable in the Speech tab as well, should you want to listen to a different voice or at a different pace.

Further down, you will see the matched intent, with a link to open the Dialogflow intent page, in case you want to edit this.

Below this, there's a block with action and parameters. Through entity extraction, the values collected will be sent as key-value pairs to a back end if fulfillment is enabled. When extracting entities, you typically would work with fulfillments.

That's also why there is a **Diagnostic Info** button. When you hit this button, you will get a raw API JSON response (Figure 3-17). This could be good for testing/debugging; this is what your back-end code should expect when it's integrated with the Dialogflow SDK.

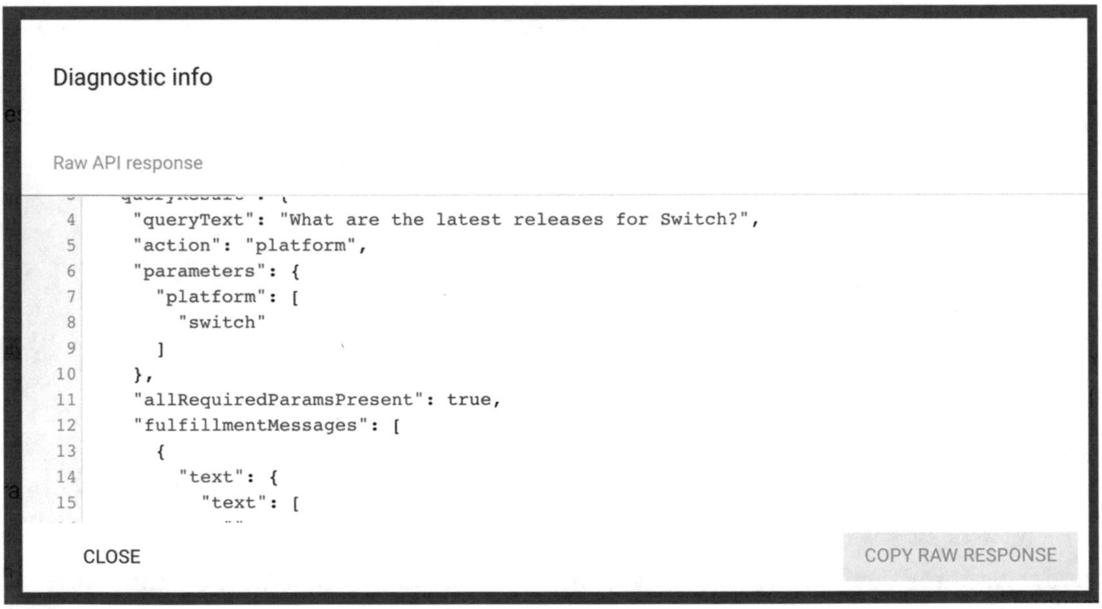

Figure 3-17. *A preview of the Diagnostic info ➤ API RAW response*

Summary

This chapter gave you all the information on the concepts of Dialogflow Essentials.

It addresses the following tasks:

- You want to add conversation parts to your Dialogflow agent to train the Dialogflow model by using intents.

- You want to create custom predefined variable objects (entities).

- You want to extract variable objects from a conversation by using predefined entities.

- You want to allow turn-taking and keep context in a conversation.

- You want to test to see if your Dialogflow agent is properly working.

In case you want to build this example, the source code for this book is available on GitHub via the book's product page, located at `www.apress.com/978-1-4842-7013-4`. Look into the _dialogflow-agent folder.

The intents that I have been using for the intent examples are

- Collect_Current_Playing_Game

- Collect_Fav_Game

- Collect_Fav_Multiplayer_Game

The intents that I have been using for the entity examples are

- Get_Release_Games

- Get_Favorite_FPS_Games

- Buy_Console

The intents that I have been using for the context examples are

- GetWalkthrough-Context-FollowUp

- MyFirstGame-SetContext

- MyFirstGame-Console-GetContext

Further Reading

- Dialogflow documentation on intents

  `https://cloud.google.com/dialogflow/es/docs/intents-overview`

- Dialogflow documentation on training phrases

  `https://cloud.google.com/dialogflow/es/docs/intents-training-phrases`

- Dialogflow documentation on events

  `https://cloud.google.com/dialogflow/es/docs/events-overview`

- Dialogflow documentation on custom events

  `https://cloud.google.com/dialogflow/es/docs/events-custom`

- Dialogflow documentation on slot filling

  `https://cloud.google.com/dialogflow/es/docs/fulfillment-webhook-slot-filling`

- Dialogflow documentation on entities

  `https://cloud.google.com/dialogflow/es/docs/entities-overview`

- Dialogflow documentation on custom entities

  `https://cloud.google.com/dialogflow/es/docs/entities-custom`

- Dialogflow documentation on system entities

  `https://cloud.google.com/dialogflow/es/docs/entities-system`

- Documentation on automated expansion

  `https://cloud.google.com/dialogflow/es/docs/entities-options#expansion`

- Documentation on composite entities

  `https://cloud.google.com/dialogflow/es/docs/entities-options#comp`

- Documentation on list entities

  `https://cloud.google.com/dialogflow/es/docs/intents-actions-parameters#lists`

- Documentation on regex entities

  `https://cloud.google.com/dialogflow/es/docs/entities-regexp`

- Syntax RE2 regular expressions

  https://github.com/google/re2/wiki/Syntax

- Dialogflow documentation on context

  https://cloud.google.com/dialogflow/es/docs/contexts-overview

- Dialogflow documentation on input and output contexts

  https://cloud.google.com/dialogflow/es/docs/contexts-input-output

- Dialogflow documentation on follow-up intents

  https://cloud.google.com/dialogflow/es/docs/contexts-follow-up-intents

  https://cloud.google.com/dialogflow/es/docs/reference/follow-up-intent-expressions

- SDK documentation on setting and getting contexts

  https://cloud.google.com/dialogflow/es/docs/reference/rpc/google.cloud.dialogflow.v2beta1#google.cloud.dialogflow.v2beta1.Contexts

CHAPTER 4

Building Chatbots with Templates

There are a few tools that can help to build an agent quickly; these are like template components. There are out-of-the-box agents that you can enable (prebuilt agents); there is the ability to enable small talk to allow a casual conversation. And it's possible to import FAQs from a (private) CSV or public website, with the knowledge base feature. This chapter will cover all of these.

Creating Prebuilt Agents

A **prebuilt agent** typically consists of example intents with parameters and entities configured. It will be configured for various languages, so that makes it very interesting. It won't contain fulfillment webhook logic since this requires a Cloud Function or a back-end. But it can be useful to quickly kickstart a project with some examples in various languages!

As you can see in Figure 4-1, when you click **Prebuilt Agents** in the Dialogflow ES menu, you will get an overview of all prebuilt agents. It's like a marketplace! There are over 40 prebuilt agents to choose from. There are prebuilt agents such as a Currency Converter, Banking, Food Delivery, Flights, and so on.

© Lee Boonstra 2021
L. Boonstra, *The Definitive Guide to Conversational AI with Dialogflow and Google Cloud*,
https://doi.org/10.1007/978-1-4842-7014-1_4

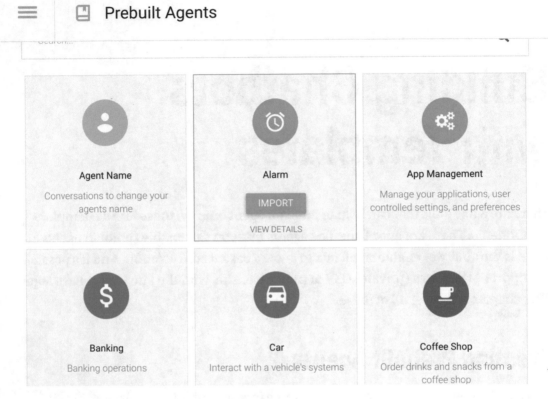

Figure 4-1. *An overview of all prebuilt agents*

When you click a prebuilt agent, you can request details, which will show up the sample intents within a pop-up screen (Figure 4-2).

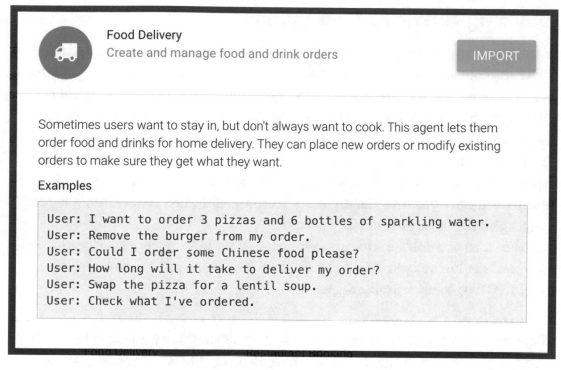

Figure 4-2. *An example of a prebuilt agent*

Hover over the prebuilt agent you want to use and click **Import**.

Choose to **create a new Dialogflow Project** and click **OK**.

Note   You can't add prebuilt agents to existing Dialogflow agents. If you want those intents, you could export/import the intents from the Settings screen.

Once an agent has been imported, you might need to go to the **Settings** screen **to add a service account to the project**. You will be prompted if this is required.

Once your agent is imported, you will have a new agent added to your Dialogflow projects, and you can refine and add new intents on top of what's already there.

Enabling Small Talk Modules

Small Talk is an excellent addition to your own intents, although they do work a little differently than manual intents. With intents, you can provide training phrases, which means you can train your chatbot to answer questions even when they are asked in a different way. Small Talk and FAQ Knowledge Base Connectors (see further in this chapter) don't provide you with the option to provide training phrases. It uses the Natural Language Understanding from Dialogflow to understand what was asked. Typically, this works fine; for example, the small talk sentence "You are funny" will also be answered when you say: "Haha, you are hilarious." But when you ask "Do you exist?", it won't give you the answer to "Are you real?".

Even when you don't provide answers on the Small Talk customization page, it will use out-of-the-box answers. Customization basically means you are overruling the standard Dialogflow small talk answers.

Caution   Although it's very nice to create a humanlike conversation in the chatbot additional to your own intents, you will have to be careful with specific small talk phrases, for example, confirmation phrases such as "Yes," "No," and "Cancel." These can answer like "Good!", but they don't execute code out of the box and don't keep the conversation going. They do set a POST action, such as smalltalk. confirmation.yes, so it's up to you to listen in your fulfillment code or webhook to these intents.

People often answer "Yes" or "No" to a question, while the answer didn't expect a Yes or No. A small talk answer is likely not what the user expects. In that case, it's very important that each intent that provides follow-up questions or contexts also provide a proper fallback.

At the time of writing this, small talk is only supported for English (en), Russian (ru), French (fr), and Italian (it), and it won't work for mega agents.

Note   Based on the **Actions on Google** policy, enabling Small Talk in its entirety will cause your action to be rejected.

To enable small talk for your Dialogflow agent, you can click the menu item: **Small Talk**. On the Small Talk settings page, you will find a switch to toggle the **Enable** switch. This will enable all the small talk topics.

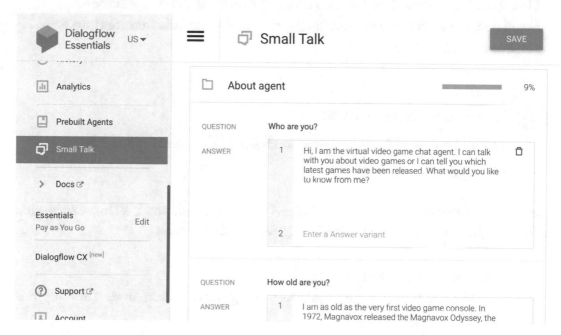

Figure 4-3. *Enabling the small talk module*

Click one of the topics you want to modify the response text for. For example, click **About agent**; this will unfold the **question** to be matched with a user utterance and the text response **answer** pairs. (See Figure 4-3.)

Click **Save**.

Creating an FAQ Knowledge Base

A **knowledge base** represents a collection of knowledge documents that you provide to Dialogflow ES. A knowledge document could be an FAQ or a text block.

Knowledge connectors complement defined intents. It is common for an agent using knowledge connectors also to use defined intents. Knowledge connectors offer less response precision and control than intents similar to Small Talk. It uses the Natural Language Understanding from Dialogflow to understand what was asked. Typically, this works fine, but sometimes, especially when you are asking questions in a very different way, it won't find the answer. You should define your intents to handle complex user requests and let knowledge connectors handle simple requests.

First, click the cogwheel next to the agent title to open the **Settings screen**.

Scroll down to **Beta Features** and flip the switch: **Enable beta features and APIs**. (See Figure 4-4.) Click **Save**.

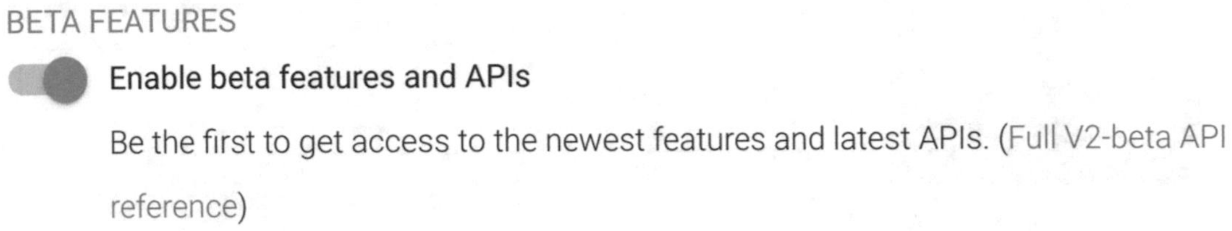

BETA FEATURES

 Enable beta features and APIs

Be the first to get access to the newest features and latest APIs. (Full V2-beta API

reference)

Figure 4-4. *In order to use the Knowledge Base Connector, you will have to enable the beta features and APIs from the Settings ➤ General screen*

Click the menu on **Knowledge**.

In the top bar, you can click the **Create Knowledge Base** button, to start adding your first knowledge base (Figure 4-5).

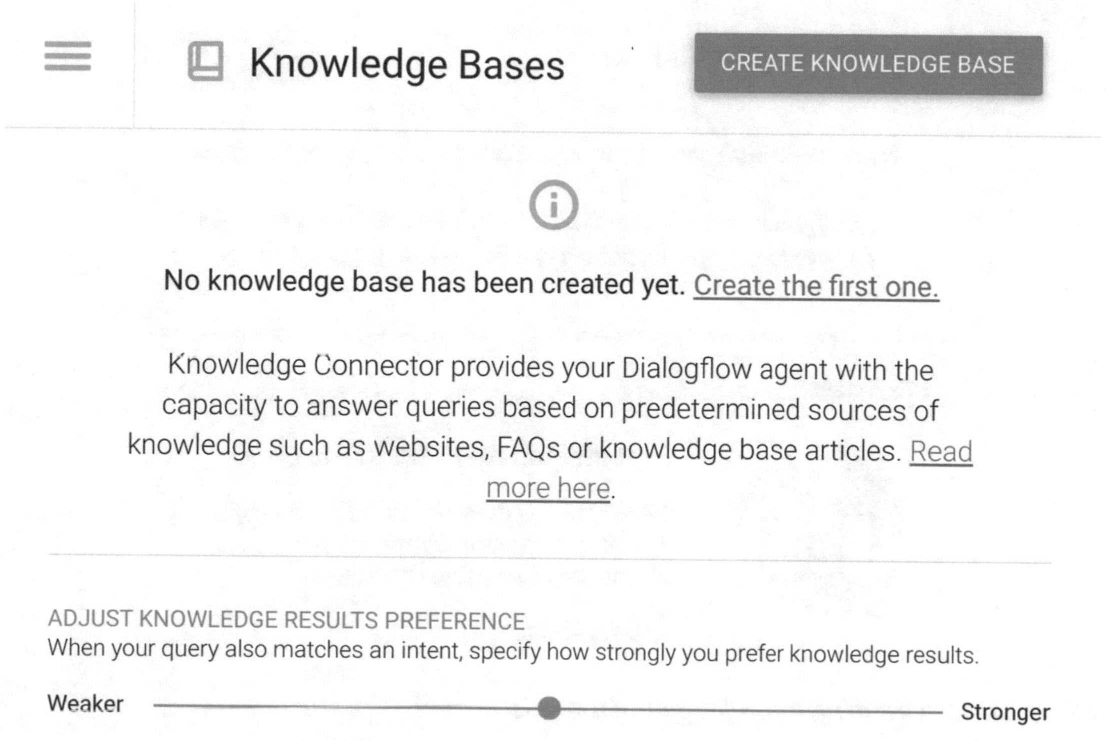

≡ | 📖 **Knowledge Bases**   CREATE KNOWLEDGE BASE

ⓘ

No knowledge base has been created yet. Create the first one.

Knowledge Connector provides your Dialogflow agent with the
capacity to answer queries based on predetermined sources of
knowledge such as websites, FAQs or knowledge base articles. Read
more here.

ADJUST KNOWLEDGE RESULTS PREFERENCE
When your query also matches an intent, specify how strongly you prefer knowledge results.

Weaker ──────────────────⬤───────────── Stronger

Figure 4-5. *Creating a knowledge base*

Give the knowledge base a name, for example, *Video Games FAQs*, and click **Save**.
A knowledge base can contain multiple documents. Click the link **Create the first
one** (Figure 4-6).

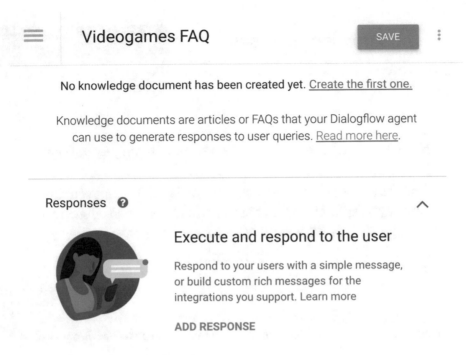

Figure 4-6.   *Creating knowledge documents*

In the pop-up screen (Figure 4-7), you can add the following information:

- You can give the document a name, for example, *Internal VideoGames FAQs* or *Public VideoGame FAQs from IGN.com*.

- You can select a knowledge type:

  - **FAQ**: A question with an answer

  - **Extensive Question Answering**: Let Dialogflow understand the question based on an article/text block

- Mime type

  - **text/html**: In case you want to import FAQs from a public website.

  - **text/csv (CSV files)**: This could be a database export.

- As a data source, you can choose between the following:

  - **File on Cloud Storage**: This is meant for private CSV files (secure) stored in Google Cloud Storage.

- **URL**: The URL to a public website to import FAQs from.

- **Upload file from a computer**: To upload a private CSV file from your disk.

- There's an **Enable Auto Reload** checkbox that allows Dialogflow to automatically reload the public website FAQs to ensure you are fetching FAQs that are new or changed.

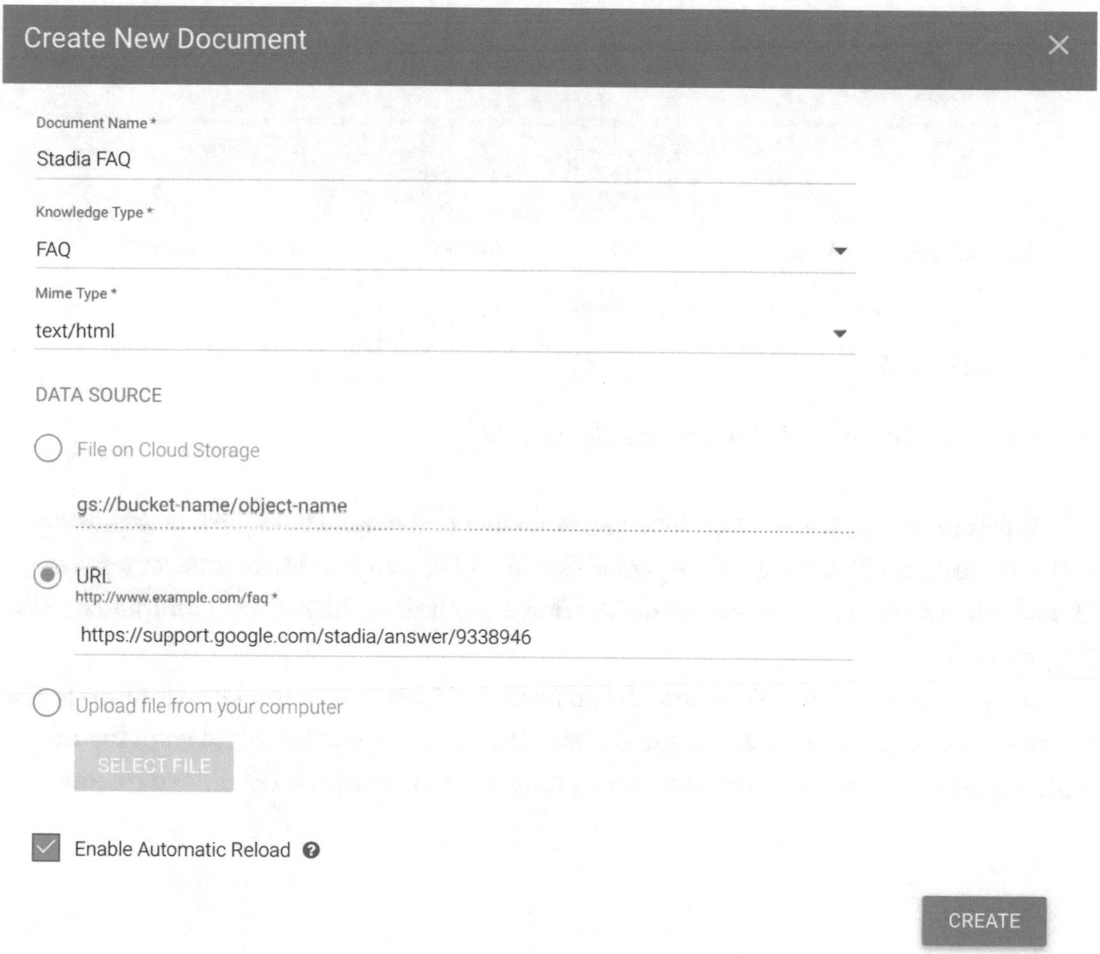

Create New Document   ✕

Document Name *

Stadia FAQ

Knowledge Type *

FAQ   ▼

Mime Type *

text/html   ▼

DATA SOURCE

◯ File on Cloud Storage

    gs://bucket-name/object-name

◉ URL
    http://www.example.com/faq *

    https://support.google.com/stadia/answer/9338946

◯ Upload file from your computer

    SELECT FILE

☑ Enable Automatic Reload ❷

                                                               CREATE

Figure 4-7.   *The document settings pop-up screen*

When you press the **Create** button, Dialogflow will start crawling/importing the Questions and Answer pairs. When it's done, you will see the document in the knowledge base documents overview. (See Figure 4-8.) In this view, it's possible to delete or add more documents.

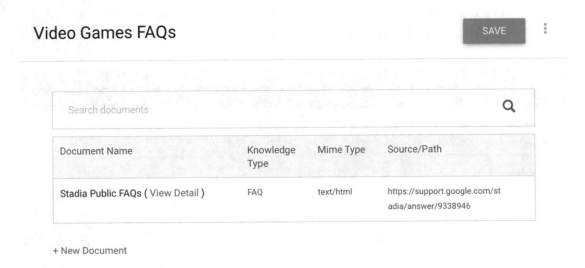

Figure 4-8. *Overview of knowledge documents*

At this moment, you are not done yet. You will need to tell Dialogflow what answer it should return. Click the **Add Response** link. It will already prefill an answer for you, `$Knowledge.Answer[1]`, which means the first answer with the highest confidence level (Figure 4-9).

But you might want to fine-tune the answers for different channel integrations (e.g., to return the response on the Google Assistant in a card). And you might want to end with a question to keep the conversation going/steer the conversation. Then hit **Save**.

Responses ❷   ⌃

DEFAULT   GOOGLE ASSISTANT   ✛

Text or SSML Response   🗑

| 1 | $Knowledge.Answer[1] |
| 2 | Enter a text or SSML response variant |

Text or SSML Response   🗑

| 1 | $Knowledge.Answer[2] |
| 2 | Enter a text or SSML response variant |

Text or SSML Response   🗑

| 1 | $Knowledge.Answer[3] |

Figure 4-9. *Fine-tune the knowledge base document responses*

By default, a knowledge base is configured with a default text response populated with the best matching knowledge answer: $Knowledge.Answer[1]. But knowledge responses may contain multiple answers, and you can reference these answers in your configured responses. The index for $Knowledge.Question and $Knowledge.Answer starts at *1*, so increase this index when adding more responses.

When defining responses, you should consider these points:

- If the number of defined responses is greater than the number N of knowledge connector response matches, only N responses will be returned.

- Given that the accuracy could be lower than matching explicitly defined intents, we recommend returning three or more responses to your users when possible.

Once you are ready with importing all the Questions and Answers, you can test the knowledge connector in the Dialogflow simulator (Figure 4-10).

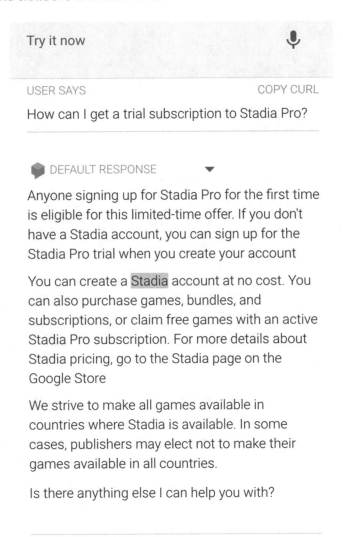

Figure 4-10. *Test the knowledge base in the simulator*

Dialogflow Trial and Enterprise Essentials allow a maximum of 10MB as total document size, 1000 requests per month and 100 requests per day.

When you choose the Dialogflow Enterprise Plus tier, this all will be unlimited.

Back on the knowledge base page (when you click **Knowledge** in the Dialogflow menu), you will notice an adjustment slider (Figure 4-11). When an end user expression also matches an intent, you can specify how strongly you prefer knowledge base results. Adjust the slider from weaker (preference given to intent) to stronger (preference given to knowledge).

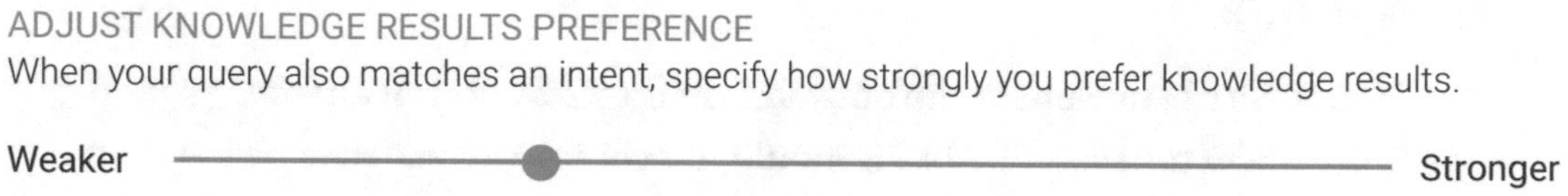

ADJUST KNOWLEDGE RESULTS PREFERENCE
When your query also matches an intent, specify how strongly you prefer knowledge results.

Weaker ——————————————●———————————————— Stronger

Figure 4-11. *Adjusting the weakness of the knowledge base*

Best Practices

For best results, here are a couple of best practices.

In general:

- CSV files must use commas as delimiters.

- The ML Settings Confidence score is not calibrated between FAQs and Knowledge Base Articles, so if you use both FAQs and Knowledge Base Articles, the best result may not always be the highest.

- Dialogflow removes HTML tags from content when creating responses. Because of this, it's best to avoid HTML tags and use plain text when possible.

- Google Assistant responses have a 640-character limit per chat bubble, so long answers are truncated when integrating with Google Assistant.

- The maximum document size is 50MB.

- When using Cloud Storage files, you should either use public URIs or private URIs that your user account or service account has access to.

Note   In the past, I have seen a few of my public knowledge base FAQs from (my own) web pages failing. By reverse-engineering the Google implementation, I've figured out that the public FAQ website will need to allow Google robots. You should add the public FAQ website to the Google Search engine via the Google Search Console, and have been crawled by the search indexer, so it exists in the search index. Therefore, websites like `https://pages.github.com` won't work.

Specific to FAQ:

- Your CSV file must have the questions in the first column and the answers in the second. Also, it should not contain a header.

- Use CSV whenever possible, because CSV is parsed most accurately.

- Public HTML content with a single QA pair is not supported.

- The number of QA pairs in one document should not exceed 2000.

- Duplicate questions with different answers are not supported.

- If possible, use valid HTML5 markup for Q&As and base it on the FAQPage schema.org notation.

Specific to Extractive QA:

- Content with dense text works best. Avoid content with many single sentence paragraphs.

- Tables and lists are not supported.

- The number of paragraphs in one document should not exceed 2000.

- If an article is long (> 1000 words), try to break it down into multiple, smaller articles. If the article covers multiple issues, it can be broken into shorter articles covering the individual issues. If the article only covers one issue, then focus the article on the issue description and keep the issue resolution short.

- Ideally, only the core content of an article should be provided (issue description and resolution). Additional content like author name, modification history, related links, and ads are not important.

Note   Extractive QA is, at the time of writing, experimental. It is based on similar technologies that have been tried and tested at Google in products like Search and Assistant.

Convert Knowledge Base Questions to Intents

It is possible to convert a knowledge base question to an intent, allowing you to provide more training phrases. When you click the **View Detail** link in the knowledge base document overview, you will see all the Questions and Answers which are imported.

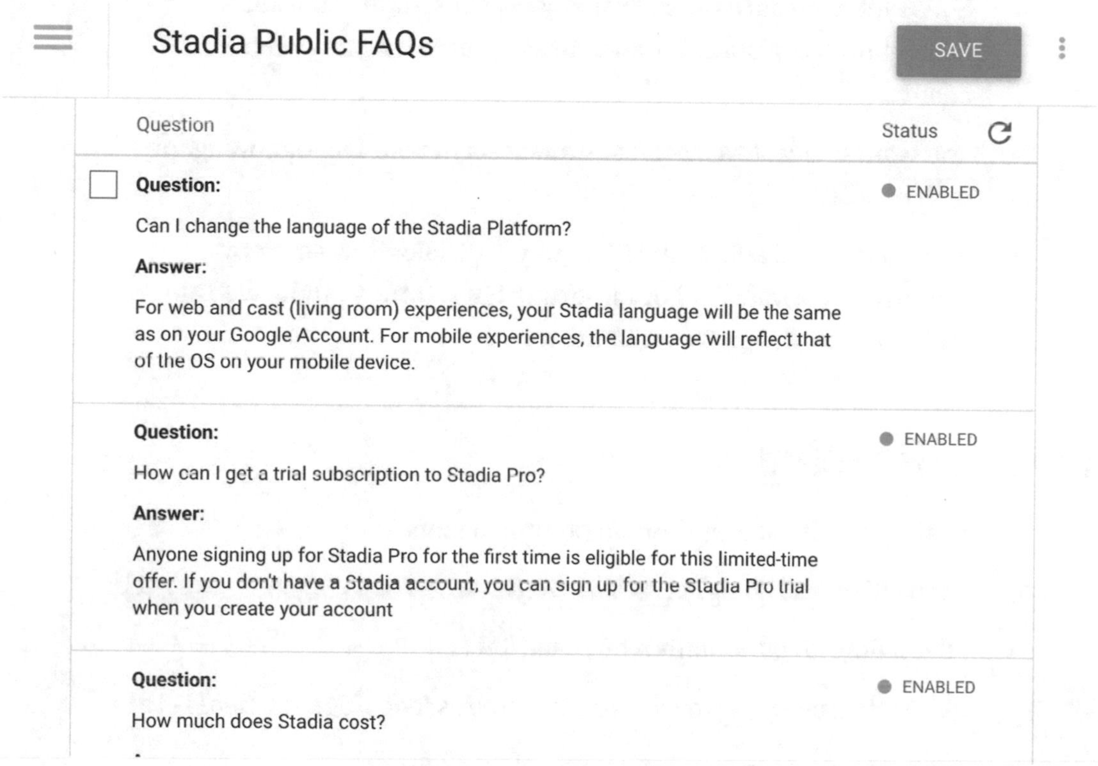

| ☰   Stadia Public FAQs | SAVE | ⋮ |

Question	Status	⟳
☐ **Question:** Can I change the language of the Stadia Platform? **Answer:** For web and cast (living room) experiences, your Stadia language will be the same as on your Google Account. For mobile experiences, the language will reflect that of the OS on your mobile device.	● ENABLED	
Question: How can I get a trial subscription to Stadia Pro? **Answer:** Anyone signing up for Stadia Pro for the first time is eligible for this limited-time offer. If you don't have a Stadia account, you can sign up for the Stadia Pro trial when you create your account	● ENABLED	
Question: How much does Stadia cost?	● ENABLED	

Figure 4-12. *Overview of all the imported FAQs*

From this screen, you can disable individual questions. It's also possible to manually reload the questions and answers. It's also the place where you can select an individual question and convert it to a real intent. (See Figure 4-12.)

Summary

This chapter gave you all the information on building Dialogflow agents from templates and knowledge bases to build a Dialogflow agent without creating intents quickly. This chapter addresses the following tasks:

- You want to create a quick Dialogflow agent imported from a Dialogflow template solution to use as a base by using prebuilt agents.

- You want to enable a casual conversation in your Dialogflow agent with small talk.

- You want to add additional FAQs to your Dialogflow agent by importing a private CSV or importing FAQs from a public website with the Knowledge Base Connector.

Further Reading

- Dialogflow documentation on prebuilt agents

  `https://cloud.google.com/dialogflow/es/docs/agents-prebuilt`

- Dialogflow documentation on Small Talk

  `https://cloud.google.com/dialogflow/es/docs/agents-small-talk`

- Dialogflow documentation on knowledge bases

  `https://cloud.google.com/dialogflow/es/docs/how/knowledge-bases`

- Google Webmasters Tool

  `https://www.google.com/intl/en/webmasters`

CHAPTER 5

Bot Management

Dialogflow not only provides great tools for writing conversations and **bot building** but it also provides features for bot management. **Agent Validation** and **Agent Training** are such features. It makes life much easier for conversational designers who are building complex bots in an enterprise environment.

Agent Validation reviews your agent out of the box, and with Agent Training your agent can learn new knowledge during conversations. Although the intent training is fixed beforehand, you can influence the intent classification score by up- and downvoting or reassigning intents to previously captured user utterances.

This chapter will show you how to enable validation and understand the validation results and how to influence your bot model based on user data.

Agent Validation

When you build a chatbot that becomes a little bit more advanced, you will easily end up with lots of intents and entities. Maybe, you are even working with a team within your Dialogflow project—various UX designers working on multiple intents. Where people work, mistakes are made. This can become a problem when you are training your Dialogflow model.

Common mistakes that can be made in Dialogflow are

- No or not enough training phrases in an intent.

- The intent has training phrases that are too similar to each other or other intents' training phrases.

- Variations of entities are not used enough in training phrases.

- Text is annotated within some training phrases but not in others.

- No negative examples for the fallback intents.

© Lee Boonstra 2021
L. Boonstra, *The Definitive Guide to Conversational AI with Dialogflow and Google Cloud*,
https://doi.org/10.1007/978-1-4842-7014-1_5

What's good to know is that Dialogflow has an automatic validation feature built in the Dialogflow console and API, which can validate on those common mistakes. The results are available whenever the agent training is completed.

Click the menu on **Validation**. The agent validation feature is, by default, enabled. Should you not find it, you can enable the Agent Validation toggle setting in the **Settings ➤ ML Settings** tab.

Once you click Validation in the Dialogflow menu (and the agent has been trained), you will see the results of the validation (as shown in Figure 5-1).

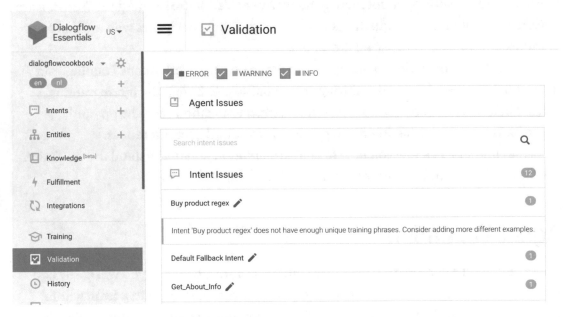

Figure 5-1. *Out-of-the-box validation*

Understanding Validation Results

The validation results are available automatically whenever agent training is performed and completed. You can access the results of the validation from either the Dialogflow Console or the API.

The validation results provide a list of warnings and errors that you should correct to improve your agent's quality and performance. It can find issues on the (global) agent level, in intents, or entities. If your agent has info or warnings, you can choose to ignore them and launch your agent.

It's for informational purposes only, but you would rob yourself of agent quality by not using this feature; basically, this is a Dialogflow Agent Review out of the box, for free!

Issues can represent various levels of severity. Only **Info**, **Warning**, and **Error** messages are shown on the Validation screen. The settings **Critical** and **Unspecified** are available in the SDK (or on the specific intent/entity pages). They are all described in Table 5-1.

Table 5-1. *The various severity levels*

Level	Description
INFO	The agent doesn't follow the best practice.
WARNING	The agent might not behave as expected.
ERROR	The agent may experience partial failures.
CRITICAL	The agent may completely fail.
SEVERITY UNSPECIFIED	Not specified. This value should never be used.

Figure 5-2 shows some validation examples.

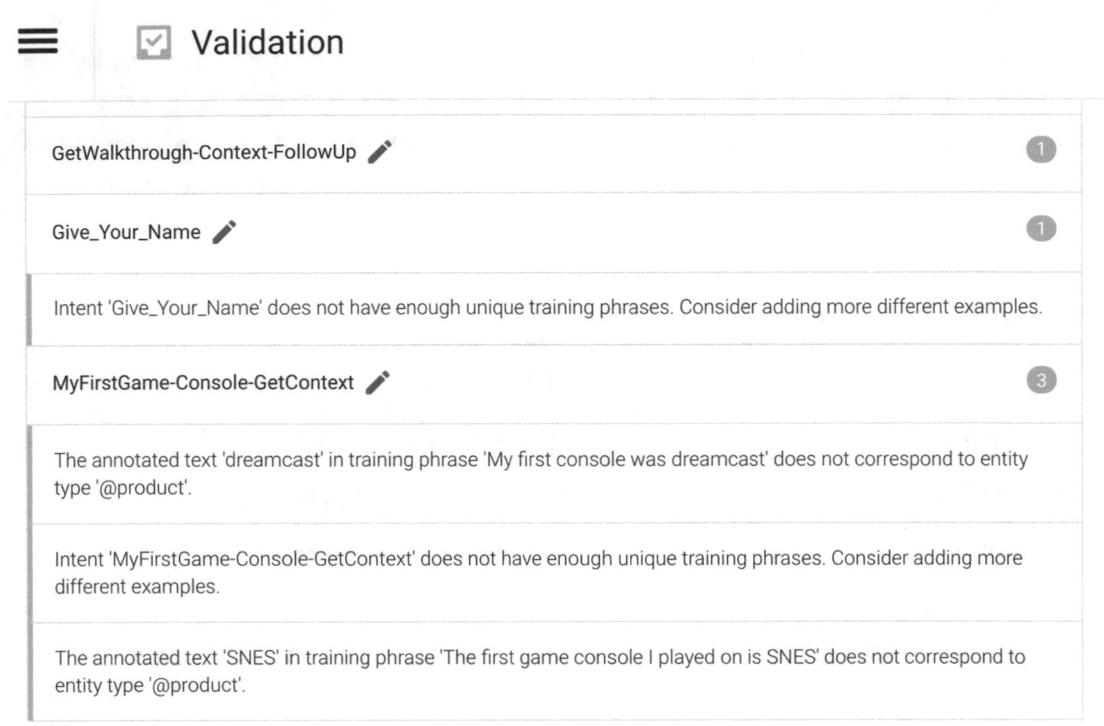

Figure 5-2. *Validation examples*

In this example, I am highlighting the following criteria:

- The *Give_Your_Name* intent shows a warning that I will need to add more training phrases with diverse examples to improve the NLU model.

- The *MyFirstGame-Console-GetContext* contains an entity, **Dreamcast**, and **SNES**, which hasn't been defined in the *@product* custom entity. Besides this, it also needs more training phrases.

The previous examples were examples of warnings, which you could ignore. But when you have errors, it's better to fix these right away.

Note   At most, 5000 issues are shown at a time. If you have over 5000 problems, you may not see a count reduction until less than 5000 remain.

Besides the validation screen, when you visit either the intents list or the entities list pages, any intents or entities with validation errors show an error outline indicator (a ! icon) next to the name.

When you visit a page for a specific intent or entity with validation errors, an error outline indicator is shown near the Save button.

Clicking this indicator shows a list of errors for the intent or entity. By default, only errors with a severity of **CRITICAL** or **ERROR** are shown.

Validation via the SDK

It's also possible to run the validation from your code through the SDK (ValidationResult). This might be handy if you are building your own CI/CD pipelines, and before bringing your agent to production, you might want to run the agent validation first.

Here's an example of how you could implement this for Node.js.

The ValidationResult response could look like Listing 5-1.

Listing 5-1. The implementation of a Cloud Function

```
{
"validationErrors": [
{
"severity": "ERROR",
   "entries": [
       "projects/my-project/agent/intents/58b44b2d-4967-
       4a81-b017-   12623dcd5d28/parameters/bf6fdf55-b862-4101-b5b1-
       36f1423629d0"
   ],
"errorMessage": "Parameter 'test' has an empty value."
},
{
"severity": "WARNING",
   "entries": [
       "projects/my-project/agent/intents/271e3808-3c91-4e6b-89e8-
       47951abcec8d"
   ],
```

```
"errorMessage": "Intent 'app.current.update' does not have enough unique
training phrases. Consider adding more different examples."
},
{
"severity": "ERROR",
   "entries": [
       "projects/my-project/agent/intents/26e64b1b-eaa7-4ce2-be46-
       631a501fccbe/trainingPhrases/a650375e-083c-4bb5-9794-ba9453e51282",
       "projects/my-project/agent/intents/58b44b2d-4967-4a81-b017-
       12623dcd5d28/trainingPhrases/1d947780-22d3-4f80-8d7a-3f86efbf0be3"
],
"errorMessage": "Multiple intents share training phrases which are too
similar:\n - Intent 'app.notifications.open': training phrase 'open all
notifications settings'\n - Intent 'app.current.notifications.open':
training phrase 'open notifications settings'"
}
]}
```

As you have seen, Dialogflow provides an out-of-the-box agent review and validation feature. It's enabled by default, and you can access it via the Dialogflow console or through the API.

This will give you an overview of errors and warnings, which you should fix to improve your agent quality.

When a large number of issues are found, you should consider fixing the issues in small batches, based on similarity. It might be that fixing one issue may solve similar issues after you retrain the agent. So, now you know. Before bringing your chatbots to production, always check the validation page!

Improve the Dialogflow Machine Learning Model with Built-in Training

Dialogflow has a training tool, which you can use to improve your Dialogflow machine learning model. You can up- and downvote or change the matched intent. Dialogflow matches based on the data it has seen before, so it knows how to handle the conversation better next time.

Select the **Training** menu item in the Dialogflow menu.

When you open the tool (see Figure 5-3), it shows the conversation history in reverse chronological order (latest utterance first).

It will showcase the user utterance, the number of requests (conversational turns in the conversation), the number of times for which no match was found, the date when the conversation happened, and a refresh button (you will use this when you overrule the training processes for content like this).

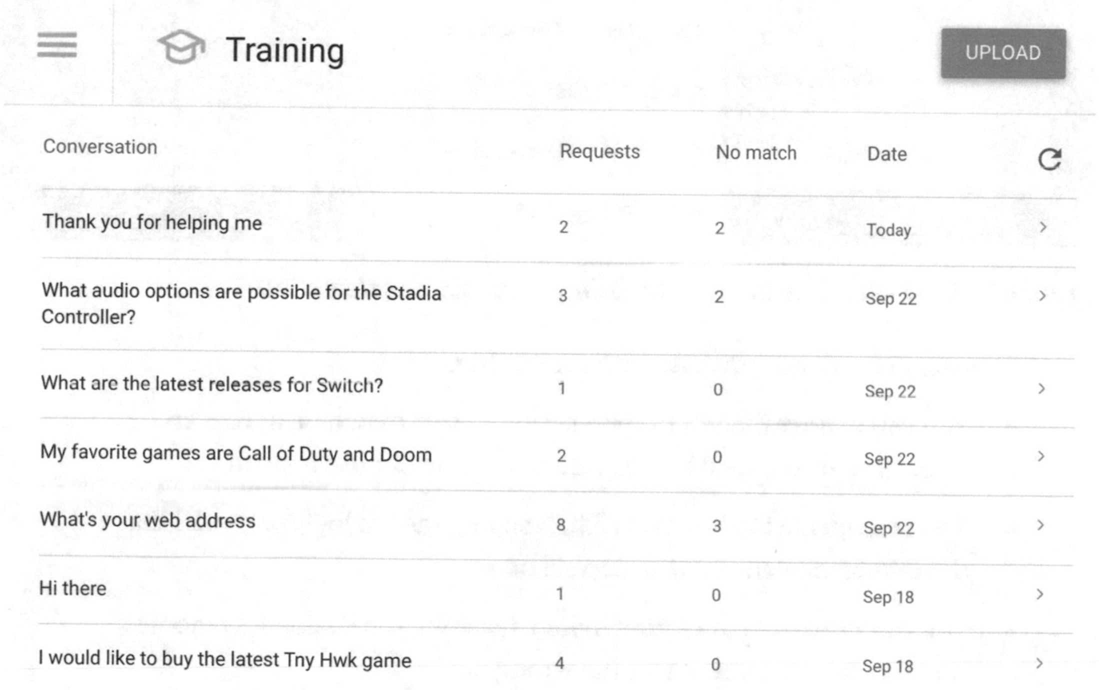

☰ 🎓 Training				UPLOAD
Conversation	Requests	No match	Date	↻
Thank you for helping me	2	2	Today	>
What audio options are possible for the Stadia Controller?	3	2	Sep 22	>
What are the latest releases for Switch?	1	0	Sep 22	>
My favorite games are Call of Duty and Doom	2	0	Sep 22	>
What's your web address	8	3	Sep 22	>
Hi there	1	0	Sep 18	>
I would like to buy the latest Tny Hwk game	4	0	Sep 18	>

Figure 5-3. *Dialogflow built-in training*

When you click a row in the conversation list, it opens the conversation in a training view as seen in Figure 5-4. The training view shows a list of conversational turns and provides controls to add this data to your training data.

Figure 5-4. *Dialogflow built-in training, improve the detection*

This is the place where you can do the following:

- You can change the intent (or if no intent was matched, assign an intent), so next time it knows which intent to choose instead.

- You can upvote the intent match, teaching the Dialogflow model that the detected intent was the correct one.

- You can downvote the intent match, teaching the Dialogflow model that the detected intent was the wrong one.

- You can remove the data. Maybe because it was bogus data, and you don't want to train your model with it.

- You can select the user utterance and annotate certain words, for example, when you have a user utterance: *I want to order the latest Star Wars Battlefront game.* You could select the name *Star Wars Battlefront* and teach Dialogflow that it's actually the entity *@fps_ games*.

You can use the training tool during agent development before your agent is released or made changes. It's also great to use the tool after production to examine if real conversations are behaving as expected.

With the upload button in the top-right corner of the screen, you can upload conversations as plain text files. One .txt file should have every user utterance phrase per line (delimited by newlines). It's possible to upload multiple (up to 10) .txt files, or you can upload a zip archive with .txt files, as long as it doesn't exceed 3MB.

Requests are not sent to the detect intent API. Therefore, no contexts are activated, and no intents are matched. Ideally, files should only include data that is useful as training phrases. The order of the end user expressions is not important.

What kind of data should you upload? Think of conversation logs; maybe you have human-to-human chat logs or online customer support conversations with questions from an email, forum, or FAQ, basically everything relevant for the chatbot. Maybe you are tracking social media, such as Twitter, to see what people are asking. Or maybe you have contact center audio recordings, which you can convert to text via the Speech-to-Text API in Google Cloud. However, try to avoid long-form, nonconversational user utterances. And try to avoid things that haven't been said by end users (e.g., responses of human agents).

Note   The training tool uses agent history data to load conversations, so logging must be enabled in the settings panel. This is enabled by default, but working with regulated companies such as banks and insurances in Europe might want to disable this feature.

The training tool only shows end user expressions. To view both agent and end user conversation data, see the more complete agent history.

Summary

This chapter explains how you can review your Dialogflow ES agent configuration (such as intents and entities) by validating your agent. With this out-of-the-box feature, you can monitor your agent quality. We have also looked into how you can run validation via the SDK; this might be handy, in case you are building your own CI/CD pipelines.

The last section of this chapter explains how your Dialogflow agent can continually learn from user data and how you can improve the underlying machine learning model. The training tool is used to review conversations your agent has had with end users and to improve your training data.

Further Reading

- Dialogflow documentation on Agent Validation

  ```
  https://cloud.google.com/dialogflow/es/docs/
  agents-validation
  ```

- Dialogflow documentation on best design practices

  ```
  https://cloud.google.com/dialogflow/es/docs/agents-design
  ```

- Validation result object in the SDK

  ```
  https://cloud.google.com/dialogflow/docs/reference/rpc/
  google.cloud.dialogflow.v2beta1#google.cloud.dialogflow.
  v2beta1.ValidationResult
  ```

- Dialogflow training tool

  ```
  https://cloud.google.com/dialogflow/es/docs/training
  ```

CHAPTER 6

Deploying Your Chatbot to Web and Social Media Channels

There are lots of out-of-the-box integrations available in Dialogflow ES. You can enable these to bring your agents to (multiple) channels. This chapter will highlight the following (text-based) integrations.

The **Dialogflow Hangouts integration** lets you create text chatbots you can include in Google Chat (formerly known as Google Hangouts), for one-on-one chats as well as chatbots in chat rooms. This integration is only available to Google Workspace (formerly known as G Suite) users, and a Google Workspace admin must allow users to install bots from the Google Workspace admin panel (https://admin.google.com/).

The **web demo implementation** is a simple web implementation that allows you to use the chat via your keyboard and even via a browser microphone. It's a quick and easy way to implement a chatbot on your website, or you could include static HTML websites or site generators (such as Google Sites). However, this solution doesn't allow you to change the look and feel of the chatbot. It also won't respond with custom rich messages such as Google Maps, hyperlinks, or rich cards. If that's what you want, you are better off by implementing the Dialogflow Messenger widget (see the last section of this chapter). If you are a developer or have a developer in your team, implement an advanced web chat on your site (see Chapter 11).

The **Dialogflow Messenger** integration provides a customizable chat dialog for your agent that could be embedded in your website via a web component. The chat dialog is implemented as a dialog window that can be opened and closed by your end user. When opened, the chat dialog appears above your content on the lower-right side of the screen.

© Lee Boonstra 2021
L. Boonstra, *The Definitive Guide to Conversational AI with Dialogflow and Google Cloud*,
https://doi.org/10.1007/978-1-4842-7014-1_6

Integrating Your Agent with Google Chat

Google Chat is Google's communication software, part of Google Workspace, built for teams. It's similar to Slack along with group messaging functions that allows Google Drive content sharing.

In the Dialogflow console, click the menu on **Integrations**.

Click the integration: **Hangouts Chat**.

Select **everyone in your domain** to ensure everyone within your Google Workspace domain can access the chatbot. (Optionally, select the agent environment.) Click **Start**.

Next, click the **Configure Bot Details** button; it will navigate to the Google Cloud Console (`https://console.cloud.google.com`) as seen in Figure 6-1. (Make sure you are logged in with the same Gmail/Google account as with Dialogflow.)

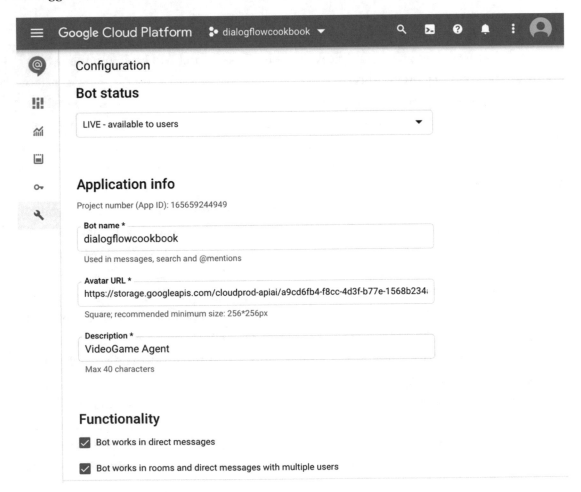

Figure 6-1. *Google Chat/Hangouts API settings*

If correct, everything is filled in already, but you could change the fields. Table 6-1 shows an overview of all the settings.

Table 6-1. *Google Chat settings*

Setting	Description
Bot name	The name that your users will see when interacting with the chatbot.
Avatar URL	An HTTPS URL pointing to a square image (PNG or JPEG), at least 128x128, which will appear as the avatar for your chatbot.
Description	A description of the chatbot's functionality.
Functionality	The way how you want to interact with the chatbot: — Add to the room — Message: Direct messaging the chatbot
Connection Settings	The endpoint for the chatbot. Since we are using Dialogflow, select **Dialogflow**.
Permissions	Permissions who can install your chatbot; everyone in your domain or specific people/groups within your domain.

Click **Save**. You can close the Google Cloud Console.

Enabling Your Agent in the Google Chat

From the chat interface (`https://chat.google.com`), you can click the + button next to the Bots header to add bots to your conversation. See Figure 6-2.

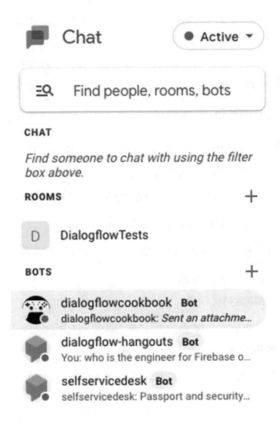

Figure 6-2. *Adding bots in Google Chat*

You will see a catalog as seen in Figure 6-3, and from there, you can search for the Dialogflow chatbot you have created. The **Add** button will show a small pop-up to choose an interaction style. You can add the chatbot to the room with **Add to room** or you can choose **Message**.

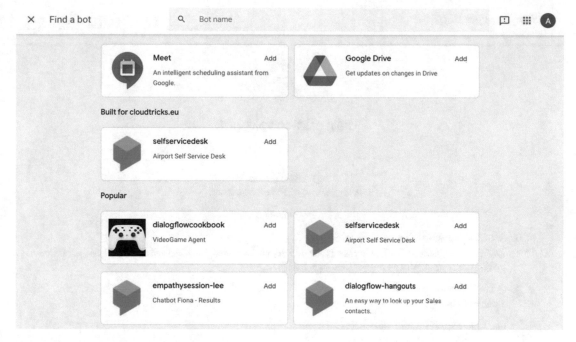

Figure 6-3. *Google Chatbot catalog*

A *bot as a message* means that you are talking directly to the bot; there is no chat room required. Add the bot as a message, and notice in Figure 6-4, when double-clicking the bot name which is presented in the left menu, you will start a conversation.

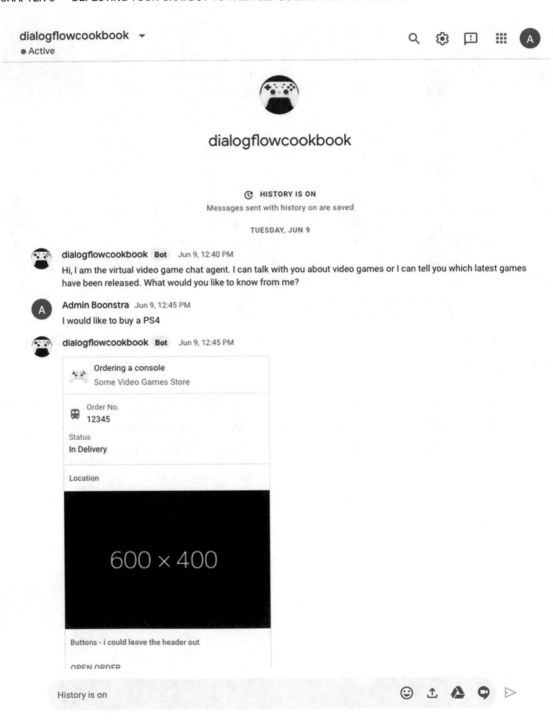

Figure 6-4. *With the message interaction, you don't need a chat room; you can directly talk to the bot*

When you add the *bot to the room*, you can talk to every user in the chat room, but when you dedicate the message to the bot, you will use the @ notation, such as *@dialogflowcookbook*. See Figure 6-5.

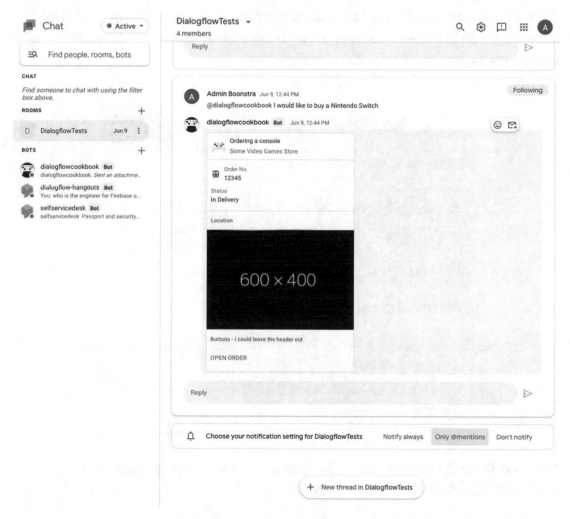

Figure 6-5. *Talking to a bot in a Google Chat room by using the @ notation*

Rich Messages Support

To send Google Chat messages other than text responses, you can use a *custom payload* from the **Hangouts Responses tab** in the Dialogflow console for a particular intent. You will first need to add Hangouts as an integration response, which you can do by hitting the + tab in the responses section of an intent, and then you can click the **Add Responses** button, which you can see in Figure 6-6.

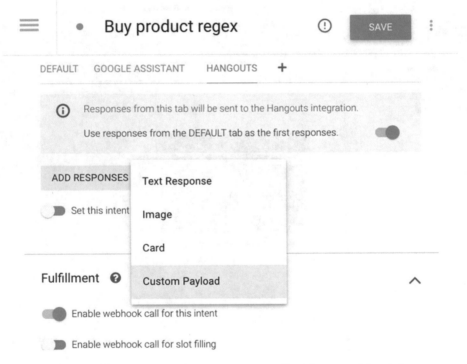

Figure 6-6. *Select Add Responses ➤ Custom Payload to enable rich messages in the Hangouts integration tab of an intent*

Hangouts Custom Payload allows you to create more advanced message types, such as cards. One card can have one or many sections. Each section could have a header. You can look into the **Hangouts message formats cards reference guide** from the Google Chat documentation to see some of the combinations you can create with this. However, using custom payloads means that you will have to provide the JSON format. You can find an example in Listing 6-1.

Listing 6-1. Google Chat custom payload

```
{
  "hangouts": {
    "header": {
      "title": "Ordering a console",
      "subtitle": "Some Video Games Store",
      "imageUrl": "https://lh3.googleusercontent.com/v8c6Jn1Aa7s6YO-5Qy6hM4
      yQ5K4onxgjYDOfzxpOKA7m1Z_OrqOJcXuncd17_W7CeqOcL6d6RfTAAUr10uHl8uk=rw"
    },
    "sections": [{
      "widgets": [{
        "keyValue": {
          "icon": "TRAIN",
          "topLabel": "Order No.",
          "content": "12345"
        }
      },
      {
        "keyValue": {
          "topLabel": "Status",
          "content": "In Delivery"
        }
      }]
    },
    {
      "header": "Location",
      "widgets": [{
        "image": {
          "imageUrl": "https://dummyimage.com/600x400/000/fff"
        }
      }]
    },
    {
      "header": "Buttons - i could leave the header out",
      "widgets": [{
```

```
    "buttons": [{
      "textButton": {
        "text": "OPEN ORDER",
        "onClick": {
          "openLink": {
            "url": "https://example.com/orders/..."
          }
        }
      }
    }]
  }]
}]
  }
}
```

Note   When you copy and paste the examples of the reference guide to the custom payload box in Dialogflow, you will need to be aware of the following:

- The first key can't be called `cards`, but it has to be named hangouts.

- The `hangouts` key points to an object, not an array (of cards).

- Make sure the editor doesn't contain any linting errors.

- And you can't test the results in the Dialogflow simulator; you will have to test it directly in Hangouts Chat.

More Text-Based/Open Source Integration Options

Dialogflow also supports integrations with **Slack**, **Telegram**, **Line**, **Facebook Messenger**, **Facebook Workplace**, **Kik**, **Skype**, **Twitter**, **Viber**, **Spark**, and **Twilio**. For what's worth, the integration with Slack is somewhat similar to Google Chat as the applications are quite similar.

In Figure 6-7, you will see an overview of all the text-based/open source integrations. Google has been adding new integrations all the time.

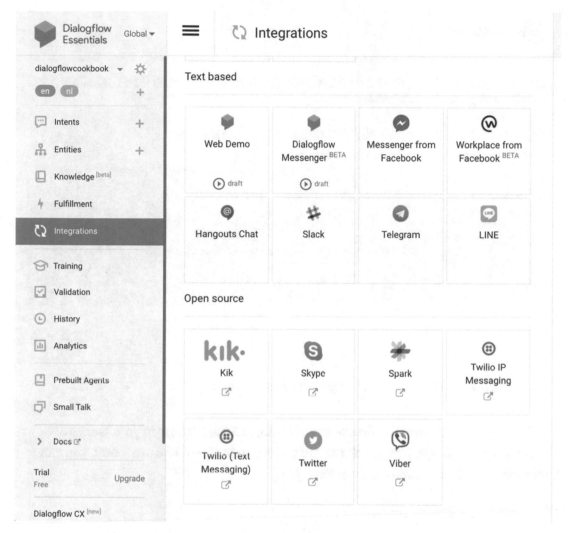

Figure 6-7. *Overview of text-based integrations*

Integrating Your Agent with a Web Demo

The Dialogflow Web Demo is a simple widget you can place in your website, which connects to your Dialogflow agent. It can make use of text and microphone streams. The look and feel of this component is fixed, and therefore this component is often used for testing purposes rather than implementing it in (enterprise) websites or web apps.

In the Dialogflow console, click the menu on **Integrations**.

Click the integration: **Web Demo**.

This will show a pop-up; see Figure 6-8.

Web Demo

Test the agent on its own page. Share the link to the page or embed the ` widget in other websites to get more conversations going. More in documentation.

https://bot.dialogflow.com/0892aa5c-b1d4-43de-be6f-9ca29b5c151b ✏

Add this agent to your website by copying the code below:

```
<iframe
    allow="microphone;"
    width="350"
    height="430"
    src="https://console.dialogflow.com/api-client/demo/embedded/0892aa5c-b1d4-43de-be
6f-9ca29b5c151b">
</iframe>
```

CLOSE   DISABLE

Figure 6-8. *Web Demo iframe implementation to copy*

The pop-up will show the iframe code (Listing 6-2) to include in your website. You can click the link to test the chatbot in the browser. When you are ready, you can implement the iframe code on a website.

Listing 6-2. Iframe example

```
<iframe
    allow="microphone;"
    width="350"
    height="430"
    src="https://console.dialogflow.com/api-client/demo/embedded/b2797be1-
    6a81-4897-918f-1d8b286dab15">
</iframe>
```

Typically, web developers put this in a website pop-up which can be opened from a button on the bottom of a website. Figure 6-9 shows how the chatbot on your website looks like.

Figure 6-9. *Web Demo example*

You can customize the top logo and the description underneath the name of your Dialogflow agent from the Dialogflow **settings** screen. Here (see Figure 6-10) you can upload an avatar or change the description of your agent.

General   Languages   ML Settings   Export and Import   Environments   Speech   Share

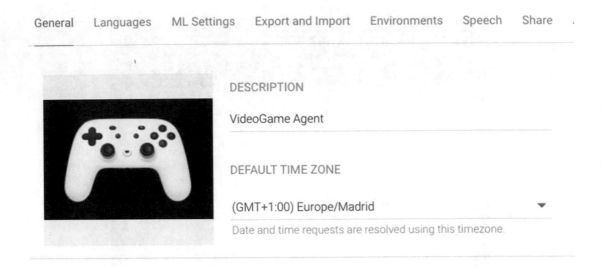

Figure 6-10. *The Web Demo component uses a few configuration settings*

Integrating Your Agent with a Dialogflow Messenger

The Dialogflow Messenger integration is a more advanced widget you can place in your website, which connects to your Dialogflow agent. It only works for text chats. The look and feel of this component is customizable, although some enterprises prefer to build their web integration themselves (e.g., so they can connect to more systems), many businesses like the Dialogflow Messenger component as it's an easy and fast way to integrate with your website or web app.

In the Dialogflow console, click the menu on **Integrations**.

Click the integration: **Dialogflow Messenger**.

A pop-up will appear (Figure 6-11), which will show a (JavaScript) code snippet, which you can copy and paste into your website.

Dialogflow Messenger

Dialogflow Messenger brings a rich UI for Dialogflow that enables developers to easily add conversational agents to websites. More in documentation.

> ⓘ End-user interactions with the Dialogflow Messenger widget may be billed to your GCP account, depending on your Dialogflow edition.

Add this agent to your website by copying the code below

```
<script src="https://www.gstatic.com/dialogflow-console/fast/messenger/bootstrap.js?v
=1"></script>
<df-messenger
  chat-icon="https:&#x2F;&#x2F;storage.googleapis.com&#x2F;cloudprod-apiai&#x2F;a9cd6
fb4-f8cc-4d3f-b77e-1568b234ad99_x.png"
  intent="WELCOME"
  chat-title="dialogflowcookbook"
  agent-id="0892aa5c-b1d4-43de-be6f-9ca29b5c151b"
  language-code="en"
></df-messenger>
```

Active environment: Draft ❷

CLOSE   DISABLE   TRY IT NOW

Figure 6-11. *Dialogflow Messenger implementation*

When you click the **Try it now** button in the pop-up, you will see how the implementation looks like. It will show a pop-up button on the bottom of the screen (Figure 6-12, with the avatar that has been set in the Settings of Dialogflow).

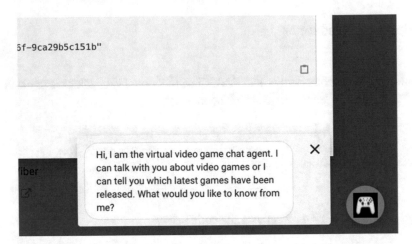

Figure 6-12. *Dialogflow Messenger pop-up button*

This button will open a chat pop-up (Figure 6-13), which actually is a web component (df-messenger).

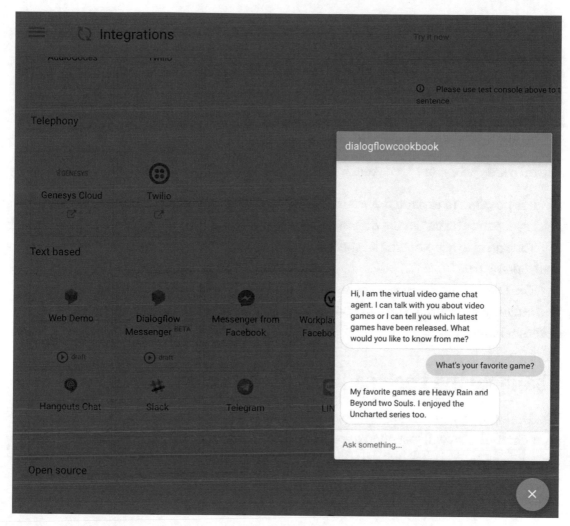

Figure 6-13. *Dialogflow Messenger web component*

Listing 6-3 shows the JavaScript code which can be implemented on your website. Paste the embed code you copied earlier in a web page on your website. The <script> and <df-messenger> HTML elements should be in the <body> element of your web page.

Listing 6-3. Dialogflow Messenger implementation example, web component

```
<script src="https://www.gstatic.com/dialogflow-console/fast/messenger/
bootstrap.js?v=1"></script>
 <df-messenger
 chat-icon="a9cd6fb4-f8cc-4d3f-b77e-1568b234ad99_x.png"
```

```
intent="WELCOME"
chat-title="Dialogflow Cookbook - Videogames"
agent-id="0892aa5c-b1d4-43de-be6f-9ca29b5c151b"
language-code="en"
></df-messenger>
```

To allow for responsive layouts, also add the following to your page:

```
<meta name="viewport" content="width-device-width, initial-scale=1">
```

It is possible to expand the web component without clicking the button with the setting expand="true" in the df-messenger component.

You can also keep the initial speech bubble closed when you load a web page, with wait-open="true".

The Dialogflow Messenger component won't support voice. Also, it can only support one language. However, you can use a *mega agent* and create multiple sub-agents in different languages.

Changing the Look and Feel of the Chatbot Component

The Dialogflow web component provides a wide range of settings to override styles in your chatbot. You will just need to add a style tag above the <df-messenger> component, and you can include the CSS variables of choice, as shown in Listing 6-4.

Listing 6-4. Dialogflow Messenger styles of the web component

```
<style>
    df-messenger {
        --df-messenger-bot-message: #282828;
        --df-messenger-button-titlebar-color: #ff9000;
        --df-messenger-button-titlebar-font-color: #ffffff;
        --df-messenger-chat-background-color: #121212;
        --df-messenger-font-color: white;
        --df-messenger-send-icon: #878fac;
        --df-messenger-user-message: #535353;
        --df-messenger-input-font-color: #000;
```

```
        --df-messenger-input-placeholder-font-color: #cccccc;
        --df-minimized-chat-close-icon-color: #ff9000;
    }
</style>
```

Figure 6-14 shows how these style settings will look like once the chatbot is rendered in the browser.

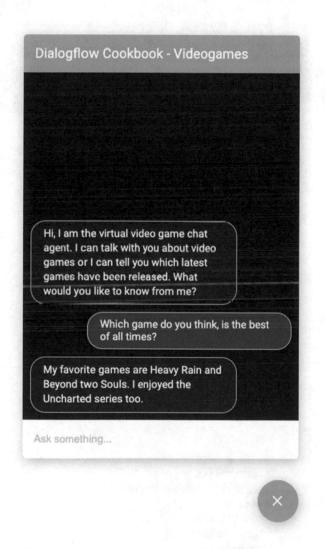

Figure 6-14. *Dialogflow Messenger with custom styling*

Rich Messages Support

You can add rich messages responses by adding code to the **Default custom payload** box in the Intent in Dialogflow, as shown in Figure 6-15.

Figure 6-15. *Dialogflow Messenger custom payload*

The rich messages that are supported are Info **Responses**, **Images**, **Lists** (as seen in Figure 6-16), **Accordions** (boxes that can expand), **Buttons**, and **Suggestion Chips**. Note the richContent field that can hold arrays. You can find the implementation examples in the Dialogflow documentation.

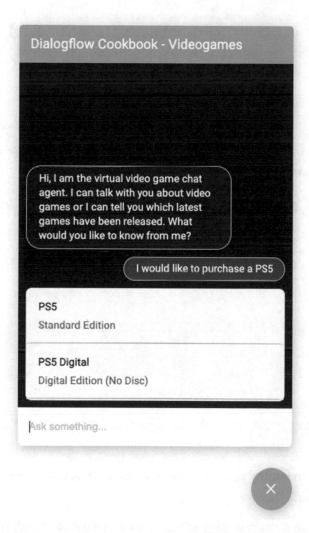

Figure 6-16. *Dialogflow Messenger custom payload example*

There are also JavaScript event triggers available, for example, to render more custom rich messages or to make links clickable.

The event target for these events is either the df-messenger element (see Listing 6-5) or the window global variable.

To add an event listener for the df-messenger element, add the following JavaScript code, where eventType is one of the event names described in Listing 6-5.

Listing 6-5. Dialogflow Messenger creating event listeners on the web component

```
const dfMessenger = document.querySelector('df-messenger');
dfMessenger.addEventListener('eventType', function (event) {
  // Handle event
  ...
});
```

To add an event listener for window, add the following JavaScript code (Listing 6-6), where eventType is one of the event names described.

Listing 6-6. Dialogflow Messenger creating event listeners on the window element

```
window.addEventListener('eventType', function (event) {
  // Handle event
  ...
});
```

Summary

This chapter describes some out-of-the-box (text-based) integrations that address the following tasks:

- You want to deploy your chatbot to Google Chat with the Hangouts integration.

- You want to quickly deploy your chatbot to a website with the web demo.

- You want to quickly deploy your chatbot to a website and change the look and feel with Dialogflow Messenger.

The source code for this book is available on GitHub via the book's product page, located at `www.apress.com/978-1-4842-7013-4`. Look into the deploying-integrations-webcomponent and _dialogflow-agent (**Buy_Console intent**) folders.

Further Reading

- Google Workspace documentation for allowing bots

  `https://support.google.com/a/answer/7651360`

- Dialogflow documentation on Google Chat

  `https://cloud.google.com/dialogflow/es/docs/integrations/hangouts`

- Google documentation on Google Chat API

  `https://developers.google.com/hangouts/chat` and `https://developers.google.com/hangouts/chat/how-tos/bots-publish`

- Google Chat card documentation

  `https://developers.google.com/hangouts/chat/reference/message-formats/cards`

- Dialogflow documentation on integrations

  `https://cloud.google.com/dialogflow/es/docs/quick/integration`

- Dialogflow documentation on Dialogflow Messenger

  `https://cloud.google.com/dialogflow/es/docs/integrations/dialogflow-messenger`

- More information on web components

  `https://developers.google.com/web/fundamentals/web-components/shadowdom`

CHAPTER 7

Building Voice Agents

Let's discuss voice bots. Typically, when we think of chatbots for voice, we would think of smart assistants, such as the Google Assistant, Alexa, or Siri. But there's actually another famous business case where you can use virtual agents for—bots in contact centers and telephony lines.

Since **Google Assistant** and Dialogflow are both Google products, you wouldn't be surprised that deploying voice bots to the Google Assistant is so easy.

The **Dialogflow Phone Gateway** feature provides a telephone interface to your agent. This is great for creating inbound simple interactive voice responses tied to a service number, such as telephone reservation systems or simple information lines.

Users who call the phone number will be connected to the Dialogflow voice agent. A conversation can be handled very naturally through Speech to Text (STT) and Text to Speech (TTS) with humanlike voices.

Google Cloud has a solution called **Contact Center AI**. This is an out-of-the-box solution for telephony contact centers to use artificial intelligence to automate conversations and help live assistants in real time. No machine learning expertise is required since Contact Center AI will be delivered and enabled through well-known telephony partners, such as Genesys, Avaya, Mitel, Twilio, Cisco, Five9, and more. It's using popular Google Cloud components, including Dialogflow, Speech-to-Text, and Text-to-Speech.

This chapter will include all of this, including how to improve your voice bots.

© Lee Boonstra 2021
L. Boonstra, *The Definitive Guide to Conversational AI with Dialogflow and Google Cloud*,
https://doi.org/10.1007/978-1-4842-7014-1_7

Building a Voice AI for a Virtual Assistant Like the Google Assistant

Let's start with an easy-to-build Voice AI solution, building a Voice AI for the Google Assistant. Both are Google products, and it's integrated out of the box when using Dialogflow. Getting this to work is just a matter of enabling the service and using the same Google user account for both services. Once it's enabled, your Dialogflow agent is available to the Google Assistant as an action (Google Assistant app). End users can invoke the action through their wake word: *Hey Google, talk to <action-name>*. Under the hood, it will open your Dialogflow agent, letting the Google Assistant deal with the Speech to Text and Text to Speech. Dialogflow will be used for Natural Language Understanding, intent matching, entity recognition, and content management. See the diagram in Figure 7-1.

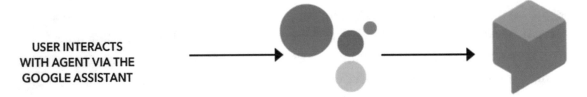

USER INTERACTS WITH AGENT VIA THE GOOGLE ASSISTANT

Figure 7-1. *The user interacts with the Google Assistant, and through Actions on Google, the Google Assistant connects to the Dialogflow agent. It all works out of the box*

1. First, click **Integrations ➤ Google Assistant ➤ Integration Settings**. This will open a pop-up; see Figure 7-2. Click the ***Test*** button. This will open the Actions on Google console (`https://console.actions.google.com/`). Pay attention; you are logged in on Actions on Google with the same Google account as Dialogflow. If this gives you problems, often due to having multiple Google accounts, log out on all accounts, and try to log back in.

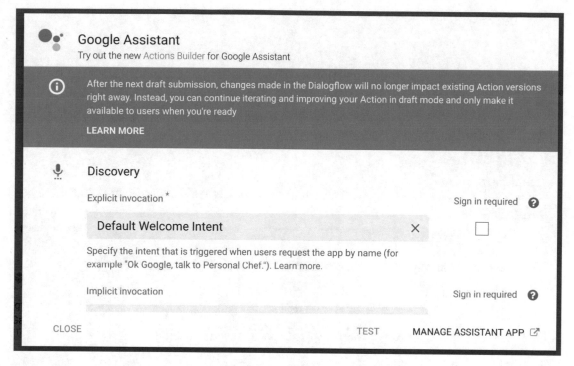

Figure 7-2. *Set up Google Assistant integration*

2. When you are new to Actions on Google, you will need to go
    through a form to agree on the services (see Figure 7-3).

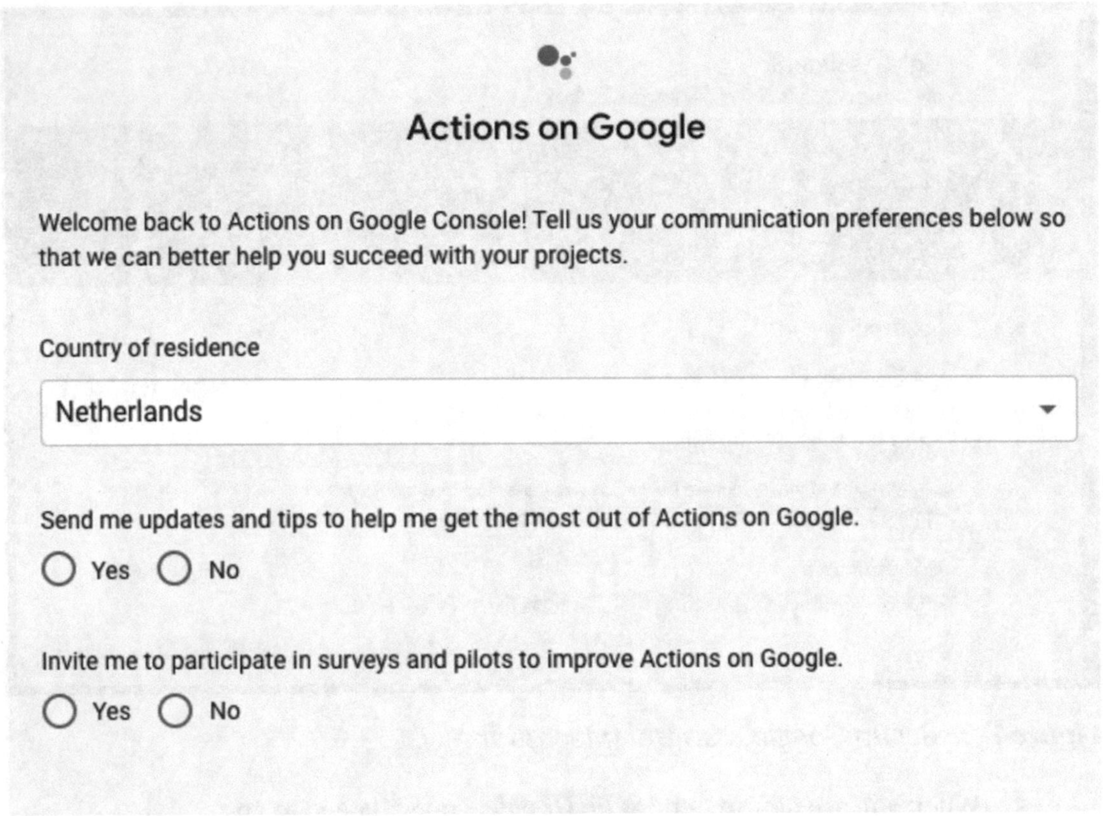

Figure 7-3. *When you are new to Actions on Google, you have to fill out this form*

3. Now you are in the simulator. Make sure the simulator is set to English (United States), select a device (e.g., phone), and click **Talk to my test-app**.

The action will greet you with the basic Dialogflow default intent. That means that setting up the integration with Actions on Google worked! See Figure 7-4.

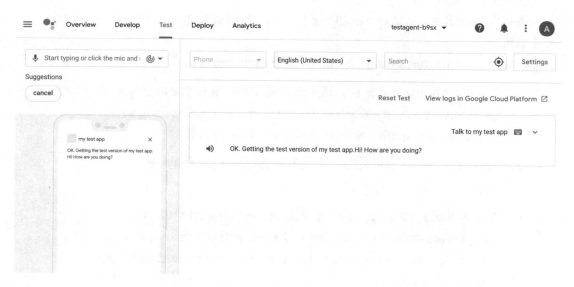

Figure 7-4. *Your Dialogflow agent in action, in the Actions on Google simulator*
(`https://console.actions.google.com`)

Rich Messages

When you are building actions for the Google Assistant, you might want to use the
particular rich messages that Actions on Google offers. Once you have set up the Google
Assistant integration in Dialogflow, you will notice that there's a new tab in the response
block of your intents (Figure 7-5).

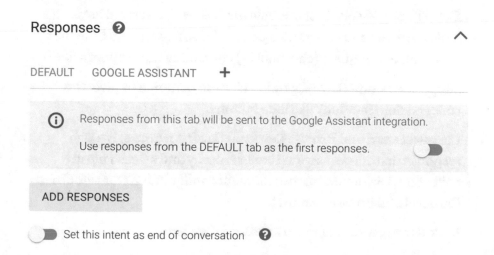

Figure 7-5. *Custom Google Assistant responses*

When it's not there, you can easily add this tab to your response block by clicking the + tab.

There are three main settings in the Google Assistant tab:

1. You can choose not to override the *DEFAULT* tab. For example, if the default text response is the same as the Google Assistant text response, you might want to enable the first switch.

2. The **Add Responses** button to add rich messages (custom payloads) to your agent.

3. A switch to set the intent at the end of the conversation. On Google Assistant, it means that you are leaving the scope of your action. For example, you could create a Goodbye intent and have this switch enabled.

When you click the **Add Responses** (Figure 7-6) button, you can choose between the following custom payload responses:

- **Simple Response**: Simple responses take the form of a chat bubble visually and use Text to Speech (TTS) or Speech Synthesis Markup Language (SSML) for sound.

- **Basic Card**: Use basic cards mainly for display purposes. They are designed to be concise, to present key (or summary) information to users, and allow users to learn more if they choose (using a weblink).

- **List**: The single-select list presents the user with a vertical list of multiple items and selects a single one. Selecting an item from the list generates a user query (chat bubble) containing the list item's title.

- **Suggestion Chips**: Use suggestion chips to continue or pivot the conversation; they look like little buttons.

- **Carousel Card and Browse Carousel Card**: A carousel is a rich response that allows users to scroll vertically and select a tile in a collection. Dialogflow has two different configurations for carousels, Carousel and Browse Carousel.

- **Link out suggestion**: Link to an external website.

- **Media Content**: Media responses let your Actions play audio content with a playback duration longer than the 240-second limit of SSML.

- **Table Card**: Table cards allow you to display tabular data in your response (e.g., sports standings, election results, and flights). You can define columns and rows (up to 3 each) that the Assistant is required to show in your table card. You can also specify additional columns and rows along with their prioritization. Tables are different from vertical lists because tables display static data and are not interactable, like list elements.

- **Custom Payload**: You can write your JSON in the format how Actions on Google expects it, for example, when you want more buttons or sections in a card.

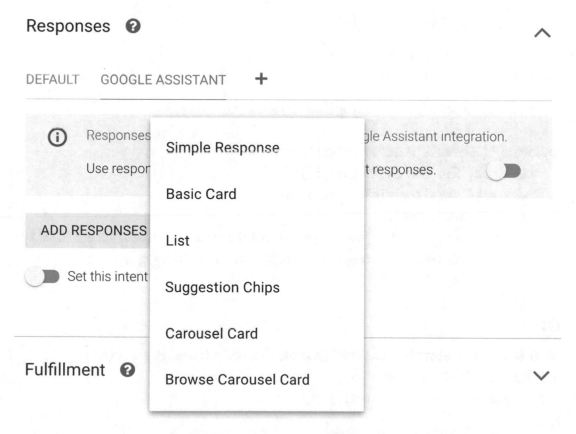

Figure 7-6. *Click the Add Responses button to show a pop-up for selecting between the various custom Google Assistant responses*

Fulfillment and Webhooks

For developers, Actions on Google has its own client library; it's available in Node Package Manager (NPM) under the name **actions-on-google-nodejs**.

This client library makes it easy to create Actions for the Google Assistant and supports Dialogflow, Actions SDK, and Smart Home fulfillment. You can deploy the code on your own server or use the Dialogflow inline editor. For more information on fulfillments and webhooks, see Chapter 10. Listing 7-1 shows an example of an Actions on Google webhook:

Listing 7-1. Actions on Google webhook example

```
const {
    dialogflow,
    Image
} = require('actions-on-google')

// Create an app instance
const app = dialogflow();

// Register handlers for Dialogflow intents

app.intent('Default Welcome Intent', conv => {
    conv.ask('Hi, how is it going?')
    conv.ask(`Here's a picture of a cat`)
    conv.ask(new Image({
        url: 'https://developers.google.com/web/fundamentals/accessibility/
        semantics-builtin/imgs/160204193356-01-cat-500.jpg',
        alt: 'A cat',
    }));
});

// Intent in Dialogflow called `Goodbye` which closes the action
app.intent('Goodbye', conv => {
    conv.close('See you later!')
});
```

```
app.intent('Default Fallback Intent', conv => {
    conv.ask(`I didn't understand. Can you tell me something else?`)
});
```

In this sample piece of code, you see that Dialogflow will be loaded from the actions-on-google library. Once you have a Dialogflow app instance, you can register handlers that listen to intents invoked in Dialogflow.

With the conv() object, you can return content. This can be text, which will be synthesized to speech, but it also can contain rich UI responses, such as Images, Basic Cards, Lists, and so on.

The actions-on-google library contains many more functions and helper classes, for example, to request a location, user information, account login, detecting a screen, and so on.

Invoke Your Action on the Google Assistant with Explicit and Implicit Invocation

Explicit invocation occurs when a user tells the Google Assistant to use your Action by name, such as *Hey Google, talk to* (trigger phrase) → *<my-action-name>* (invocation name specified by the developer) → *to do x y z* (invocation phrase specified by the developer). See Figure 7-7. Optionally, the user can include an invocation phrase at the end of their invocation that will take them directly to the function they're requesting.

Figure 7-7. Google Assistant Explicit invocations

It's also possible to choose one or more **Implicit invocation** intents. This is how users can invoke your app without specifying its name. For example, if your app can locate nearby concerts, users can say, *"Ok, Google, I want to find concerts around me."* The Google Assistant attempts to match the user's request to a proper fulfillment, such as an Action, search result, or mobile app, then presents recommendations to the user. To find matching Actions, Google uses signals such as users telling the Assistant to do something similar to an invocation phrase for one of your configured intents or when the user is in a context where your Action would be appropriate.

This interaction occurs as follows:

1. A user asks the Assistant to perform a task.

2. The recommendation algorithm determines that your Action can complete the user's task.

3. The Assistant recommends your Action to the user.

To set up Explicit and Implicit intents, click Dialogflow on the **Integrations ➤ Google Assistant ➤ Integration Settings** link (Figure 7-8). And select the intents in both discovery dropdowns.

Figure 7-8. *Setting up invocations in Dialogflow*

Submitting an Action via Actions on Google

Google has a framework that includes a UI toolkit, SDK, a simulator, and tools to deploy your actions to the Google Assistant. It's called *Actions on Google*.

You can open the Actions Console with `https://console.actions.google.com/`.

When you are logged in on the same Gmail/Google account in Dialogflow, Actions on Google, and your Google Assistant device, then it's possible to test your application on a physical device, out of the box.

Before submitting your Action for approval, we recommend you go through a prelaunch checklist. Using a checklist catches many of the issues we see during the approval process and improves your project's chances of approval. Every subsequent time you update the Action package after submission, it must go through another approval cycle.

Tip   With Dialogflow ES, it is possible to create different versions of your agent to create an immutable version of your Dialogflow agent before Action submission. This approach gives you the ability to create multiple versions of your Dialogflow agent, publish them to separate environments, and roll back to previous versions if necessary.

You can deploy your action from within the **Deploy** tab of the Actions on Google console.

Building an Action with the Actions SDK

Ninety percent of all the actions that are available on the Google Assistant are actually built with Dialogflow. The reasoning behind this is simple; both are Google products, and publishing an action through the Dialogflow integration tab is so easy. Why would you choose a different way?

There is another way to deploy your actions, and that's through the Actions SDK. It's a lot more complicated as you have to build the integration yourself, but there are some advantages to doing so. Instead of letting Actions on Google talk to Dialogflow out of the box, you might want to let Actions on Google connect to your own back-end layer where the back-end layer connects to Dialogflow; see Figure 7-9.

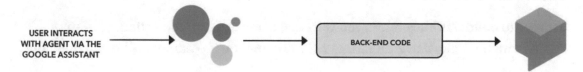

Figure 7-9. *Actions on Google connects to your codebase, and your codebase connects to the Dialogflow agent to do intent detection*

Enterprises that are building large customer experience platforms that support many platforms as channels might want to use Dialogflow as the NLU intent detection layer, which will be written and maintained in one place; all the channels, including Actions on Google, will be middleware. The only purpose of that middleware is to capture the user input (typed text or spoken audio transcribed to text), send the response text or audio, and present it in the right format. For example, your synthesized voice should not contain any hyperlinks, and maybe you also want to support Google Assistant UI widgets, like cards. The architecture would look like Figure 7-10.

Figure 7-10. *Actions on Google connects to your codebase which has a middleware layer for handling the Actions SDK and returning SSML or Assistant views, and it has a script that connects to the Dialogflow agent to do intent matching. Other channels can reuse this last part*

Tip   In case you are using Dialogflow CX instead of Dialogflow Essentials, the Actions SDK solution is, by the time of writing this, the only way to bring your conversations to the Google Assistant.

By using the Actions SDK, you will need to bring your own NLU/intent detection. When you pick Dialogflow (Essentials or CX), you benefit from the fast Google backbone connection, as both Actions on Google and Dialogflow are Google products using Google networks, and of course Google's great NLU which also powers the Google Assistant.

Using the Actions SDK Solution

In order to build this integration, you will need to make use of the Actions SDK npm library and the Dialogflow API. Listing 7-2 will show you an example of how to build this.

Listing 7-2. Code implementation

```
// 1)
const { actionssdk } = require('actions-on-google');
const dialogflow = require('@google-cloud/dialogflow');
const uuid = require('uuid');

// 2)
const app = actionssdk();

// 3)
app.intent('actions.intent.MAIN', async (conv) => {
    // 4)
    var queryInput = {
        event: {
            name: 'WELCOME',
            languageCode: 'en'
        }
    };
    var response = await dialogflowDetection(queryInput);

    // 5)
    conv.ask(response.response.queryResult.fulfillmentText);
})

app.intent('actions.intent.TEXT', (conv, input) => {
    // 6)
    var queryInput = {
        text: {
            text: input,
            languageCode: 'en'
        }
    };
    var response = await dialogflowDetection(queryInput);
    conv.ask(response.queryResult.fulfillmentText);
});
```

```
async function dialogflowDetection(){
    // 7)
    const sessionId = uuid.v4();
    const sessionClient = new dialogflow.SessionsClient();
    const sessionPath = sessionClient.projectAgentSessionPath(projectId,
    sessionId);

    // 8)
    const request = {
        session: this.sessionPath,
        queryInput: qInput,
        queryParams: null
    };

    // 9)
    const [response] = await this.sessionClient.detectIntent(request);
    return response;
}
```

1. Import the libraries.

2. Create a Google Assistant app instance.

3. Register handlers for Actions SDK intents.

4. `actions.intent.MAIN` will be triggered when the Action is started. We will fetch the Default Welcome Intent by passing in the event name "WELCOME".

5. Let the Google Assistant speak out the fulfillmentText.

6. We will use the `actions.intent.TEXT` as a catch-all to pass every incoming user input (spoken text, transcribed by the Google Assistant Speech to Text, or written text) as text intent detection in Dialogflow.

7. To create a Dialogflow Session Client and a Session Path, we will need a unique ID and the Dialogflow Project ID. Steps 7 to 9, the Dialogflow SDK usage, will be further explained in Chapters 10, 11, and 12.

8. This is the request which will be formed with either a text object or an event object.

9. Now we call the detectIntent method from the sessionClient, and we pass in the request. It will return a promise; once the promise is fulfilled, it returns the response (fulfillment text).

The Actions SDK requires an *action package file* (action.json), which is a kind of a JSON manifest file, describing the intents to "listen" to and telling the Google Assistant what to do once such intent is triggered. See Listing 7-3.

Listing 7-3. The action.json file maps intents to fulfillment

```
{
  "actions": [
    {
      "description": "Default Welcome Intent",
      "name": "MAIN",
      "fulfillment": {
        "conversationName": "welcome"
      },
      "intent": {
        "name": "actions.intent.MAIN",
        "trigger": {
          "queryPatterns":["talk to CCAIDemo"]
        }
      }
    },
    {
      "description": "Dialogflow Intents",
      "name": "TEXT",
      "fulfillment": {
        "conversationName": "dialogflow_intent"
      },
```

```
      "intent": {
        "name": "actions.intent.TEXT",
      }
    }
  ],
  "conversations": {
    "welcome": {
      "name": "welcome",
      "url": "https://www.leeboonstra.dev/webhook/"
    },
    "dialogflow_intent": {
      "name": "dialogflow_intent",
      "url": "https://www.leeboonstra.dev/webhook/"
    }
  },
  "locale": "en"
}
```

Every Actions project must have a welcome intent that acts as an entry point for users to start conversations. The welcome intent is triggered when users explicitly invoke an Action by uttering its name (e.g., "Hey Google, talk to the video game agent"). This welcome intent is identified with the `actions.intent.MAIN` intent name.

You can create additional entries in your Action package with intents that you define yourself. However, for Dialogflow projects, you will need the `actions.intent.TEXT` intent, which will work like a catch-all. All spoken or typed inputs are sent as `actions.intent.TEXT` intents. Notice bullet 6, in Listing 7-2, and the `actions.intent.TEXT` block in Listing 7-3. You can simply grab the raw text and forward it along to your fulfillment server. From there, you can process the text with Dialogflow and build a response to send back to Actions on Google.

You can pretty much ignore everything else about the Actions SDK. However, there are other nice features, such as triggers. This allows users to invoke specific functionality by saying an Action name along with an intent (e.g., "Hey Google, talk to ExampleAction to find some shoes").

In the next listing, Listing 7-4, note the `trigger` block. The `queryPatterns` works as a speech adaptation list with hints to bias the Speech to Text model in order to make sure the correct parameters marked in the parameter block are sent to your NLU detection layer. Without these hints, the STT model could hear something like "buy some blue sweat shoes" instead of "buy some blue suede shoes." Your NLU layer won't understand "sweat shoes."

Listing 7-4. Bias the STT model in the action.json file

```json
{
  "description": "Direct access",
  "name": "BUY",
  "fulfillment": {
    "conversationName": "ExampleAction"
  },
  "intent": {
    "name": "com.example.ExampleAction.BUY",
    "parameters": [
      {
        "name": "color",
        "type": "org.schema.type.Color"
      }
    ],
    "trigger": {
      "queryPatterns": [
        "find some $org.schema.type.Color:color sneakers",
        "buy some blue suede shoes",
        "get running shoes"
      ]
    }
  }
}
```

The `conversations` block works as a router; it will need access to public HTTPS URLs for retrieving the fulfillments. Your back-end fulfillment receives requests from the Assistant, processes the request, and responds. You can host this back-end code wherever you want to—on-premise or within Google Cloud. Chapter 10 will discuss the various computing solutions as long as you listen for POST requests.

In case you build a back-end server with express, your POST route will look like this:

```
var assistant = actionssdk();
expressApp.post('/webhook/', assistant);
```

In case you want to run it locally, you will need a tool like **ngrok** to create a secure tunnel. This is because the Google Assistant works in the Cloud, and so is Dialogflow. Your fulfillment needs to be available via a nonlocal URL on HTTPS. Chapter 10 discusses ngrok in more detail.

Actions on Google also offers a command-line tool called **gactions**. With the command `gactions init`, you can generate boilerplate code, similar to Listing 7-3.

Deploying Your Action

To upload your Action package, you will need the gactions command-line tool and run the following command, replacing `PACKAGE_FILE` and `PROJECT_ID` with the relevant values for your project:

```
gactions update --action_package PACKAGE_FILE --project PROJECT_ID
```

Building a Callbot with a Phone Gateway

The Dialogflow ES Phone Gateway is an easy way to set up an inbound voice agent for telephony. You will get a toll-free number; when you call that number, the Dialogflow agent will talk to you. The use case would be more for simple phone bots (like a reservation system) or testing purposes. In case you want to integrate robots in your IVR/contact center or already have an existing contact center (telephony partner), enabling Dialogflow via Contact Center AI (as described in the next section) would be a better solution for you.

When you use the Dialogflow trial version, you won't have access to a toll-free number. And you will get limited quotas, such as 3 total phone minutes per minute, 30 phone minutes per day, 500 phone minutes per month, and the phone number will be reserved for only 30 days. The enterprise tiers will include 100 call minutes per minute. In other words, the Dialogflow trial is excellent for testing the Phone Gateway, but you would like to move to a paid enterprise tier to have it working in production. When you receive a busy signal or call drops during phone calls, it will mean that you have exceeded your quota.

Let's enable the phone gateway.

1. At the time of writing, this feature is beta. In case you can't find the speech tab in the settings panel, you will need to enable the beta features first (see Figure 7-11). This can be found in the **Settings ➤ General** tab.

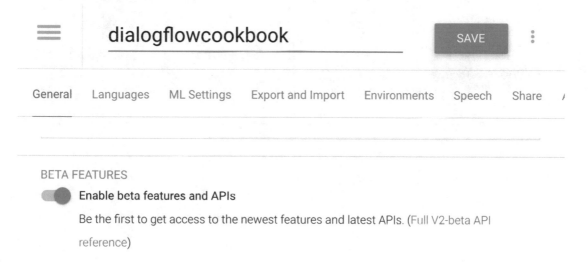

Figure 7-11. *Enable beta features and APIs in the settings panel*

2. Click **Integrations**.

3. Click **Telephony Phone Gateway** (Figure 7-12).

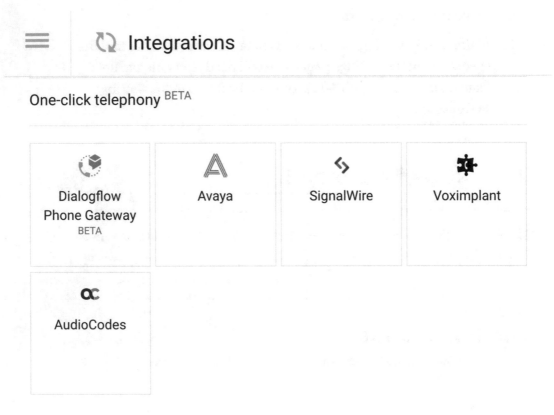

Figure 7-12. *Enable the Dialogflow Phone Gateway*

4. A pop-up will appear; here's where you can configure the telephony gateway (see Figure 7-13).

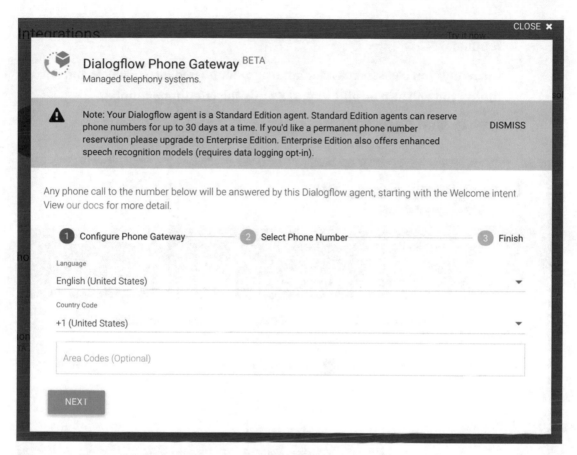

Figure 7-13. *Dialogflow Phone Gateway pop-up, pick a country and an area code*

5.   It's possible to select a **language** and a **country code**.

Note   While this feature is still in beta, the only languages and phone numbers currently supported for the telephony gateway integration are English United States/Spanish United States, +1 United States.

---

6.   Optionally, you can specify an American **area code**, such as 516, the area code for New York. Once you start typing, a select box will let you pick the area codes. You can also request a phone number with an 833 area code, which is a toll-free number. Note that toll-free numbers are priced higher.

7.   Click **Next**.

8. From here, you can choose from some preselected phone numbers.

    Currently, you can select a telephone number hosted by Google. In the future, you will also be able to port an existing telephone number.

9. Click **Create** (Figure 7-14).

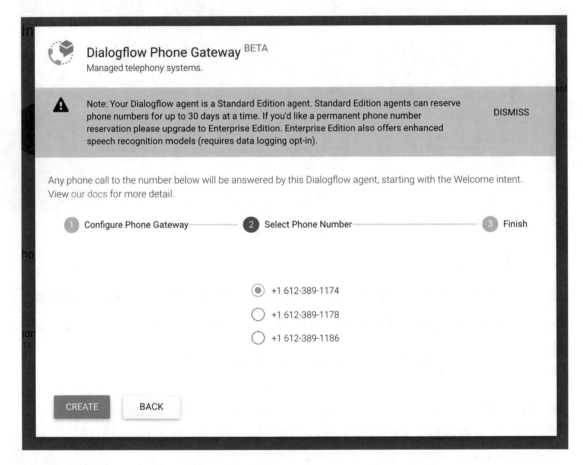

Figure 7-14. *Dialogflow Phone Gateway pop-up, pick a number*

Now the telephone number is connected to your voice bot. Additionally, you can select an environment. You can now call the number and follow the voice prompts provided by your Dialogflow intents. After that, you will also see the call history and analytics in the **History** and **Analytics** tabs.

Response Messages for the Phone Gateway

In the Dialogflow console, you can customize the voice responses to use rich (audio) response messages via the responses block in each intent. You can click the + button to enable the Dialogflow Phone Gateway. (See Figure 7-15.)

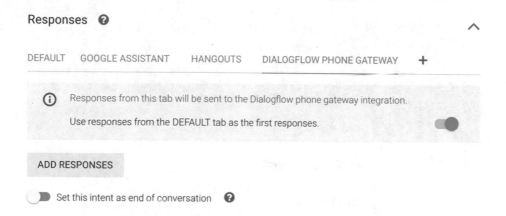

Figure 7-15. *Dialogflow Phone Gateway, click the + to add custom responses*

By default, it uses the responses from the **Default** tab.

When you click the **Add Responses** button, there's a choice of three different rich messages. Note Figure 7-16.

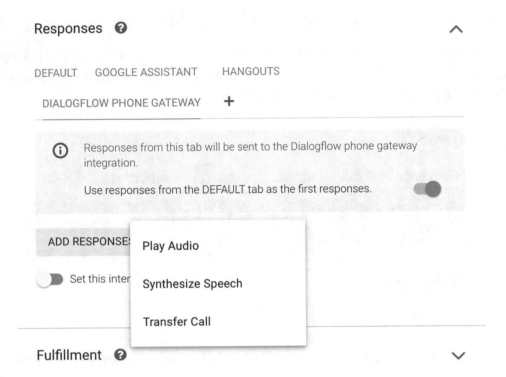

Figure 7-16. Dialogflow Phone Gateway custom responses

- **Play Audio**: It's possible to play a supplied audio file. This audio file has to be hosted in Google Cloud Storage. You can enter the Google Cloud Storage URI in this field, for example, *gs://bucket/object*. The object must contain a single channel (mono) of linear PCM audio (2 bytes/sample) at 8kHz.

- **Synthesize Speech**: Instead of using the text from the Default tab, you can enter the text in the Synthesize Speech tab. Therefore, you can return a different spoken voice than written text. Sometimes, your spoken dialogues might differ from written text. You can also use this block to write **SSML** (Speech Synthesis Markup Language) in your responses. You will read more in this chapter about this feature to tweak the TTS voices to make it sound more natural.

- **Transfer Call**: It is possible to transfer a call to another (during the beta, American) phone number, for example, to have a human hand-over. When this response is filled in, it will transfer the call once the intent has been detected.

Figure 7-17 shows how it will look like once you have them all enabled.

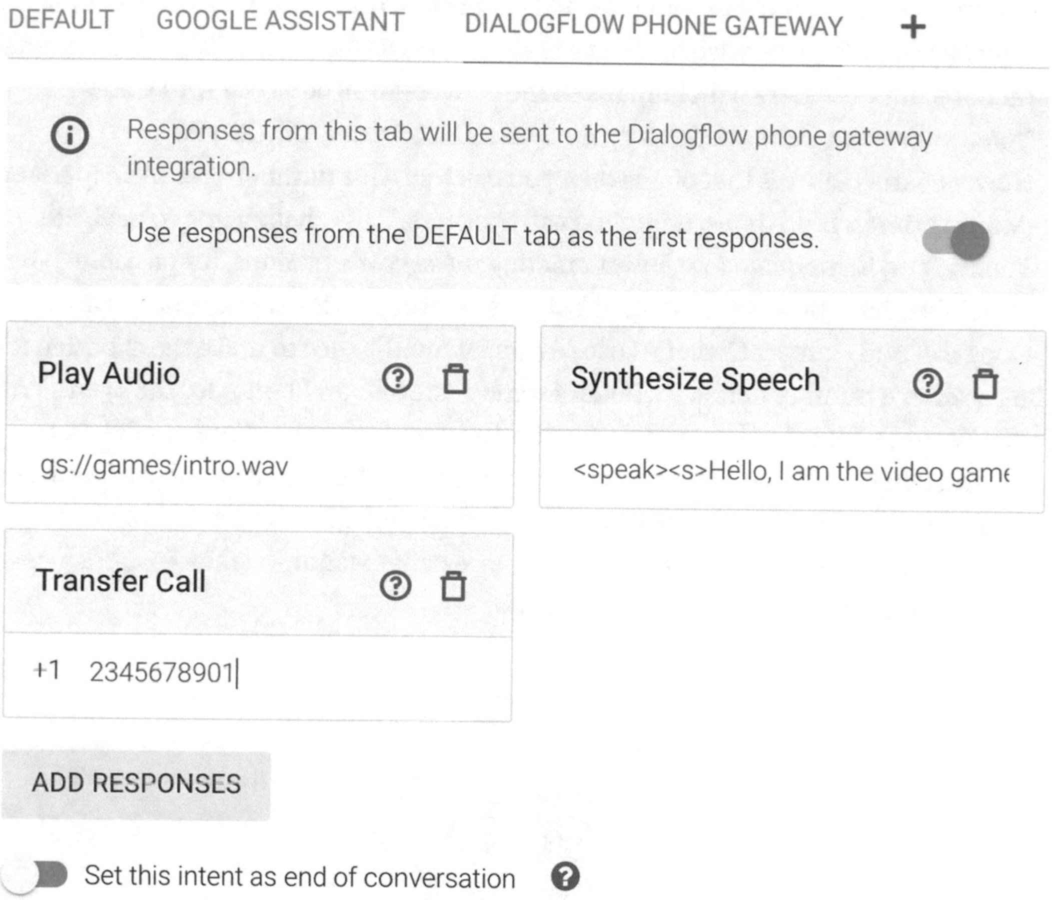

Figure 7-17. *Dialogflow Phone Gateway custom response examples*

There's also a switch in the Dialogflow Phone Gateway block to set the intent at the end of the conversation. Once the intent has been detected, it can terminate the call.

Building Bots for Contact Centers with Contact Center AI

Various researches have been shown that chatbots can trim business costs billions per year. Contact centers are a huge cost item, so there's a lot to win in this space.

When customers' call experience is pleasant, customers are willing to pay the premium price, stay loyal to your service, and share good experiences. Customers expect great, flexible, and personal experiences. 60% of the customers want easier access to self-service solutions, 64% wish to receive real-time assistance, and 75% prefer personal interactions not necessary with humans so the conversation could be with a bot.*

Source: Zendesk, Statista, Strategy Analytics, HBR, Ovum, CISCO VNI

However, the reality is that often when you call a service number, you will experience long waiting times, hold times, unlimited call transfers, IVRs challenging to navigate, availability, and inadequate info. By automating these conversations, it's possible to be 24/7 available, have no more waiting or hold times, and provide homogeneous answers.

Google Cloud Contact Center AI uses Artificial Intelligence to make the experience of calling a service number better. It's better for the customer and better for the agent. With Contact Center AI (CCAI), bots can understand and reply to your questions (**Virtual Agent**) and can listen in and give on-screen advice to the human agent (**Agent Assist**). Live agents will always provide the right answer to the question, and it can automatically prefill forms. Businesses can get analytics on these conversations via the **Insights** component. Figure 7-18 shows the architecture.

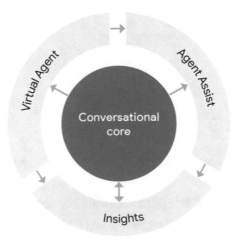

Figure 7-18. *Contact Center AI architecture*

Note Figure 7-19 and see how it works:

1. Contact Center AI integrates with your current telephone IVR system. Users can call a service number. Telephony partners such as Avaya, Genesys, Cisco, Mitel, and Twilio have implemented the Google Cloud components for Speech-to-Text, Text-to-Speech, and Dialogflow on top of their own infrastructure to handle the call. It uses special IVR features such as **barge-in** (interrupt the chatbot flow), **silence detection** (how long we wait till we figure out nothing has been said), **DTMF tone recognition** (parse tones to numeric entities), and **async fulfillment** (allows for long-running operations on the customer back-end to extend the 5-second fulfillment response time).

2. A robot will pick up the telephone; it can understand your speech, even on phone quality (8kHz mono), with background noises and interruptions from each other.

3. It will detect the intents in **Dialogflow**, query the information from a knowledge base, or fetch the data from systems through (asynchronous) fulfillment **webhooks**.

4. The responses will be spoken out via **Text-to-Speech**. It uses WaveNet models to make the voices sound humanlike.

5. When the bot doesn't know the right answer, it can hand over the conversation to a live human agent. The bot will still listen in to provide suggestions on the screen. This feature is called **Agent Assist**; it will help agents to reduce call and waiting times.

6. This solution will show **transcripts**, agent modeling, and **analytics** so businesses can get insights and learn from past conversations.

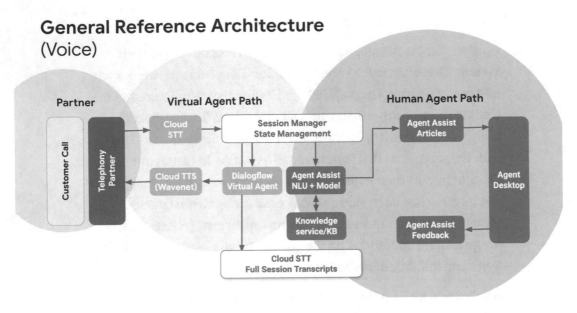

Figure 7-19. *Contact Center AI architecture explained*

If this sounds interesting to you, either contact your current telephony provider or use the one-click telephony integrations from Dialogflow. Even when these are future plans, it's already good to start now. You can build multichannel chatbots that include all customer journeys (inbound and outbound), telephony calls, hybrid chats, social media, or smart assistance.

Enabling Contact Center AI

Enterprises with existing telephony/IVR hardware can contact telephony providers to enable Contact Center AI. It is possible to hand over the Dialogflow project ID to use a current Dialogflow agent in their contact center.

Enterprises or companies new to this technology can either contact an IVR provider of choice or use the **one-click telephony integrations** (Figure 7-20) available on the Dialogflow **integrations** page. This allows you to follow the various wizards of **Avaya, SignalWire, Voximplant, AudioCodes, Genesys Cloud,** or **Twilio**.

Google Cloud provides documentation to make use of the Agent Assistant and Insights APIs in case you want to integrate these parts in your own employee-facing applications.

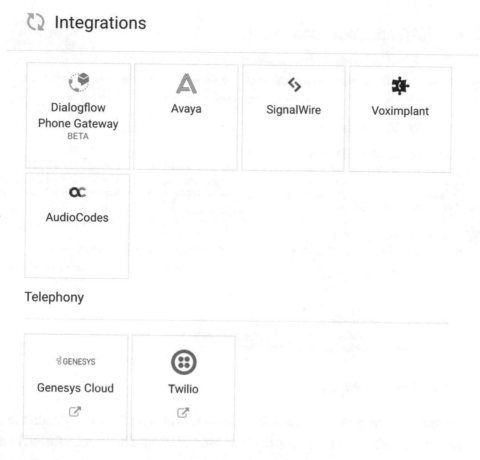

Figure 7-20. *Various telephony integrations to choose from*

Improving Speech to Text Quality

When we talk about Speech Machine Learning models, Speech to Text models have been trained by large datasets. Based on the audio examples it heard before, it tries to match text phrases out of it. With that being said, mishearing speech is not only hard for humans; it can be difficult for machines as well. However, we can bias the machine learning model by providing tips. In Dialogflow, when building voice agents, it's actually easy; you just need to enable **the auto speech adaptation switch,** which can be found in the **Settings ➤ Speech** tab (Figure 7-21). Intents and (marked) entities will be used as hints.

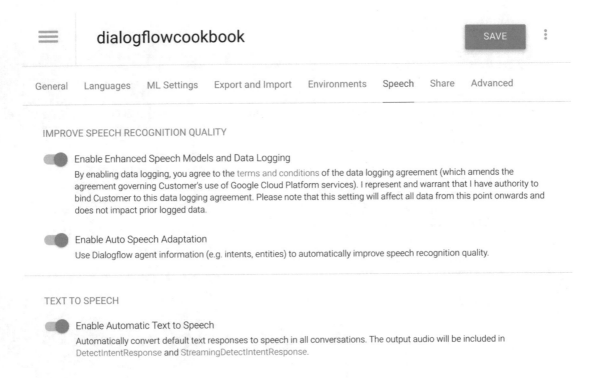

Figure 7-21. Speech settings

At the time of writing, this feature is beta. In case you can't find the speech tab in the settings panel, you will need to enable the beta features first. This can be found in the **Settings ➤ General** tab.

Once you have enabled auto speech adaptation, you can build your Dialogflow voice agents in ways to take advantage of it. You can test it in the simulator by using your microphone. If you are a developer, I would suggest using my Dialogflow speech recognition example because it will give you access to more debug information.

For best results, you'll also want to enable enhanced models: `https://cloud.google.com/dialogflow/docs/data-logging`.

Note   Auto speech adaptation does not work for Actions on Google (Google Assistant). With the AoG framework, speech recognition is performed by Actions on Google before sending data to Dialogflow.

The following examples show how speech recognition may be improved with certain changes to your agent.

Custom Entities Hints

If you define entities for product or service names offered by your company, and the end user mentions these terms in an utterance, they are more likely to be recognized. For example, without Speech Adaptation enabled and without having a custom entity for the rare video game console, *Ouya,* it would have understood "Oh yeah" instead of *Ouya*.

System Entities Hints

The previous example makes use of custom entities. But it will work similarly with system entities such as **@sys.number**. Think about user speech expressions when the user says "two"; it may be recognized as "to," "too," "2," or "two." And "for 4 to 5" could be understood as "425," "four four two five," and so on. When the Speech Adaptation function is enabled, the system entities will be used as hints.

Intent Hints

If you define training phrases with a phrase like "We are going to Ibiza," a similar-sounding user utterance is reliably recognized as "We are going to Ibiza" and not "We are going to eat pizza."

Overriding Speech Hints in Your Code

You can also tweak the speech adaptation in your code. That's handy when you are implementing integrations through the API. Providing explicit **speech_contexts** in the **inputAudioConfig** will override the implicit speech context hints generated by auto speech adaptation for input audio (speech-to-text) configuration in the Dialogflow Console. The speechContexts takes an object with an array of phrases[] containing words and phrases that the speech recognizer should recognize with a higher likelihood.

The speechContexts object can also take an optional boost (float) property. Boost for this context compared to other contexts:

- If the boost is positive, Dialogflow will increase the probability that the phrases in this context are recognized over similar-sounding phrases.

- If the boost is unspecified or nonpositive, Dialogflow will not apply any boost.

Dialogflow recommends that you use boosts in the range (0, 20) and that you find a value that fits your use case with binary search.

Here, you can find an example. Consider the following chat flow:

> "When will I get notified when the PlayStation 5 is in your store?"

> > I can send it to you by e-mail or text message.

> "Mail"

To make sure that the agent understands "Mail" and not "Male" or "Nail," I have provided speechContexts in the code of Listing 7-5.

Listing 7-5. Biasing the speech model with the speechContexts

```
const uuid = require('uuid');
const df = require('dialogflow').v2beta1;

const sessionId = uuid.v4();
const sessionClient = new df.SessionsClient();
const sessionPath = sessionClient.sessionPath(projectId, sessionId);

let request = {
  session: sessionPath,
  queryInput: {
    audioConfig: {
      sampleRateHertz: 16000,
      encoding: 'AUDIO_ENCODING_LINEAR_16',
      languageCode: 'en-US',
      speechContexts: [
          {
            phrases: [
              'mail',
              'email'
            ],
            boost: 20.0
          }
      ]
    },
```

```
    singleUtterance: singleUtterance
  }
}

request.inputAudio = audio;
const responses = await sessionClient.detectIntent(request);
```

Tip   What do I bias toward? You can favor the Dialogflow speech model for strong context or weak context examples.

Strong context use cases are, for example, when voice is used in an IVR/telephony system to make sure certain expected "flows" or common commands will work.

User history or important named entities could be fair use cases too. For example, when the flow is asking for a phone number, make sure your bias for numbers.

Weak context use cases are use for misspellings. You might want to correct, the not common but important named entities that are often misunderstood by the STT model.

Speech Adaptation will work for all Dialogflow languages that support voice.

Fine-Tuning the Text to Speech Output of Voice Bots with SSML

The Text to Speech (TTS) output of voice bots, voice assistants, and callbots (bots in contact centers) can be tweaked to make it sound more natural. We can use **SSML** for this, which stands for **Speech Synthesis Markup Language**. It's a markup language, like HTML (HyperText Markup Language) is for websites. In HTML, you would put all the markup *tags* in the <body> tag of an HTML document; with SSML, you will put all specific SSML tags for building pauses or emphasis in the <speak> tag.

SSML is an XML-based markup language for speech synthesis applications. It is a recommendation of the W3C's voice browser working group.

When you have **Automatic Text to Speech enabled** in your Dialogflow settings, you can start writing SSML tags in your intent response tabs.

In Figure 7-22, you can see the **Default** tab returning SSML as a response.

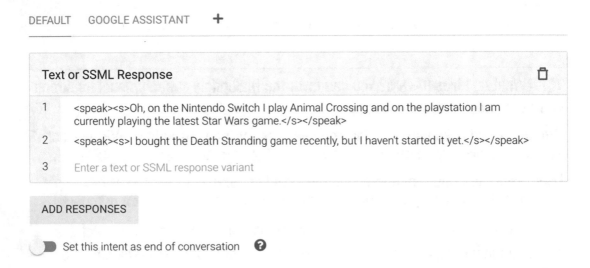

Figure 7-22. *Writing SSML code in the DEFAULT tab*

Some integrations such as the **Dialogflow Phone Gateway** or the **Google Assistant** provide their own response boxes to enter text and SSML versions of answers. You can see how this works for the Google Assistant in Figure 7-23.

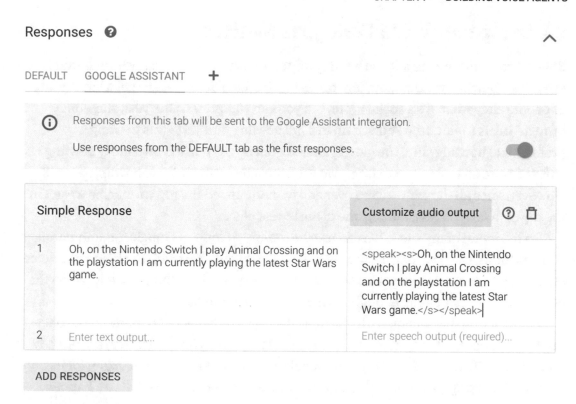

Figure 7-23. *Writing SSML code in the Google Assistant tab by customizing the audio output*

Caution   Be aware of writing SSML code in the Default Responses tab. Although this works excellent for single-channel integrations, it might not be ideal for cross-channel agents where you will have to support text and voice as both solutions. As then, the text version will include the SSML tags, which will be somewhat odd.

A better approach would be to use the Integration Response tabs, such as the Google Assistant or Dialogflow Phone Gateway tabs, to provide a spoken version of your answer when your implementation is not available as an out-of-the-box integration. For example, you are integrating voice in a website. You could also differentiate between the SSML and text version through fulfillment code.

UX Design for Voice Dialogues Matters!

Before I continue, let me tell you a funny off-topic story. Every year, my friends and I organize a bowling tournament. You can bring in other friends, so we get a large group of people altogether. It's a social event, but you can win prizes. One year, somebody brought in his friend, who showed up in a full bowling outfit. He was wearing a professional bowling shirt, the gloves, and he even brought in his own lucky bowling ball. We were all looking up to him; "wow, he must be a professional bowling player!" However, once all the games were over and we announced the top winner, he wasn't in the top 3. In fact, he was holding one of the lowest places.

So the moral of my story: We can use the top-notch tools of Google for automating conversations, but if we don't write great dialogue that fits best with the belonging voice channel, you won't deliver your users a good user experience. Unfortunately, when the user experience isn't good enough, your users won't come back.

I am starting this section with this topic because I have seen too many voice chat implementations, where chatbots initially built for the Web (text interface) are directly passed to the Text to Speech output of Google, without rewriting the dialogue for its channel. By taking this approach, here are some examples of things that can happen:

- **Long stories when it's the bot's turn to talk**: On a screen, text can be long and contain multiple paragraphs. You can skip the parts that are not interesting to you. But hearing a bot talking for too long won't make your users happy.

- **No follow-up questions**: It's great to include FAQ knowledge base questions in your voice chats. Typically, on web interfaces, it ends by providing the answer to a question. On the phone, you're used to asking and taking turns. "Is there anything else I can help you with?" It would be odd if the person on the other end suddenly becomes quiet.

- **Hyperlinks, tables, images, abbreviations, and so on**: On a screen, you can refer to an image or click a link. You can't do this on a device without a screen.

- **Error codes**: It's not a great experience and doesn't make sense to hear Error 404. In conversations, there are no errors. Your users will raise their voice and repeat the same answer, which won't work.

So with this in mind, let's have a look at best voice practices:

- Write compact dialogues that are easy to understand for your audience.

- Always end with a question to steer the conversation and to get the interactions going.

- Don't use hyperlinks, tables, images, abbreviations. You could refer to a website when data is tabular, return the best match, and ask if the user wants to hear alternative options.

- Don't abbreviate words but mention the full naming.

- When something goes wrong, it's better to provide a fallback dialogue that everyone understands. Help users to be successful; steer them to tell them precisely what you would like to hear as an answer. For example, if you provide options, don't ask "Would you like A or B?"— because then a user could answer "yes."

- Instead, ask: "I have A, and I have B. Which one do you prefer?"

- Start with a welcome message, explain that you are a virtual agent, and explain the type of questions the virtual agent will address. For example, "Hey there, I am the virtual agent of video games dot com. I can tell you which game releases are upcoming, and you can purchase video games. How can I help?" And not: "Good morning, I am Lee. What would you like to know?" With the last example, you risk the chance that your users are asking questions that the virtual agent wasn't trained on. A user could ask: "Which cities near me have arcade halls?" Your chatbot will return a fallback answer. The user could ask the question differently, but it still won't know the answer. It will give an impression that your chatbot doesn't know anything. It does; it just doesn't have that particular flow.

- It also means that you would want to collect analytics on what your users are asking to implement those flows by providing that training data. Your chatbot will become smarter over time. That also means that you can go to production with your virtual agent as soon as possible and continue improving the experience by learning as long as you set your boundaries.

- Create a persona for your virtual agent. It's the face where your customers are talking to. So you can think of the style, the gender, how the voice will sound, the tone of voice, what word and phrase choices you use, and so on. You can imagine a video game virtual agent might target youth and young adults. For the elderly, you might have a different word choice or style.

- Use SSML to change the intonation of your sentences, so your voices will sound more natural.

Text to Speech Voices

Dialogflow and the Google Assistant use WaveNet voices to make the voices sound humanlike and less like robots.

When building virtual agents for IoT, web pages, or contact centers, there is a wide selection of custom voices available for you to pick from in Dialogflow. When you build agents for the Google Assistant, it will use the Text to Speech synthesizer from the Google Assistant, and therefore you will have to choose the voices from within Actions on Google.

All the voices differ by language, gender, and accent (for some languages). Some languages have multiple voices to choose from. In Dialogflow, you can configure the voice by setting the agent language, voice choice, speaking rate, pitch, and volume gain from the **Settings ➤ Speech** tab. (See Figure 7-24).

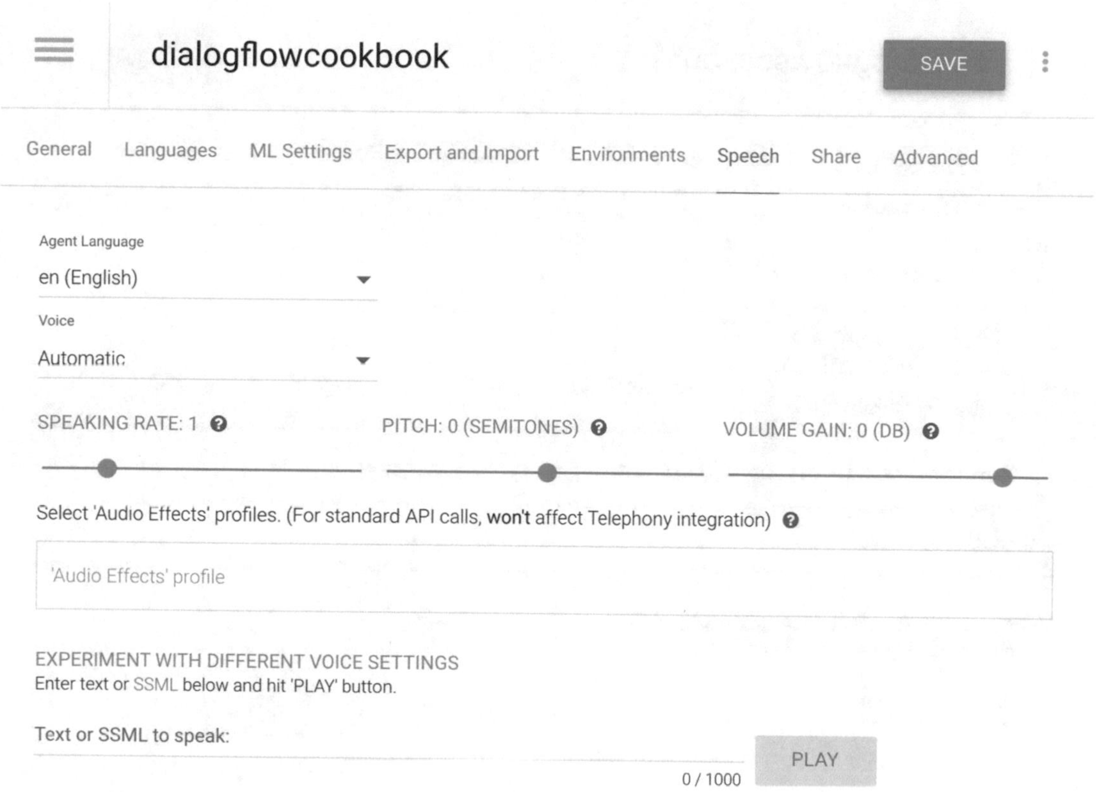

≡   **dialogflowcookbook**   SAVE   ⋮

General   Languages   ML Settings   Export and Import   Environments   **Speech**   Share   Advanced

Agent Language
en (English)   ▼

Voice
Automatic   ▼

SPEAKING RATE: 1 ❷   PITCH: 0 (SEMITONES) ❷   VOLUME GAIN: 0 (DB) ❷

Select 'Audio Effects' profiles. (For standard API calls, **won't** affect Telephony integration) ❷

'Audio Effects' profile

EXPERIMENT WITH DIFFERENT VOICE SETTINGS
Enter text or SSML below and hit 'PLAY' button.

Text or SSML to speak:
                                                              PLAY
                                            0 / 1000

Figure 7-24. *Voice settings*

It's also possible to change the **audio effects profile** as seen in Figure 7-25. When you deploy your voice on a headphone or medium speaker, you might want to have the best voice quality. On a handheld device, you could lower the quality. That reduces the audio stream's size, and it will be smaller, and thus it will be faster to play.

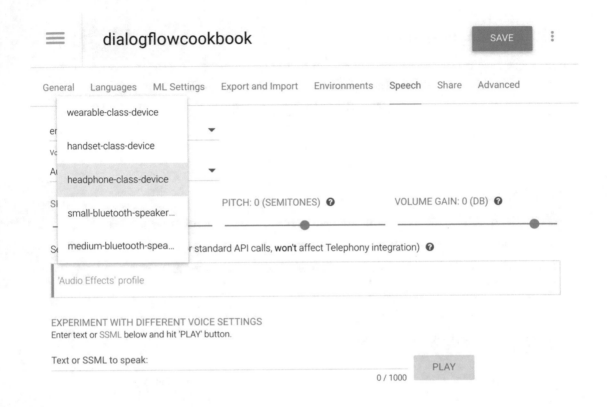

Figure 7-25. *Changing the audio profiles*

On the bottom of the **Settings ➤ Speech** tab, there is an SSML text box (Figure 7-26), which allows you to test your SSML writing, so you can play around with the tags and see if the sound is optimal.

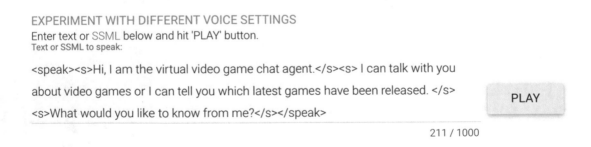

Figure 7-26. *Trying out SSML in the speech editor*

Controlling the Intonation

With SSML, you can give more structure or intonation to your sentences.

The definition of **intonation** is how your voice pitch goes up and down as you talk or recite something by singing it. An example of intonation is the way your voice raises in pitch at the end of a question. With intonation, you can give sentences with different meanings and emotions.

You will write all your SSML tags in the parent `<speak>` tag.

You can cluster paragraphs and sentences with `<p>` and `<s>` tags. By clustering those sentences, you can build in more pauses. By grouping sentences with a paragraph, the pause will be a little longer than between sentences.

Specific punctuation marks will also change the intonation. For example, a comma will create a little pause and raise the intonation. A question mark will make sure that the sentence will sound more like a question because it increases the intonation at the end.

With the `<break>` tag, you can control the time in seconds (s) or milliseconds (ms) of a pause manually.

The `<say-as>` element lets you indicate information about the type of text construct within the element. You can make sure that words will be pronounced as **cardinals**, **ordinals**, **characters**, **fractions**, **units**, **telephone numbers**, **verbatims**, **dates,** and **times.** You can even bleep out censored text.

Here's an example spoken as "Twelve thousand three hundred forty five" (for US English) or "Twelve thousand three hundred and forty five" (for UK English):

```
<speak><say-as interpret-as="cardinal">12345</say-as></speak>
```

`<sub>` indicates that the text in the alias attribute value replaces the contained text for pronunciation. This is handy for abbreviations, but you could also use it to "tweak" the pronunciation if you feel that the TTS synthesizer doesn't pronounce your word in a certain language the right way.

```
<sub alias="World Wide Web Consortium">W3C</sub>
```

`<prosody>` is used to customize the **pitch**, **speaking rate**, and **volume** of the element's text.

There are also tags for playing audio files or controlling media with the `<audio>` and `<media>` elements. In contact centers, you can use these to play audio recordings or music clips while waiting. Or you could use short audio sounds as feedback after collecting answers from your users.

Summary

This chapter gave a lot of information on building voice bots for smart assistants such as the Google Assistant and building voice bots for telephony systems. The last sections of this chapter included ways on how you can improve the Speech to Text and the Text to Speech of voice bots:

- You want to build a conversation for the Google Assistant.

- You want to build a simple conversation for a telephone with the telephony gateway to create an inbound toll-free number.

- You want to have AI in your contact centers to provide advanced automated conversations with Contact Center AI.

- You want to improve the Speech to Text quality for voice and callbots.

- You want to make your voice conversations Text to Speech output to make it sound more natural.

Further Reading

- Actions on Google documentation

  https://developers.google.com/assistant/conversational/overview

- Actions on Google console

  https://console.actions.google.com

- Actions on Google documentation on rich message response types

  https://developers.google.com/assistant/conversational/rich-responses

- Actions on Google documentation on submitting an action

  https://developers.google.com/assistant/conversational/submit-project

- Checklist for submitting your action

  ```
  https://developers.google.com/assistant/conversational/
  checklist
  ```

- Dialogflow documentation on the Actions on Google integration

  ```
  https://cloud.google.com/dialogflow/es/docs/integrations/aog
  ```

- Dialogflow documentation on versioning

  ```
  https://cloud.google.com/dialogflow/es/docs/agents-
  versions
  ```

- Actions on Google Node.js client library

  ```
  https://github.com/actions-on-google/actions-on-google-
  nodejs
  ```

- Conversational Actions tool

  ```
  https://developers.google.com/assistant/conversational/
  overview
  ```

- Define Actions with the Actions SDK

  ```
  https://developers.google.com/assistant/conversational/df-
  asdk/actions-sdk/define-actions
  ```

- gactions command-line tool

  ```
  https://developers.google.com/assistant/conversational/df-
  asdk/actions-sdk/gactions-cli
  ```

- ngrok

  ```
  https://ngrok.com/
  ```

- actions-sdk on npm

  ```
  https://www.npmjs.com/package/actions-on-google
  ```

- Dialogflow documentation on telephone gateway integration

  ```
  https://cloud.google.com/dialogflow/es/docs/integrations/
  phone-gateway
  ```

- Dialogflow pricing on Phone Gateway usage

  `https://cloud.google.com/dialogflow/pricing`

- Contact Center AI documentation

  `https://cloud.google.com/solutions/contact-center`

- How Contact Center AI works by Genesys

  `https://www.youtube.com/watch?v=3PWd52OW6ns`

- Dialogflow documentation on Speech Adaptation

  `https://cloud.google.com/dialogflow/es/docs/speech-adaptation`

- Speech Adaptation in SDK

  `https://cloud.google.com/dialogflow/es/docs/reference/rpc/google.cloud.dialogflow.v2beta1#google.cloud.dialogflow.v2beta1.SpeechContext`

- Google Assistant guide on best practices for voice dialogues

  `https://designguidelines.withgoogle.com/conversation/conversation-design/`

- Google Assistant documentation on SSML

  `https://developers.google.com/assistant/actions/reference/ssml`

CHAPTER 8

Creating a Multilingual Chatbot

Dialogflow supports many languages; it is possible to create multilingual chatbots. When you create a Dialogflow agent, you have to pick your default language, for example, English. Afterward, you can add other languages.

This chapter will give you an overview of the languages that Dialogflow Essentials support. It will show you how to build a multilingual virtual agent. It will explain how an export looks like for a multilingual bot and how you can programmatically detect languages through the Dialogflow API. This chapter will end with using a translation service to translate your bot answers on the fly automatically.

Agent Languages

There are two categories of languages:

- **Root languages**: These are languages like *English (en)* that do not specify a locale.

- **Locale-specific languages**: These are languages like *English-US (en-US)* that specify a locale as a specific region or country.

You should primarily design your agent for root language multi-language and only customize for locale-specific languages as needed. Figures 8-1 and 8-2 will show you the languages which are supported by the time of writing.

© Lee Boonstra 2021
L. Boonstra, *The Definitive Guide to Conversational AI with Dialogflow and Google Cloud*,
https://doi.org/10.1007/978-1-4842-7014-1_8

Name	Tag *	Text	STT	TTS	Phone	Knowledge	Sentiment	SmTalk
Chinese - Cantonese	zh-HK	✔	✔	✔				
Chinese - Simplified	zh-CN	✔	✔	✔	✔		✔	
Chinese - Traditional	zh-TW	✔	✔				✔	
Danish	da	✔	✔	✔	✔			
Dutch	nl	✔	✔	✔	✔			
English	en	✔	✔	✔	✔	✔	✔	✔
English - Australia	en-AU	✔	✔	✔	✔	✔		
English - Canada	en-CA	✔	✔	✔	✔	✔		
English - Great Britain	en-GB	✔	✔	✔	✔	✔		
English - India	en-IN	✔	✔	✔	✔	✔		
English - US	en-US	✔	✔	✔	✔	✔	✔	
French	fr	✔	✔	✔	✔		✔	✔
French - Canada	fr-CA	✔	✔	✔	✔			
French - France	fr-FR	✔	✔	✔	✔		✔	
German	de	✔	✔	✔	✔		✔	

Figure 8-1. *Overview of all the languages and supported features that are available in Dialogflow Essentials (part 1)*

Hindi	hi	✔	✔	✔	✔		
Indonesian	id	✔	✔	✔	✔		
Italian	it	✔	✔	✔	✔	✔	✔
Japanese	ja	✔	✔	✔	✔	✔	
Korean	ko	✔	✔	✔	✔	✔	
Norwegian	no	✔	✔	✔	✔		
Polish	pl	✔	✔	✔	✔		
Portuguese - Brazil	pt-BR	✔	✔	✔	✔		
Portuguese - Portugal	pt	✔	✔	✔	✔	✔	
Russian	ru	✔	✔	✔	✔		✔
Spanish	es	✔	✔	✔	✔	✔	
Spanish - Latin America	es-419	✔	✔				
Spanish - Spain	es-ES	✔	✔	✔	✔	✔	
Swedish	sv	✔	✔	✔	✔		
Thai	th	✔	✔				
Turkish	tr	✔	✔	✔	✔		
Ukrainian	uk	✔	✔	✔	✔		

Figure 8-2. Overview of all the languages and supported features that are available in Dialogflow Essentials (part 2)

Note   As a best practice, you should complete your agent in the default language before adding additional languages.

Building a Multi-language Agent

To add a language, click the + button next to the existing languages (bullets, see Figure 8-3). This takes you to the **Languages** tab of agent settings. Alternatively, you can go to the **Dialogflow Settings** panel and choose the Languages tab.

Figure 8-3. *The language bullets to switch agent language*

Choose a language from the **Select Additional Language** dropdown menu. (You can scroll with your mouse through over 20 different languages; see Figure 8-4.)

Figure 8-4. *Choosing languages*

Click **Save** .

You can switch between languages by clicking the **blue and grey language bullets** under the agent name.

The Dialogflow agent will share all its settings, but what's unique to a language are the **Intent training phrases**, **Intent Responses**, and **Entity entries**. Those you will need to localize to make your multilingual agent work.

You can use the simulator by selecting the language of choice before testing your conversations.

It depends on the integration of choice, how languages are supported and presented to the user, for example:

- When building a bot for **Google Assistant**, Actions on Google will take the Dialogflow language and can deploy the Assistant action in a certain language for a defined region.

- The built-in **Web Demo** integration only supports English, so no multilingual agents, but the built-in **Dialogflow Messenger** web integration does support multilingual agents, as long as you set the HTML element language-code while integrating the snippet to your website. With server-side coding, for example, you could build a switch that presents the chatbot in the correct language based on a button click or IP address.

- When you build your own custom integration, for a website or mobile app, you will have to detect the intent, through the SDK. The detectIntent calls take a language code as a parameter as part of the TextInput QueryInput object. You will see an example later in this chapter.

Note   Do not mix training phrases with different languages in the same agent, like in the following example. You will likely damage the Machine Learning model by doing so.

User: I want to buy an Xbox series X (English)

Agent: How many controllers do you need?

User: mujhe 2 kantrolar chaahie (Hindi)

Agent: Ok, I will order an Xbox series X with two controllers.

Exporting a Multi-language Dialogflow ES Agent

When you export a Dialogflow agent via the settings panel (Figure 8-5), you will retrieve a zip file. This zip file will contain intents and entity JSON files.

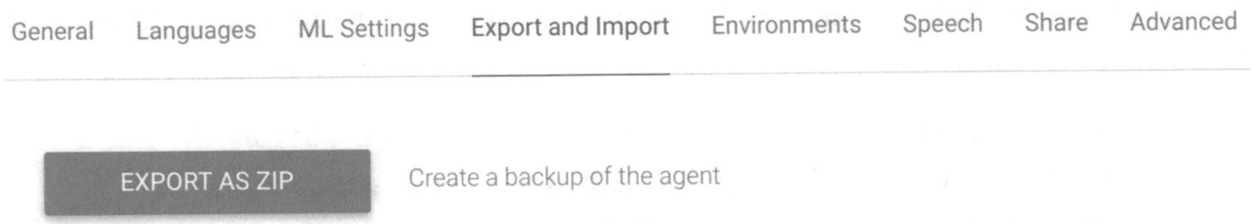

| General | Languages | ML Settings | Export and Import | Environments | Speech | Share | Advanced |

EXPORT AS ZIP   Create a backup of the agent

Figure 8-5. *Exporting the zip to preview language files in your editor*

For intents, the intent settings, as well as the responses, are in the *x_Intent.json* file. The training phrases for each particular language are in the *x_Intent_ usersays_<languagecode>.json* file.

- *intents/Default Welcome Intent.json*

- *intents/Default Welcome Intent_usersays_en.json*

- *intents/Default Welcome Intent_usersays_nl.json*

For entities, the entity settings are in the entity JSON file. The keys and values of an entry in their particular language are in the *x_entries_<languagecode>.json* file.

- *entities/product_color.json*

- *entities/products_color_entries_en.json*

- *entities/products_color_entries_nl.json*

Tip   When you are handy with a code editor and are comfortable reading JSON files, it might save you some time to translate Dialogflow agents via a coding editor.

Detecting Multi-language Intents via the SDK

In case you want to build your conversational AI in a custom web integration (see Chapter 11), it's good to know that you can set the languageCode field in the detectIntent call, when defining the text input within a queryInput:

```
const responses = await sessionClient.detectIntent({
  queryInput: {
    text: {
      // The query to send to the dialogflow agent
      text: 'hello',
      // The language used by the client (en-US)
      languageCode: 'en-US',
    },
  },
}
});
```

When Dialogflow receives a detectIntent request and a language wasn't passed in, Dialogflow handles the request using the default language.

When Dialogflow receives a detectIntent request that does not supply a language supported by the agent, the following rules apply:

- When a request supplies a locale-specific language that the agent does not support, but the agent's associated root language is supported, Dialogflow handles the request using the root language.

- System entity extraction is an exception to the previous rule. System entity extraction uses the supplied locale-specific language, even if the agent does not support the locale-specific language.

Working with the Translation Service

Suppose you want to use a different language in Dialogflow than the supported Dialogflow languages. In that case, it might be possible to manually build a solution that translates every incoming user utterance to a base language before detecting the intent with Dialogflow. This typically works in not too difficult dialogues, assuming that the translated user utterances will be somehow similar to the training phrases the intent was trained on. The responses could be translated by you directly in the Dialogflow console or maybe come from a database through a fulfillment.

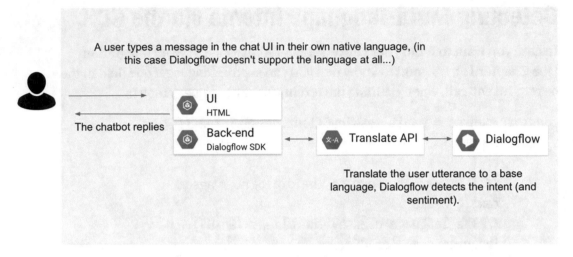

Figure 8-6. *The architecture of a real-time language service*

To build a solution like this (see the architecture in Figure 8-6), you will need to create a custom integration. See Chapter 11 to read more about this topic. In case you are interested in building and optimizing your webhooks for multi-language support, have a look at Chapter 10.

Summary

This chapter shares all the information on building a chatbot that supports multiple languages. We have examined the file structure of a multi-language agent export, how to detect multi-language intents with the SDK, and how you can integrate this with a translate service.

Further Reading

- Dialogflow documentation on multilingual chatbots

  https://cloud.google.com/dialogflow/es/docs/agents-multilingual

- Dialogflow supported languages

  https://cloud.google.com/dialogflow/es/docs/reference/language

## CHAPTER 9

Orchestrate Multiple Sub-chatbots from One Chat Interface

When you are building a chatbot with Dialogflow, you might notice that at some moment, you will reach the point that your chatbot performs less and becomes hard to maintain. If you have 1500 intents in one agent, likely you will have intents with training phrases that are quite similar to each other. The way you can solve this is in the Dialogflow settings panel, the **ML Settings** tab, to change the Machine Learning threshold for the confidence score. If the returned value is less than the threshold value, then a fallback intent will be triggered, or if there are no fallback intents defined, no intent will be activated. This might solve your problem for then, but what if your agent has more than 2000 intents?

And how would you maintain that, especially when working with large teams?

Imagine you would work for a large enterprise, such as a bank. The chatbot needs to address Bank Accounts, Mortgages, and General Banking questions. When you add all these intents to one Dialogflow agent, you will likely have intents colliding with each other. In fact, at a traditional bank, people work in teams. There is a team working on chatbots for Bank Accounts vs. Mortgages and so on. These teams don't know about the existence of each other's Dialogflow intents.

Data governance is essential. The mega-agent feature could solve these problems because each team can work on their own chatbot. This means rapid changes without breaking the training phrases from other teams, better debugging, version control, and agent reviews. But for the end user, it looks like one single chatbot which can address many features through one interface.

© Lee Boonstra 2021
L. Boonstra, *The Definitive Guide to Conversational AI with Dialogflow and Google Cloud*,
https://doi.org/10.1007/978-1-4842-7014-1_9

As with all Dialogflow agents, you can only create only one agent per Google Cloud project, so each sub-agent and the mega-agent will be associated with its own Google Cloud project. The small talk feature won't work, but you can include Knowledge Base Articles per sub-agent. A mega-agent can have at most ten sub-agents. Each Dialogflow agent can have 2000 intents. So this will give you a maximum of 20k intents.

Creating a Mega-Agent

The mega-agent feature allows you to connect various sub-Dialogflow agents to one single Dialogflow agent connected to your integration channels, so your users can interact with one chatbot interface instead of many.

Imagine you are a media retailer (see Figure 9-1). Your shop sells video games and movies. The chatbot users can ask questions about video games that will be answered by the video games chatbot or about movies, which will be answered by a movie chatbot.

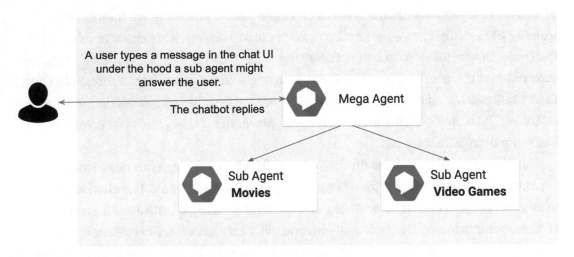

Figure 9-1. *An architectural overview of how a mega-agent works*

To set up the mega-agent feature, you will need to have (or create) "normal" Dialogflow agents first, which later will become a sub-agent.

1. **Create a new agent** from the dropdown menu under the logo. (See Figure 9-2.)

   You will give the new agent a name such as *mega-agent-media-retailer* and then flip the switch, **Set as mega-agent**, then hit **save**.

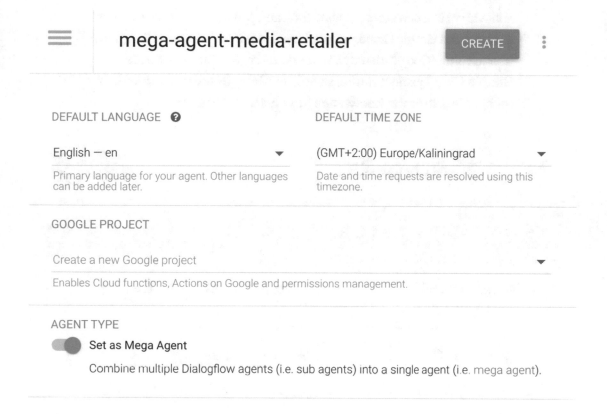

Figure 9-2. *Setting up a mega-agent*

2. After you have created the mega-agent, you will see a new menu item, *Sub Agents*, in your Dialogflow menu. Additionally, if your mega-agent name doesn't take too many characters, you will see the word "MEGA" next to the agent name. (Notice Figure 9-3.)

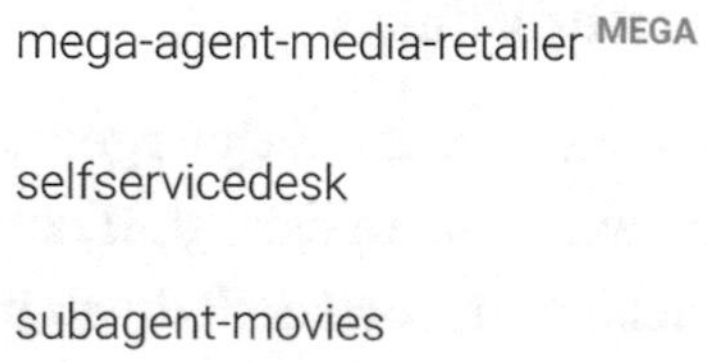

mega-agent-media-retailer ^{MEGA}

selfservicedesk

subagent-movies

Figure 9-3. *How a mega-agent is shown in the menu*

When it's your first time setting up the mega-agent, you will need to assign the sub-agents. Click No sub-agents yet. **Add the first one**.

You will get in a new screen (Figure 9-4), and you can start to select other agents (from Google Cloud projects) that are available to your Dialogflow user account (Google identity). While doing so, you can also see the **Google Cloud project name**, select the **Dialogflow environment**, or **include/exclude the knowledge base feature**. Hit **save**.

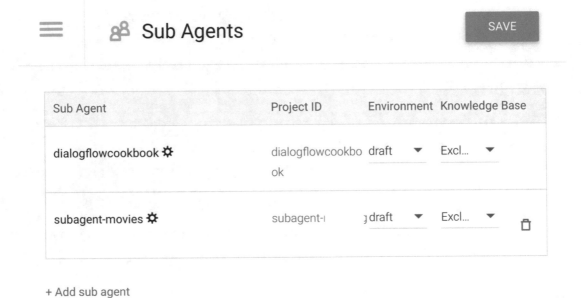

Figure 9-4. *Defining the sub-agents*

3. The mega-agent will need to get access to each sub-agent, and we can do this via the *IAM roles page* in the Google Cloud Console (Figure 9-5) by adding the service account email address to each sub-agent. Here's how we do this.

   While in Dialogflow, make sure the mega-agent is still active. Click the **settings cog** icon next to the mega-agent name, which will open the settings panel. When you scroll down in the **General** tab, you will see the project ID, which you can click. This will open the Google Cloud console. Navigate to the **IAM & Admin ➤ Service Accounts** page.

   Copy or make a notation of the mega-agent service account address, for example:

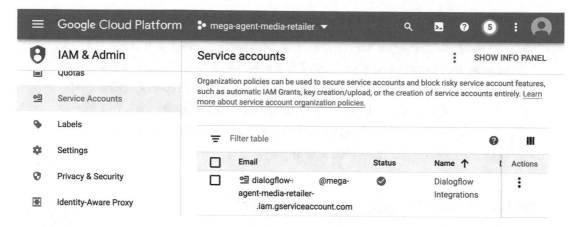

Figure 9-5. *Find the mega-agent service account address in the Google Cloud console*

```
dialogflow-<somecode>@mega-agent-media-retailer-<some
code>.iam.gserviceaccount.com
```

For what's worth, this project will need to have the Dialogflow API enabled. If it's correct, it's already enabled by default, but it's better to double-check this. First, you select the project in the blue top bar (Figure 9-6) and use the search form to search for *Dialogflow API*. When you see the blue *Disable API link*, you will know it's enabled.

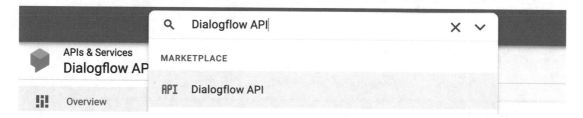

Figure 9-6. *Make sure the Dialogflow API is enabled*

4.   We will repeat step 4 for each sub-agent by clicking the Project ID in Dialogflow to open the Google Cloud console for the sub-agent projects. But now, we will navigate to the **IAM & Admin ➤ IAM** page.

Click the **Add** button at the top.

In the next slide-out screen, you can **paste the service account email address** (from step 4, see Figure 9-7) as a member. As a role, use the filter to search for **Dialogflow API Client**. (*Project Owner, Project Editor, or Dialogflow Admin* roles would work as well, but for security reasons, it's always best to give the least/absolute necessary permissions to your service accounts.)

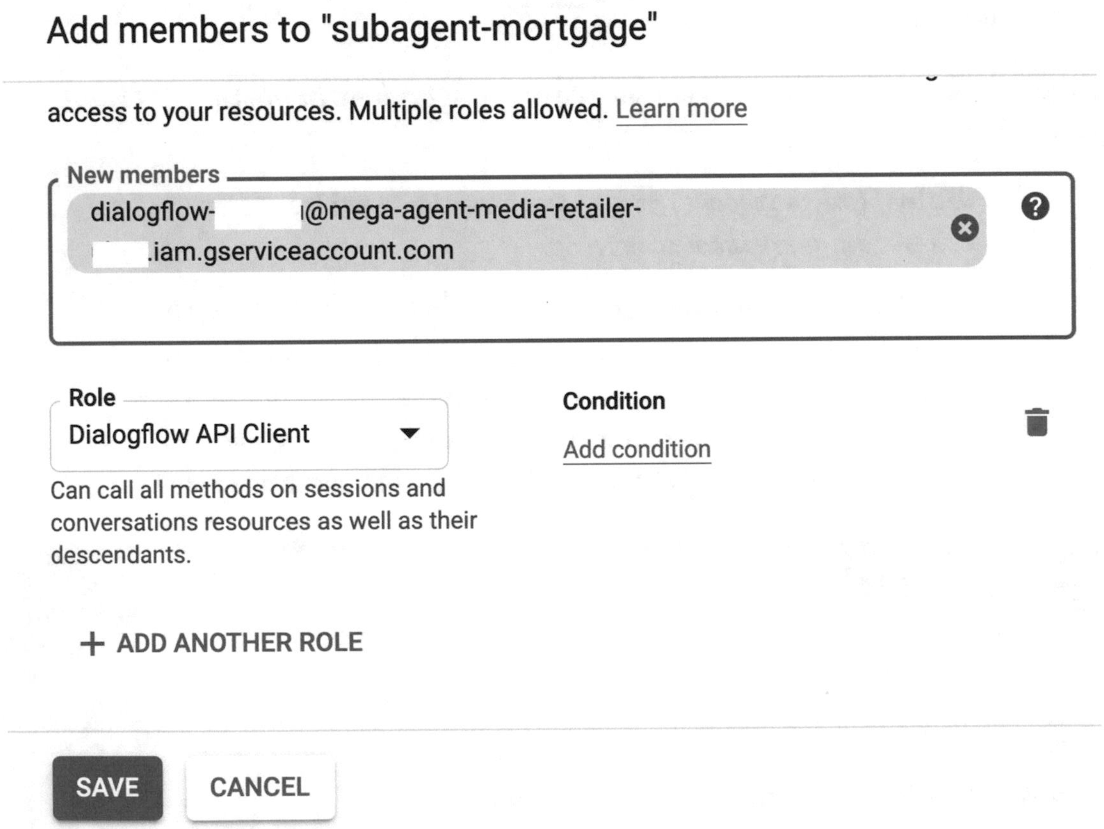

Add members to "subagent-mortgage"

access to your resources. Multiple roles allowed. Learn more

New members

dialogflow-   @mega-agent-media-retailer-
          .iam.gserviceaccount.com

Role
Dialogflow API Client   ▼

Condition
Add condition

Can call all methods on sessions and conversations resources as well as their descendants.

+ ADD ANOTHER ROLE

SAVE   CANCEL

Figure 9-7. *We add the mega-agent's service account address to each sub-agent's IAM settings, with the Dialogflow API Client role*

Repeat this step for each sub-agent and hit **Save**.

5. From here, you can test your mega-agent in the Dialogflow simulator. However, if you want to integrate this into a real application, you will likely need to download the service account to your local drive. (See Chapter 10.)

To test the mega-agent feature in Dialogflow, make sure you are still in the mega-agent project. You can start typing questions in the simulator like

- "What's your favorite videogame?" It will return the response from the video games sub-agent.

- "What movies are out on DVD?" It would return an answer from the movies sub-agent.

Tip   If you want to use the mega-agent feature while working with integrations such as the Google Assistant, you will need to add the IAM role Dialogflow Service Agent to the Service Account of each agent (mega and subs).

Using the SDK

When you detect an intent via the SDK, you would make a detectIntent call and use the mega-agent's project ID. Dialogflow will consider all of the sub-agents, and the best response from the sub-agents is returned.

However, it's also possible to specify one or more sub-agents for a detect intent request by setting the subAgents field of QueryParameters.

```
{
  "queryInput": {
    "text": {
      "text": "How can I open a new bank account?",
      "languageCode": "en-US"
    }
  },
  "queryParams": {
```

```
  "subAgents": [
    {"project": "projects/dialogflow-mortgages"},
    {"project": "projects/dialogflow-bankaccounts"}
  ]
 }
}
```

How Billing Works

The pricing is based on the number of intents used to fulfill a user request. If a request explicitly specifies sub-agents, this is the sum of all intents for the supplied sub-agents. If a request does not specify sub-agents, this is the sum of all intents for the mega-agent's sub-agents. Thus, when any request is made with the potential for any one of N intents as a match, all N intents need to be examined. Dialogflow has to search through all N of those intents, so when N is large, the price will be increased.

Summary

This chapter contains information about mega-agents. Imagine you are working in a large team, and you want to orchestrate multiple chatbots through one chatbot interface. With the mega-agent feature, you can create sub-agents and link them all together. This is great for data governance, but also you can 10x your intent limit.

The source code is available on GitHub via the book's product page, located at www.apress.com/978-1-4842-7013-4.

The agents that I have been using for these examples are

- _mega-agent-media-retailer

- _sub-agent: movies

- sub-agent: dialogflowcookbook (videogames) (_dialogflow-agent)

Further Reading

- Dialogflow documentation on mega-agents

  https://cloud.google.com/dialogflow/es/docs/agents-mega

## CHAPTER 10

Creating Fulfillment Webhooks

Fulfillment typically means that you are connecting your conversation to a web service. Companies often have web services and APIs to display content on websites in place already. In that case, although the majority of the work (like connecting to databases, security and business rules, etc.) has been done before, you will still need to work on an additional code that takes care of routing (to all your web services), and the conversational part, how you return your dialogue back to the user.

This chapter will explain how fulfillment webhook work in Dialogflow Essentials. It will show you how to write your own webhook with the actions-on-google npm package and the dialogflow npm package and how to write webhooks without using a package at all. It will discuss the various places where to run code, as a cloud function via the inline editor, as a container on Cloud Run or your own server with Express or locally. This chapter will also discuss how to build multilingual webhooks and how to secure your webhook code. It will contain lots of code examples to help you getting started.

An Introduction to Fulfillment Webhooks

Let's look into the following example; imagine I am building a banking agent for voice. Let's say it's a Google Assistant action, but it was linked to a user account. I could ask my agent:

1. "Has my salary been deposited today?"

2. Dialogflow matches the "salary intent."

L. Boonstra, *The Definitive Guide to Conversational AI with Dialogflow and Google Cloud*, https://doi.org/10.1007/978-1-4842-7014-1_10

3. I could fetch the bank account number from my employer from my user account, and the date of today's entity could be extracted by Dialogflow from the user utterance.

4. Fulfillment is enabled for the intent in Dialogflow. (Because Dialogflow doesn't transfer money, no web services of a bank do.)

5. A web request from Dialogflow to the webhook/back-end code is made.

6. Now we will do something with the request data.

    a. We will fetch the intent name, parameters, and context from the request.

    b. We will route another request to an existing banking web service for retrieving the account balance.

    c. That web service returns code, maybe JSON data like

    ```
    {
            "status": "ok",
            "bankaccount: "IBAN1234567890",
            "datetime": "1593080084",
            "amount": "3000",
            "currency": "USD"
    }
    ```

    We can't return this JSON feed to the user as this is not how you would have a conversation with your users. This is computer language, and also the date-time object is a timestamp instead of an understandable date.

    Instead, you would like to answer your users, maybe even in a Google Assistant rich message card:

    "It looks like 3000 dollars has been transferred today at 3 PM."

    So you will need a code that translates web service responses to a human-understandable conversation.

7. The webhook sends the response to the agent, so users can see and hear this.

You can see the preceding example flow exactly in Figure 10-1. In step 6, this is the additional work as seen in the webhook column. You will need a conversational UX designer to write the dialogue for the replies. You will need a developer who works in the webhook back-end code; to fetch the incoming request, call the underlying web services to translate computer responses to meaningful dialogues, and then return it to the agent.

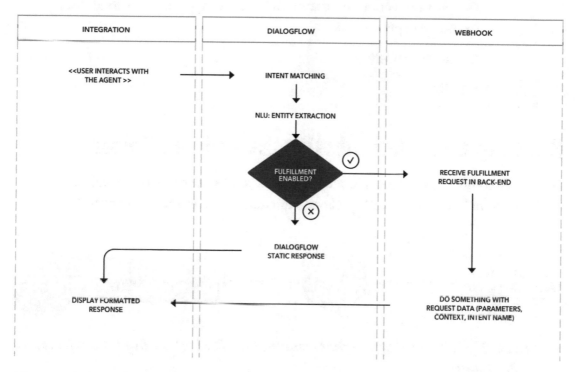

Figure 10-1. *A diagram that explains how Dialogflow fulfillment works. For simplicity of this Dialogflow, I have simplified the previous diagram. Theoretically, there should be a layer between the Dialogflow and webhook, which is your own custom implementation of the integration (which likely also includes security); that's the part that does the detectIntent calls. See Chapter 11 for more information*

Note   The webhook response must occur within 5 seconds. For Google Assistant actions, the response time can be extended to 10 seconds. Also, the webhook response must be less than or equal to 64KiB in size. If these limitations are not fulfilled, then the webhook request will time out and give the error "Webhook call failed. Error: DEADLINE_EXCEEDED", which you can see in the Fulfillment status.

There are various ways how you can execute a fulfillment with Dialogflow:

- Firebase Functions via the inline editor

- Fulfillment webhook

  - Cloud Functions

  - Google Cloud computing solutions such as App Engine, Cloud Run, Compute Engine, or GKE

  - On-premise hosting

  - Locally

Building a Fulfillment with the Built-in Editor

For simple webhook testing and implementation, you can use the inline editor. Under the hood, it makes use of serverless Cloud Functions for Firebase; see Figure 10-2.

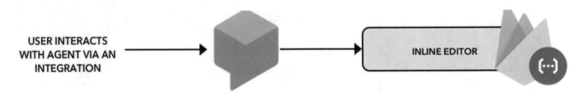

Figure 10-2. *A simple diagram that explains how Dialogflow fulfillment works for the inline editor*

Cloud Functions for Firebase is a serverless framework that lets you automatically run back-end code in response to events triggered by Firebase features and HTTPS requests. Your JavaScript or TypeScript code is stored in Google's cloud and runs in a managed environment. There's no need to manage and scale your own servers.

Note   When your web services are a little more advanced or care about the region where your code is hosted, you likely won't use the inline editor. Instead, you will enable the webhook switch, so you can specify your own web services URL.

Enable Fulfillment

You will have to enable dynamic fulfillment on the intent level. While you are on the intent page, you can enable fulfillment via the switches as seen in Figure 10-3.

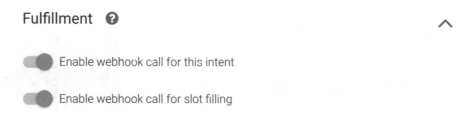

Figure 10-3. *Enable fulfillment in Dialogflow for each intent*

The enable webhook call for this intent enables dynamic fulfillment.

The second switch will enable webhooks for **slot filling**. When an intent is matched at runtime, the Dialogflow agent continues collecting information from the end user until the end user has provided data for each of the required parameters. This process is called slot filling. By default, Dialogflow does not send a fulfillment webhook request until it has collected all the data needed from the end user before posting it to the webhook back end when parameters are marked as required. (This means the agent will ask follow-up questions before calling the fulfillment back-end code.) Dialogflow will go through all the required parameters in the provided order.

However, when the webhook call for slot filling switch is enabled, Dialogflow sends a fulfillment webhook request for each conversational turn during slot filling. You might want to use this when you have a large conversation, and you want to store all the answers for each question each turn-taking turn. A technique you might be familiar with from websites that present large forms or shopping carts is they store every form field or step before submitting the total form (last page).

The next step is to tell Dialogflow where to post the data to. The webhook back-end code can be written in the editor, or you can provide one URL to a web service where Dialogflow will post. To use the editor, make sure the **enable inline editor switch** is enabled. See Figure 10-4.

Figure 10-4. *The inline editor in Dialogflow*

Using the dialogflow-fulfillment Package

By default, the editor contains some example code. It will make use of the
dialogflow-fulfillment npm library. See the **package.json** file in Listing 10-1.

Caution   The **dialogflow-fulfillment** library is no longer maintained. It doesn't
mean that it will be removed; it will work, but you won't see any updates to the
library. It should only be used when using the inline editor. Later in this chapter,
I will also show you how you can build a fulfillment without the dialogflow-
fulfillment library.

Listing 10-1. Dialogflow fulfillment in the editor, package.json

```
{
    "name": "dialogflowFirebaseFulfillment",
    "description": "This is the default fulfillment for a Dialogflow agent
    using Cloud Functions for Firebase",
    "version": "0.0.1",
```

```
  "private": true,
  "license": "Apache Version 2.0",
  "author": "Lee Boonstra",
  "engines": {
    "node": "8"
  },
  "scripts": {
    "start": "firebase serve --only functions:dialogflowFirebaseFulfillment",
    "deploy": "firebase deploy --only functions:dialogflowFircbaseFulfillment"
  },
  "dependencies": {
    "actions-on-google": "^2.12.0",
    "firebase-admin": "^5.13.1",
    "firebase-functions": "^2.0.2",
    "dialogflow-fulfillment": "^0.6.1"
  }
}
```

Firebase HTTPS functions start with the following code implementation (see Listing 10-2) to fetch data from the request.

Listing 10-2. A cloud function in Firebase

```
const functions = require('firebase-functions');
exports.helloWorld = functions.https.onRequest((request, response) => {
  response.send("Hello from Firebase!");
});
```

Under the hood, this Node.js script makes use of the Node.js web framework Express. The request parameter will give you information such as parameters from the request. body. With the response parameter, you can return the results (back to Dialogflow.)

When Firebase Functions are used in combination with the dialogflow-fulfillment package, your Dialogflow code could look like the **index.js** file of Listing 10-3. This example has an intent map for three intents: the default welcome, default fallback, and the buy product regex. It will show a response that's provided by the fulfillment code. The welcome message and fallback will show a simple message, where the buy product regex intent will show you a rich message—a card component.

Listing 10-3. Dialogflow fulfillment in the editor

```
'use strict';

const functions = require('firebase-functions');
const { WebhookClient, Card, Suggestion } = require('dialogflow-
fulfillment');

process.env.DEBUG = 'dialogflow:debug'; // enables lib debugging statements

exports.dialogflowFirebaseFulfillment = functions.https.onRequest((request,
response) => {
  const agent = new WebhookClient({ request, response });
  console.log('Dialogflow Request headers: ' + JSON.stringify(request.
  headers));
  console.log('Dialogflow Request body: ' + JSON.stringify(request.body));

  function welcome(agent) {
    agent.add(`Welcome to my agent!`);
  }

  function fallback(agent) {
    agent.add(`I didn't understand`);
    agent.add(`I'm sorry, can you try again?`);
  }

  function yourFunctionHandler(agent) {
    agent.add(`Ok. Buying product:`);
    console.log(agent.parameters);
    agent.add(new Card({
        title: agent.parameters.producttype,
        imageUrl: 'https://dummyimage.com/300x200/000/fff',
        text: `This is the body text of a card.  You can even use
        line\n  breaks and emoji! 💁`,
        buttonText: 'This is a button',
        buttonUrl: 'https://console.dialogflow.com/'
      })
    );
```

```
    agent.add(new Suggestion(`Quick Reply`));
    agent.add(new Suggestion(`Suggestion`));
    agent.context.set({ name: 'gamestore-picked', lifespan: 2, parameters:
    { gameStore: 'DialogflowGameStore' }});
}

// Run the proper function handler based on the matched Dialogflow intent name
let intentMap = new Map();
intentMap.set('Default Welcome Intent', welcome);
intentMap.set('Default Fallback Intent', fallback);
intentMap.set('Buy product regex', yourFunctionHandler);
agent.handleRequest(intentMap);
});
```

The **dialogflow-fulfillment** package does these main things:

- It wraps code around the request/responses to make the syntax of
  getting and returning a matched intent (with parameters and
  responses) easier.

  For example, **agent.add()** returns responses to Dialogflow,
  one by one. Or you could build a JavaScript intent map and use
  agent.handleRequest() to switch between the various intents.
  For example, Dialogflow detected the 'Buy product regex' intent as a
  match (it has the highest confidence level). The request object in the
  Cloud Function contains this detected intent. If the strings in the
  intent map contain the same string as the matched intent name
  (the name you used to create an intent in the Dialogflow UI),
  then it will invoke a function (in this case, yourFunctionHandler).
  That custom function will use **agent.add()** to return messages to
  your chatbot implementation, such as the web UI. You could get
  parameters or contexts from the **agent** parameter too.

- It wraps code around the various Dialogflow custom payloads for
  Dialogflow and other integrations (such as the Google Assistant) to
  implement those more quickly. Look into the yourFunctionHandler
  function. To display a rich message with a Dialogflow card, you
  don't have to write a long JSON payload; instead, you can use the
  Card() class.

Once you finish writing your code in the cloud function, you can click **deploy**. It will take a few minutes for Dialogflow to reach Firebase and build a serverless container under the hood, which will be reachable via public HTTPS.

Caution   The inline editor uses the **firebase-admin** dependencies under the hood. The **dialogflow-fulfillment** library uses the **actions-on-google** under the hood. You will have to list "actions-on-google" and "firebase-admin" in the **package.json** dependencies to deploy a cloud function with the inline editor; else, you will receive a build error.

Diagnostic Info

Requests that will be sent to the webhook can be viewed with the **Diagnostic Info** button at the bottom of the page. It will open a window as seen in Figure 10-5, which will show you the fulfillment request.

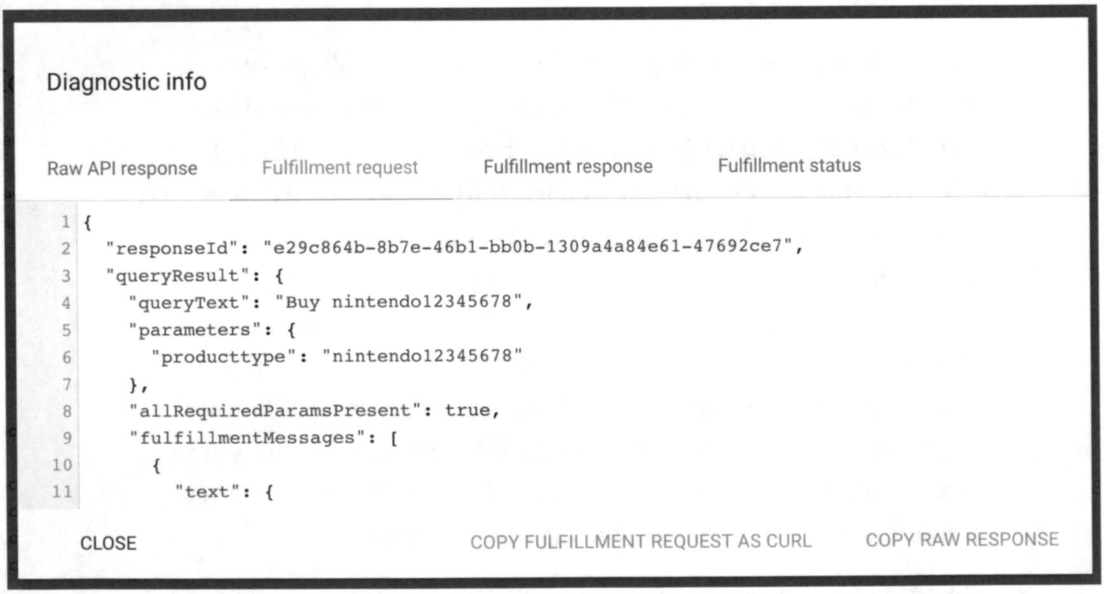

```
Diagnostic info

Raw API response      Fulfillment request      Fulfillment response      Fulfillment status

 1  {
 2    "responseId": "e29c864b-8b7e-46b1-bb0b-1309a4a84e61-47692ce7",
 3    "queryResult": {
 4      "queryText": "Buy nintendo12345678",
 5      "parameters": {
 6        "producttype": "nintendo12345678"
 7      },
 8      "allRequiredParamsPresent": true,
 9      "fulfillmentMessages": [
10        {
11          "text": {

     CLOSE                          COPY FULFILLMENT REQUEST AS CURL      COPY RAW RESPONSE
```

Figure 10-5. *Diagnostic info ➤ Fulfillment request, which will be sent to the Dialogflow API*

The fulfillment response tab as seen in Figure 10-6 will show you the response returned from the webhook (server).

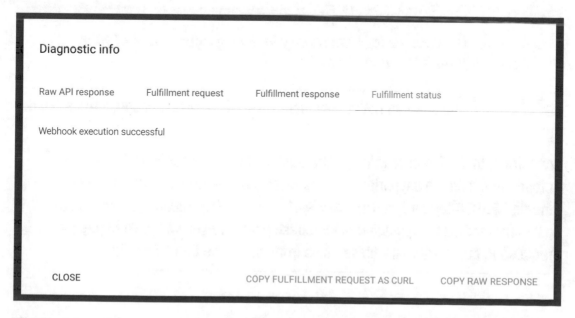

Diagnostic info

Raw API response   Fulfillment request   Fulfillment response   Fulfillment status

```
 1  {
 2    "fulfillmentMessages": [
 3      {
 4        "text": {
 5          "text": [
 6            "Ok. Buying product:"
 7          ]
 8        }
 9      },
10      {
11        "card": {
```

CLOSE   COPY FULFILLMENT REQUEST AS CURL   COPY RAW RESPONSE

Figure 10-6. *Diagnostic info ➤ Fulfillment response from the Dialogflow API*

The fulfillment status can tell you if the webhook execution was successful or not; see Figure 10-7.

Diagnostic info

Raw API response   Fulfillment request   Fulfillment response   Fulfillment status

Webhook execution successful

CLOSE   COPY FULFILLMENT REQUEST AS CURL   COPY RAW RESPONSE

Figure 10-7. *Diagnostic info ➤ Fulfillment status returned by the Dialogflow API*

Firebase Logs

Since the inline editor uses Cloud Functions within Firebase, you can get access to the logs via Firebase. This is handy for debugging when things go wrong.

Just open Firebase (`https://console.firebase.google.com/`) and click **Functions ➤ Logging**. Figure 10-8 will show you how the logs screen in Firebase will look like.

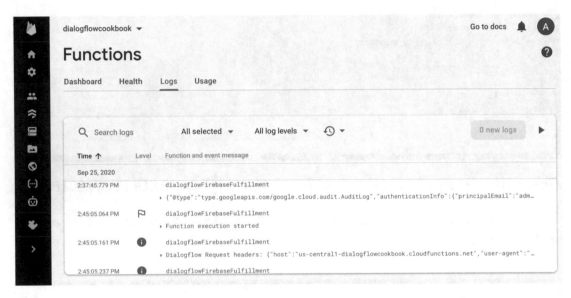

Figure 10-8. *The Firebase logs can show you the log information of your Dialogflow fulfillment from the editor*

Note   The inline editor in Dialogflow makes use of Firebase Functions (Free Spark plan).

According to the Firebase Pricing, Outbound Network connections for Firebase Cloud Functions are supported with the Blaze plan. Network Egress is free for the first 5GB. Afterward, you will pay $0.12 per GB. This means you will need a payment method by upgrading the Firebase plan, and you will have to pay for requesting other external web services from within the Cloud Function.

Besides writing JavaScript fulfillment code by the **dialogflow-fulfillment npm** package, there are other ways how you can write fulfillment code with JavaScript. As a matter of fact, you can write any fulfillment in the language you like, but this book uses JavaScript for all of the examples.

For example, you could write JavaScript fulfillments with the Actions on Google npm package (`https://www.npmjs.com/package/actions-on-google`). You could use this if you are building fulfillment for the Google Assistant.

It's also possible to manually create a webhook without any npm package at all. You would need to fetch the matched intent name, parameters, and context from the incoming webhook requests, manually build custom payloads, and return them to the agent.

Using Actions on Google for Building Dialogflow Fulfillment

Let's look into an example using the Actions on Google package; it will do the exact same thing as the code example in Listing 10-2. Since Actions on Google is an npm package, you will need a **package.json** as shown in Listing 10-4.

Listing 10-4. Actions on Google package.json

```
{
    "name": "dialogflowFirebaseFulfillment",
    "description": "This is the default fulfillment for a Dialogflow agents
    using Cloud Functions for Firebase",
    "version": "0.0.1",
    "private": true,
    "license": "Apache Version 2.0",
    "author": "Lee Boonstra",
    "engines": {
      "node": "8"
    },
    "scripts": {
      "start": "firebase serve --only functions:dialogflowFirebaseFulfillment",
```

```
    "deploy": "firebase deploy --only functions:dialogflowFirebase
    Fulfillment"
  },
  "dependencies": {
    "actions-on-google": "^2.12.0",
    "firebase-admin": "^5.13.1",
    "firebase-functions": "^2.0.2"
  }
}
```

The **index.js** of Listing 10-5 contains the implementation code.

Listing 10-5. Actions on Google index.js

```
'use strict';

const {
  dialogflow,
  BasicCard,
  Button,
  Image,
  Suggestions
} = require('actions-on-google');

const functions = require('firebase-functions');

process.env.DEBUG = 'dialogflow:debug'; // enables lib debugging statements

function welcome(conv) {
    console.log('Dialogflow Request headers: ' + JSON.stringify(conv.headers));
    console.log('Dialogflow Request body: ' + JSON.stringify(conv.body));
    conv.ask(`Welcome to my agent!`);
  }

function fallback(conv) {
    console.log('Dialogflow Request headers: ' + JSON.stringify(conv.headers));
    console.log('Dialogflow Request body: ' + JSON.stringify(conv.body));
```

```
    conv.ask(`I didn't understand`);
    conv.ask(`I'm sorry, can you try again?`);
}

function yourFunctionHandler(conv, parameters) {
    conv.ask(`Ok. Buying product:`);
    console.log(parameters);

    conv.ask(new BasicCard({
        title: parameters.producttype,
        image: new Image({
          url: 'https://dummyimage.com/300x200/000/fff',
          alt: 'Image alternate text',
        }),
        text: `This is the body text of a card.  You can even use
        line\n  breaks and emoji! 🏃`,
        buttons: new Button({
          title: 'This is a button',
          url: 'https://assistant.google.com/',
        })
    }));

    conv.ask(new Suggestions(`Quick Reply`));
    conv.ask(new Suggestions(`Suggestion`));
    conv.contexts.set({ name: 'gamestore-picked', lifespan: 2, parameters:
    { gameStore: 'DialogflowGameStore' }});
}

const app = dialogflow();

// Run the proper function handler based on the matched Dialogflow intent name
app.intent('Default Welcome Intent', welcome);
app.intent('Default Fallback Intent', fallback);
app.intent('Buy product regex', yourFunctionHandler);
```

```
// Intent in Dialogflow called `Goodbye`
app.intent('Goodbye', conv => {
    conv.close('See you later!');
});

exports.dialogflowFirebaseFulfillment = functions.https.onRequest(app);
```

Note the differences between the **dialogflow-fulfillment** npm package (Listing 10-3 vs. 10-5) and the **actions on google** npm package of Listing 10-5:

- **conv** is an instance of type DialogflowConversation.

- **app** is an instance of type DialogflowApp.

- **app** accepts options of type DialogflowOptions.

- **conv.ask** sends a text string to the device. The Google Assistant synthesizer will speak this sentence out. On a device with a screen, you will also see a text balloon, including this text.

- **parameters**: These can be received as a second argument in the function.

- **contexts**: You can get and set context from the conv.contexts object. (Notice the "s" after context.)

- **conv.close**: This will close the action and return to the native Google Assistant scope.

Besides this, the formatting for Cards and other rich messages is all according to the Actions on Google spec.

Tip   When building actions for the Google Assistant, it's best to use the Google Assistant simulator to test the experience (`https://console.actions.google.com/`).

Here's how the fulfillment response of an Actions on Google action looks like in the Dialogflow Diagnostic Info window; see Figure 10-9.

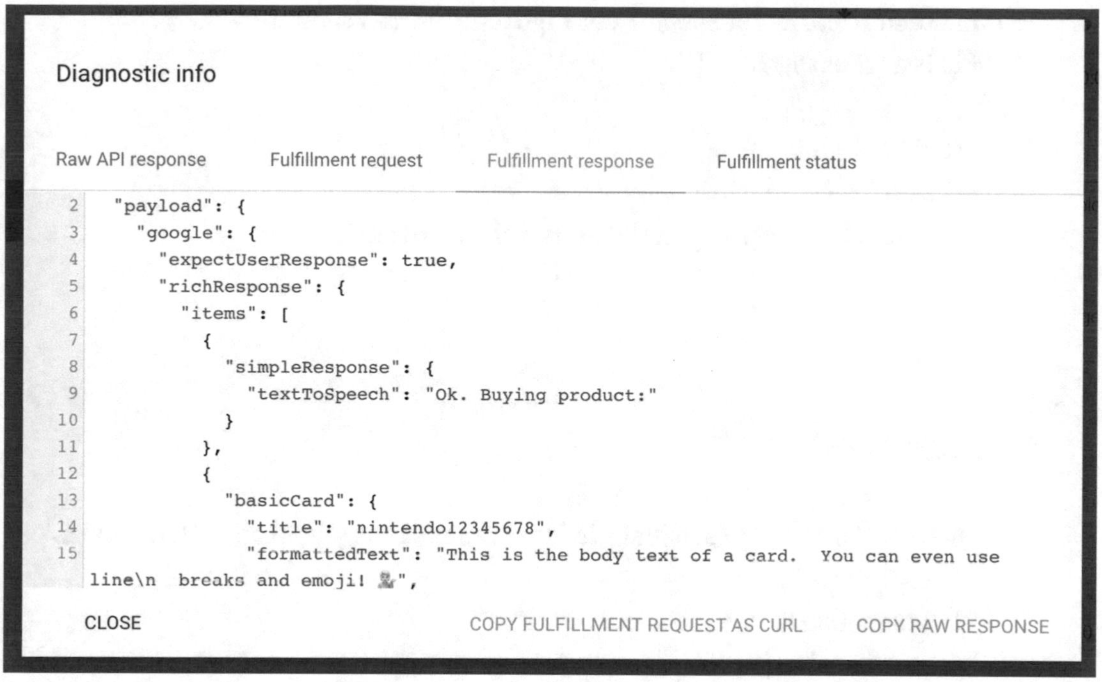

Figure 10-9. *Dialogflow fulfillment response of a Google Assistant action*

Build Your Fulfillment Webhook Manually

A webhook response that was received from Dialogflow typically looks like the following response; see Listing 10-6. Notice the intent object, which contains the matched intent name with the confidence level. It includes the outputContexts and parameters that have been used to gather the response.

Listing 10-6. Dialogflow API request to use to build fulfillment manually

```
{
  "responseId": "response-id",
  "session": "projects/project-id/agent/sessions/session-id",
  "queryResult": {
    "queryText": "End-user expression",
    "parameters": {
      "param-name": "param-value"
    },
    "allRequiredParamsPresent": true,
```

```json
    "fulfillmentText": "Response configured for matched intent",
    "fulfillmentMessages": [
      {
        "text": {
          "text": [
            "Response configured for matched intent"
          ]
        }
      }
    ],
    "outputContexts": [
      {
        "name": "projects/project-id/agent/sessions/session-id/contexts/
        context-name",
        "lifespanCount": 5,
        "parameters": {
          "param-name": "param-value"
        }
      }
    ],
    "intent": {
      "name": "projects/project-id/agent/intents/intent-id",
      "displayName": "matched-intent-name"
    },
    "intentDetectionConfidence": 1,
    "diagnosticInfo": {},
    "languageCode": "en"
  },
  "originalDetectIntentRequest": {}
}
```

In order for the virtual agent to present the results on the screen (depending on the channel/integration), you would need to send this response to your server

The response which we will need to send back to the agent should contain the format which is shown in Listing 10-7.

Listing 10-7. Dialogflow API response to use to build fulfillment manually

```
{
  "fulfillmentMessages": [
    {
      "text": {
        "text": [
          "Ok. Buying product:"
        ]
      }
    },
    {
      "card": {
        "title": "",
        "subtitle": "This is the body text of a card.  You can even use
        line\n  breaks and emoji! 🏊",
        "imageUri": "https://dummyimage.com/300x200/000/fff",
        "buttons": [
          {
            "text": "This is a button",
            "postback": "https://consolc.dialogflow.com/"
          }
        ]
      }
    },
    {
      "quickReplies": {
        "quickReplies": [
          "Quick Reply",
          "Suggestion"
        ]
      }
    }
  ],
```

```
  "outputContexts": [
    {
      "name": "projects/dialogflowcookbook/agent/sessions/0e39ecfb-881d-
      859e-6ac6-d65c8398311c/contexts/gamestore-picked",
      "lifespanCount": 2,
      "parameters": {
        "gameStore": "DialogflowGameStore"
      }
    }
  ]
}
```

Have a look at how I have implemented this; see Listing 10-8.

Listing 10-8. The index.js of a Dialogflow fulfillment without using the dialogflow-fulfillment libary

```
'use strict';

const functions = require('firebase-functions');
process.env.DEBUG = 'dialogflow:debug'; // enables lib debugging statements

function handleRequest(map, request){
    let intent;
    if(request.body && request.body.queryResult && request.body.
    queryResult.intent){
        intent = request.body.queryResult.intent.displayName;
    }

    let response;
    if (map.has(intent) !== false){
        response = map.get(intent)(request);
    } else {
        response = map.get('Default Fallback Intent')(request);
      }
    return response;
}
```

```
function fallback(request) {
 return {
    "fulfillmentMessages": [
      {
        "text": {
          "text": [
            "I didn't understand.",
            "I'm sorry, can you try again?"
          ]
        }
      }
    ]
  };
}

function welcome(request) {
  return {
    "fulfillmentMessages": [
      {
        "text": {
          "text": [
            "Welcome to my agent!"
          ]
        }
      }
    ]
  };
}

function yourFunctionHandler(request) {
  let parameters;
  if(request.body.queryResult.parameters){
    parameters = request.body.queryResult.parameters;
  }
  console.log(parameters);
  return {
    "fulfillmentMessages": [
```

```
  {
    "text": {
      "text": [
        "Ok. Buying product:"
      ]
    }
  },
  {
    "card": {
      "title": `${parameters.producttype}`,
      "subtitle": "This is the body text of a card.  You can even use
      line\n  breaks and emoji! 🏋",
      "imageUri": "https://dummyimage.com/300x200/000/fff",
      "buttons": [
        {
          "text": "This is a button",
          "postback": "https://console.dialogflow.com/"
        }
      ]
    }
  },
  {
    "quickReplies": {
      "quickReplies": [
        "Quick Reply",
        "Suggestion"
      ]
    }
  }
],
"outputContexts": [
  {
    "name": `${request.body.session}/contexts/gamestore-picked`,
    "lifespanCount": 2,
    "parameters": {
```

```
        "gameStore": "DialogflowGameStore"
      }
    }
  ]
 };
}

// parameters can be retrieved from the request
// you will need to work with custom payloads for rich messages, see:
// https://cloud.google.com/dialogflow/docs/reference/rest/v2beta1/
   projects.agent.intents
// outputContext won't work if you dont set the full session path.

exports.dialogflowFirebaseFulfillment = functions.https.onRequest((request,
response) => {
    let intentMap = new Map();
    intentMap.set('Default Welcome Intent', welcome);
    intentMap.set('Default Fallback Intent', fallback);
    intentMap.set('Buy product regex', yourFunctionHandler);
    let webhookResponse = handleRequest(intentMap, request);
    console.log(webhookResponse);
    response.json(webhookResponse);
});
```

This example uses a package.json as shown in Listing 10-9.

Listing 10-9. The package.json of a Dialogflow fulfillment without using the dialogflow-fulfillment library

```
{
    "name": "dialogflowFirebaseFulfillment",
    "description": "This is the default fulfillment for a Dialogflow agents
    using Cloud Functions for Firebase",
    "version": "0.0.1",
    "private": true,
    "license": "Apache Version 2.0",
    "author": "Lee Boonstra",
    "engines": {
```

```
      "node": "8"
    },
    "scripts": {
      "start": "firebase serve --only functions:dialogflowFirebaseFulfillment",
      "deploy": "firebase deploy --only functions:dialogflowFirebaseFulfillment"
    },
    "dependencies": {
      "actions-on-google": "^2.12.0",
      "firebase-admin": "^5.13.1",
      "firebase-functions": "^2.0.2"
    }
}
```

As you will notice, I am not using any Dialogflow npm packages. Instead, I handle the request myself with my custom `handleRequest` method, which uses a JavaScript map to retrieve the function name to execute based on the matched intent name (which was returned in the request from Dialogflow).

The `yourFunctionHandler` method implements a custom payload, which takes the correct JSON format of what's needed for a card. (You can find these formats in the Dialogflow documentation.)

Once I have formatted the JSON, I can send this back to the agent, with

```
response.json(webhookResponse);
```

Building Fulfillments Webhook

Instead of using the inline editor, you can also choose to run your fulfillment code elsewhere, as long as it runs over HTTPS. This is where you will need the webhook option for. See Figure 10-10.

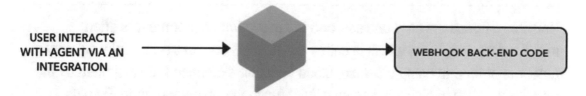

USER INTERACTS WITH AGENT VIA AN INTEGRATION

WEBHOOK BACK-END CODE

Figure 10-10. *A simple architecture of how fulfillment works with webhook code*

Where to Run My Back-End Code?

It's entirely up to you where you want to run your fulfillment code. The previous section discusses the inline editor, which runs your code under the hood in **Firebase**, serverless cloud functions. It's built-in, and it's easy to use.

For compliance reasons, you might want to run your code elsewhere, for example, **on-premise** (in-house, where you maintain your infrastructure) or in Google Cloud.

Tip   Since enterprises are using the pay-as-you-go edition of Dialogflow Essentials, they accepted the Google Cloud terms and conditions. Your code and data will be safe and secure, and you are the data owner. You will automatically get access to all the various computing/serving code options within Google Cloud. Since everything within Google Cloud uses the Google backbone undersea cable, this connection can transmit 60 terabytes of data per second. It's about 10 million times faster than your home broadband connection on a good day. Since Dialogflow is a Google Cloud solution and one of the computing options, this is the fastest way of running your code.

Here are the options within Google Cloud you can use for your webhooks.

Cloud Functions

Cloud Functions lets you automatically run back-end code in response to events triggered by Google Cloud/Firebase/Google Assistant features and HTTPS requests.

Out of the box, Cloud Functions serves your code over HTTPS. Running over an HTTPS connection requires a valid and trusted SSL certificate. Cloud Functions will set up out-of-the-box valid, secure, and trusted certificates.

> **Caution**   Functions are stateless, and the execution environment is often initialized from scratch, which is called a cold start. Cold starts can take significant amounts of time to complete. Also, Cloud Function execution time is limited by the timeout duration, which you can specify at function deployment time. By default, a function times out after 1 minute, but you can extend this period up to 9 minutes. When function execution exceeds the timeout, an error status is immediately returned to the caller. This makes Cloud Functions not always the right solution, especially when you have to connect to multiple databases and services to fetch information from.

App Engine (Flexible Environment)

Google App Engine is a cloud computing platform as a service for developing and hosting web applications in Google-managed data centers. Applications are sandboxed and run across multiple servers. There are various environments to choose from, supporting your favorite coding languages. It has no server management, which makes it easy for developers to bring their code into production. Out of the box, App Engine serves your code over HTTPS. Running over an HTTPS connection requires a valid and trusted SSL certificate. App Engine will set up out-of-the-box valid, secure, and trusted certificates.

Cloud Run

Develop and deploy highly scalable containerized applications on a fully managed serverless platform. You can write code your way using your favorite languages (Go, Python, Java, Ruby, Node.js, and more). Cloud Run will abstract away all infrastructure management for a simple developer experience. It's also very portable as it builds containers using the open standard Knative. This means you can run the containers anywhere you want (Google Cloud, other Cloud, on-premise). Out of the box, Cloud Run serves your code over HTTPS. Cloud Run will set up valid, out of the box, secure, and trusted certificates.

This chapter will show an example using webhook code on Cloud Run.

> **Caution**   Cloud Run runs containers, so for each release you have to build a container and push it to Google Cloud. Unlike App Engine Flexible Environment, Cloud Run only runs when requests come in, so you don't pay for time spent idling, but this also means you have to deal with cold starts.

Kubernetes Engine

Google Kubernetes Engine (GKE) is a secured and fully managed Kubernetes service, which means you don't need to worry about setting up and maintaining Kubernetes on an infrastructure.

> **Tip**   It's possible to build stateful applications with GKE that save data to persistent disk storage for use by the server, by clients, and by other applications. An example of a stateful application is a database or key-value store to which data is saved and retrieved by other applications. You won't have to worry about cold starts or event-driven timeouts. But you will need to set up the server yourself. In order to run GKE over HTTPS, you will need to connect a domain name and attach a valid certificate.

Compute Engine

Compute Engine lets you create and run virtual machines on Google's infrastructure.

> **Caution**   With VMs, you will need to set up and maintain everything (like the web server) yourself. In order to run over HTTPS, you will need to connect a domain name and attach a valid certificate.

This chapter will show an example using webhook code on Compute Engine to show you how to set up secure certificates.

Enable Webhooks

You will have to provide a **URL** to your fulfillment service on the **Dialogflow Fulfillment** page, as seen in Figure 10-11.

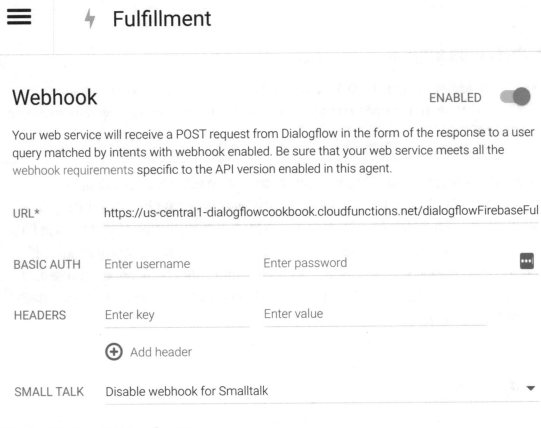

Figure 10-11. Webhook settings

Your webhook service must meet the following requirements:

- It must handle HTTPS requests. HTTP is not supported. Serverless computing solutions such as Cloud Run, Cloud Functions, and App Engine will come out of the box with a URL that runs over HTTPS.

- The webhook service can be behind basic auth or header authentication.

- It must handle POST requests with a JSON **WebhookRequest** body.

- It must respond to WebhookRequest requests with a JSON **WebhookResponse** body.

Cloud Function Implementation

Running your code from Google Cloud Functions is very similar to the inline editor. Under the hood, it even makes use of the same technology, as the inline editor is using Firebase Functions, and under the hood, Firebase Functions are Google Cloud Functions. The main difference is that Google Cloud will provide you a URL, which you can add to the webhook section in the Dialogflow Fulfillment page.

There are a few other benefits to using Cloud Functions over the inline editor. This is why many enterprises make use of the Cloud Functions instead of the Dialogflow built-in editor:

- Cloud Functions can be written in more languages than just Node.js such as Python, Go, or Java.

- Cloud Functions will be maintained in the same Google Cloud project as your Dialogflow project.

- Cloud Functions are part of Google Cloud, using the same terms and conditions, and are committed to compliances.

- Cloud Functions have integrated monitoring, logging, and debugging capability in Google Cloud.

- You can secure Cloud Functions with identity-based or network-based access control.

- Cloud Functions network settings enable you to control network ingress and egress to and from individual functions.

- Cloud Functions is regional, which means the infrastructure that runs your Cloud Function is located in a specific region and is managed by Google to be redundantly available across all the zones within that region.

Listing 10-10 shows an example of the code.

Listing 10-10. The implementation of a Cloud Function

```
// Dialogflow Fulfillment Code

exports.helloWorld = function helloWorld (request, response) {

    // get the Dialogflow request
    // do something
    // return to the agent

  res.send(`Hello from Cloud Functions!`);
};
```

A Cloud Run, App Engine, Compute Engine, GKE, or on-premise implementation could make use of the Express.js framework. It's a Node.js web application server framework, which is specifically designed for building single-page, multipage, and hybrid web applications.

Express Implementation (with Cloud Run)

Using an implementation on the Node.js Express framework can have several advantages over Cloud Functions (or Dialogflow inline editor). The main benefit will be that your code can be much more organized. Especially when you have a large codebase or are working with a large team of developers, you would instead pick this solution.

Here's an implementation solution on Cloud Run. With Cloud Run, you will make use of the following benefits:

- Write code your way using your favorite languages (Go, Python, Java, Ruby, Node.js, and more).

- Cloud Run takes any container image and pairs great with the container ecosystem: Cloud Build, Artifact Registry, Docker. This also means you could set up CI/CD pipelines.

- A simple command-line and user interface to quickly deploy and manage your services.

- No infrastructure to manage: once deployed, Cloud Run manages your services so you can sleep well.

- Cloud Run automatically scales up or down from zero to N depending on traffic.

- Cloud Run services are regional, which means the infrastructure that runs your Cloud Run app is located in a specific region and is managed by Google to be redundantly available across all the zones within that region. It can be automatically replicated across multiple zones.

- Out-of-the-box integration with Cloud Monitoring, Cloud Logging, and Error Reporting to ensure an application's health.

- Container instances run in a secure sandbox isolated from other resources.

Listing 10-11 shows an example of running a Dialogflow fulfillment as a Node.js Express implementation on Cloud Run. You will see that the implementation is similar to the inline editor implementation of the previous section, except that the implementation of Express is a little different.

Listing 10-11. Example of a Dialogflow fulfillment running as a Node.js Express application on Cloud Run. Indcx.js

```
'use strict';

const express = require('express');
const bodyParser = require('body-parser');
const basicAuth = require('express-basic-auth');

const { WebhookClient, Card, Suggestion } = require('dialogflow-
fulfillment');

process.env.DEBUG = 'dialogflow:debug'; // enables lib debugging statements

// Dialogflow Fulfillment Code

function welcome(agent) {
    agent.add(`Welcome to my agent!`);
  }
```

```javascript
function fallback(agent) {
    agent.add(`I didn't understand`);
    agent.add(`I'm sorry, can you try again?`);
}

function yourFunctionHandler(agent) {
    agent.add(`Ok. Buying product:`);
    console.log(agent.parameters);
    agent.add(new Card({
        title: agent.parameters.producttype,
        imageUrl: 'https://dummyimage.com/300x200/000/fff',
        text: `This is the body text of a card.  You can even use
        line\n  breaks and emoji! 🏋`,
        buttonText: 'This is a button',
        buttonUrl: 'https://console.dialogflow.com/'
        })
    );
    agent.add(new Suggestion(`Quick Reply`));
    agent.add(new Suggestion(`Suggestion`));
    agent.context.set({ name: 'gamestore-picked', lifespan: 2, parameters:
{ gameStore: 'DialogflowGameStore' }});
}

// Express Code

const app = express().use(bodyParser.json());

// Basic Authentication
app.use(basicAuth({
    users: { 'admin': 'supersecret' }
}));

app.use(function(req, res, next) {
    if (!req.headers['x-auth']) {
      return res.status(403).json({ error: 'No auth headers sent!' });
    }
    next();
});
```

```
app.post('/fulfillment', (request, response) => {
    const agent = new WebhookClient({ request, response });
    console.log('Dialogflow Request headers: ' + JSON.stringify
    (request.headers));
    console.log('Dialogflow Request body: ' + JSON.stringify(request.body));

    // Run the proper function handler based on the matched Dialogflow
        intent name
    let intentMap = new Map();
    intentMap.set('Default Welcome Intent', welcome);
    intentMap.set('Default Fallback Intent', fallback);
    intentMap.set('Buy product regex', yourFunctionHandler);
    agent.handleRequest(intentMap);
});

app.get('/', (req, res) => {
    res.send(`OK`);
});

const port = process.env.PORT || 8080;
app.listen(port, () => {
    console.log('Dialogflow Fulfillment listening on port', port);
});
```

This **index.js** uses the **package.json** as shown in Listing 10-12 to load the npm packages.

Listing 10-12. The required packages in package.json

```
{
    "name": "dialogflow-fulfillment",
    "description": "This is the default fulfillment for a Dialogflow agents
    using Cloud Run",
    "version": "0.0.1",
    "private": true,
    "license": "Apache Version 2.0",
```

```
    "author": "Lee Boonstra",
    "engines": {
      "node": "8"
    },
    "scripts": {
      "start": "node index.js",
      "build": "gcloud builds submit --tag gcr.io/dialogflowcookbook/
      dialogflow",
      "deploy": "gcloud run deploy --image gcr.io/dialogflowcookbook/
      dialogflow --platform managed"
    },
    "dependencies": {
      "@google-cloud/dialogflow": "^2.0.0",
      "actions-on-google": "^2.5.0",
      "body-parser": "^1.19.0",
      "dialogflow-fulfillment": "^0.6.1",
      "express": "^4.17.1",
      "express-basic-auth": "^1.2.0"
    }
}
```

You will need to include a Dockerfile to build a container; see Listing 10-13.

Listing 10-13. Dockerfile that belongs to this example to run the container in Cloud Run

```
# Use the official lightweight Node.js 12 image.
# https://hub.docker.com/_/node
FROM node:12-slim

# Create and change to the app directory.
WORKDIR /usr/src/app

# Copy application dependency manifests to the container image.
# A wildcard is used to ensure both package.json AND package-lock.json are
  copied.
# Copying this separately prevents re-running npm install on every code change.
```

```
COPY package*.json ./

# Install production dependencies.
RUN npm install --only=production

# Copy local code to the container image.
COPY . ./

# Run the web service on container startup.
CMD [ "npm", "start" ]
```

The **.dockerignore** file (Listing 10-14) makes sure that specific files won't be copied to the image. For example, the **node_modules** folder will be generated from the package. json file, no need to copy all these large files over.

Listing 10-14. Docker ignore file

```
Dockerfile
README.md
node_modules
npm-debug.log
```

With the following command-line commands, I can deploy the Cloud Run container. First, enable the container registry API:

```
gcloud services enable containerregistry.googleapis.com
```

Log in on gcloud:

```
gcloud init
```

Build the container, and give the image a tag name:

```
gcloud builds submit --tag gcr.io/PROJECT_ID/dialogflow
```

Deploy the container using the image tag name (use the managed platform, not Anthos):

```
gcloud run deploy --image gcr.io/PROJECT_ID/dialogflow --platform managed
```

This will walk you through a wizard. You can choose a region. Allow unauthenticated invocations to make the URL public available. Once you are done, it will create an HTTPS URL for your fulfillment. This is the URL you can add to the Webhook URL field in the Dialogflow console:

https://<myapp>.a.run.app

Listing 10-15 shows an example of the code.

Listing 10-15. Dialogflow fulfillment with Express

```javascript
const express = require('express');
const bodyParser = require('body-parser');

// Dialogflow Fulfillment Code

const expressApp = express().use(bodyParser.json())
expressApp.post('/fulfillment', (request, response) => {
     // Agent intent map
});
expressApp.get('/', (req, res) => {

  // get the Dialogflow request
  // do something
  // return to the agent

  res.send(`Hello from Google Cloud!`);
});

const port = process.env.PORT || 8080;
expressApp.listen(port, () => {
  console.log('Dialogflow Fulfillment listening on port', port);
});
```

Google Cloud Logging

When making use of Google Cloud products, logging comes out of the box. See Figure 10-12.

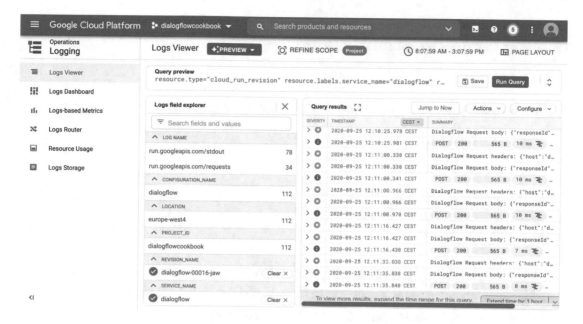

Figure 10-12. *Fulfillment webhook logs in the Google Cloud Console (previously known as Stackdriver)*

Building Multilingual Fulfillment Webhook

When working with different languages, you will likely work with other number formats, foreign currencies, or date/time strings. More tools will come in handy:

- **moment.js**: To parse, validate, manipulate, and display dates and times in JavaScript.

- **numeral.js**: A JavaScript library for formatting and manipulating numbers.

When your webhook back end is a Node.js back end, there are remarkable frameworks available that can help you better organize your code and localize your strings.

This tool will help you:

- **i18n**: Lightweight, simple translation module with dynamic JSON storage. Supports plain vanilla Node.js apps.

Dialogflow will send a language code (such as "en" for English or "nl" for Dutch), with each query result:

```
request.body.queryResult.languageCode;
```

You will use this to initialize the i18n library. Then you can refer to these multi-language text strings by using the following calls:

```
i18n.__(KEY)
```

All the text-based strings can be stored in JSON files, such as

- *locales/en-US.json*

- *locales/nl-NL.json*

The contents will look like this:

en-US.json
```
{
    "WELCOME_BASIC": "Hi, I am the virtual video game chat agent. I can talk
    with you about video games or tell you which latest games have been
    released. What would you like to know from me?"
}
```
nl-NL.json
```
{
    "WELCOME_BASIC": "Hoi, ik ben de virtual video game chat agent. Ik kan
    over video games praten en ik kan je vertellen welke games net uit zijn.
    Wat wil je weten?"
}
```

Tip   Since i18n uses JSON files to store language strings, you could store these JSON files together with your code and deploy your webhook in the cloud with, for example, Cloud Run. If you rather use the inline editor or Cloud Functions, you will likely want to store the JSON files in Google Cloud Storage.

---

i18n Code Example

Let's look into a full code example on implementing a multilingual webhook, deployed with Cloud Run.

The **package.json** file will contain these additional dependencies:

```
"i18n": "^0.10.0",
"moment": "^2.27.0",
"numeral": "^2.0.6"
```

The localized JSON files will look like Listing 10-16. Notice that certain strings can contain variables (%s).

Listing 10-16. You can create locale JSON files to use within your webhook code

locales/en-US.json

```
{
    "WELCOME_BASIC": "Hi, I am the virtual video game chat agent. I can talk
    with you about video games or tell you which latest games have been
    released. What would you like to know from me?",
    "DELIVERY_DATE": "The date is %s.",
    "PRICE": "It costs %s.",
    "TOTAL_AMOUNT": "The total is: %s.",
    "FALLBACK": "Oops, something went wrong. Would you like to try again?"
}
```

locales/nl-NL.json

```
{
    "WELCOME_BASIC": "Hoi, ik ben de virtual video game chat agent. Ik kan
    over video games praten en ik kan je vertellen welke games net uit zijn.
    Wat wil je weten?",
    "DELIVERY_DATE": "De datum is %s.",
    "PRICE": "Het kost %s.",
    "TOTAL_AMOUNT": "Het totaal is: %s.",
    "FALLBACK": "Oeps, er ging iets mis. Kun je het opnieuw proberen?"
}
```

Listing 10-17 shows how you set up your webhook code in order to make use of those JSON language files.

Listing 10-17. Dialogflow fulfillment multilingual webhook code using the i18n library

```
'use strict';

const express = require('express');
const bodyParser = require('body-parser');
const { WebhookClient} = require('dialogflow-fulfillment');

//1
const i18n = require('i18n');
i18n.configure({
  locales: ['en-US', 'nl-NL'],
  directory: __dirname + '/locales',
  defaultLocale: 'en-US'
});

//2
const moment = require('moment');
require('moment/locale/nl');

//3
const numeral = require('numeral');
numeral.register('locale', 'nl', {
  delimiters: {
      thousands: ',',
      decimal: '.'
  },
  abbreviations: {
      thousand: 'k',
      million: 'm',
      billion: 'b',
      trillion: 't'
  },
  ordinal: function (number) {
      var b = number % 10;
      return (~~ (number % 100 / 10) === 1) ? 'th' :
```

```
            (b === 1) ? 'st' :
            (b === 2) ? 'nd' :
            (b === 3) ? 'rd' : 'th';
  },
  currency: {
      symbol: '€'
  }
});

process.env.DEBUG = 'dialogflow:debug'; // enables lib debugging statements

//4
function welcome(agent) {
  agent.add(i18n.__('WELCOME_BASIC'));
}

function fallback(agent) {
  agent.add(i18n.__('FALLBACK_BASIC'));
}

function getPrice(agent) {
  agent.add(i18n.__('PRICE', numeral(399).format('($0,0)')));
}

function getDeliveryDate(agent) {
  agent.add(i18n.__('DELIVERY_DATE', moment().format('LL')));
}

function getTotalNumber(agent) {
  agent.add(i18n.__('TOTAL_AMOUNT', numeral(1000).format('0,0')));
}

// Express Code
const app = express().use(bodyParser.json());

app.post('/fulfillment', (request, response) => {
    const agent = new WebhookClient({ request, response });
    console.log('Dialogflow Request headers: ' + JSON.stringify(request.
    headers));
    console.log('Dialogflow Request body: ' + JSON.stringify(request.body));
```

```
    //5
    var lang = request.body.queryResult.languageCode;
    var langCode;
    if(lang === "nl") langCode = "nl-NL";
    if(lang === "en") langCode = "en-US";
    i18n.setLocale(langCode);
    moment.locale(lang);
    numeral.locale(lang);

    //6
    let intentMap = new Map();
    intentMap.set('Default Welcome Intent', welcome);
    intentMap.set('Default Fallback Intent', fallback);

    intentMap.set('Get_Price', getPrice);
    intentMap.set('Get_Delivery_Date', getDeliveryDate);
    intentMap.set('Get_Total_Number', getTotalNumber);
    agent.handleRequest(intentMap);
});

app.get('/', (req, res) => {
    res.send(`OK`);
});

const port = process.env.PORT || 8080;
app.listen(port, () => {
    console.log('Dialogflow Fulfillment listening on port', port);
});
```

1) First, we will require the i18n library to handle multilingual support. We will need to configure it to explain which locales we are using, where they are located, and which locale will be the default.

2) Next, we will require moment.js for date and time objects.

3) By default, it works for the English language. All the other locales
    will need to be required separately.

4) Then we require numeral.js to handle currencies and numbers. To
    make it work with other locales, we will have to register the locales
    and provide the options. For example, in European notation, the
    decimal delimiter is a "." instead of a ",".

5) Here, we assign the i18n keys to the response outputs. The i18n
    framework will find the value (the correct translated text string) in
    the locale file.

6) We will retrieve the languageCode from the Dialogflow
    queryResult object. As you have seen, i18n uses ISO language
    codes, conforming to the ISO 639-1 standard, complete with two-
    letter country codes where relevant, like ("nl-NL" or "en-US"), so
    will need to create that mapping.

7) These are the intents which will make use of multilingual
    responses.

Figures 10-13 and 10-14 will show how the result looks like in the simulator.
Figure 10-13 will show the example in English. Note also the valuta sign.

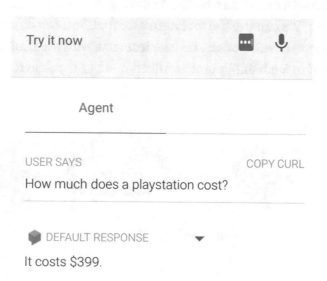

Figure 10-13. *Testing multilingual bots that make use of fulfillments, English
language*

Figure 10-14 will show the example in Dutch. Note also the valuta sign.

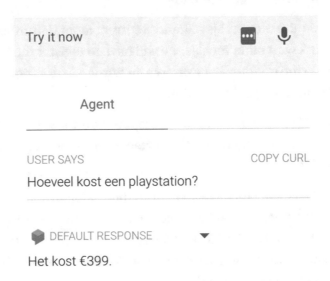

Figure 10-14. *Testing multilingual bots that make use of fulfillments, Dutch language*

Using Local Webhooks

Running your fulfillment locally can be handy during development, as you don't need to deploy your solution. We can use the tool **ngrok** for this. You can download it from npm.

Figure 10-15 shows how it works. The user interacts with the Dialogflow agent. Once Dialogflow will need to fetch fulfillment, it will connect to ngrok.io to execute your local webhook code.

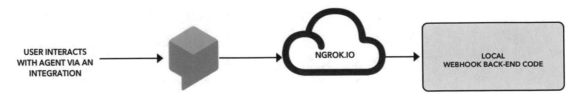

Figure 10-15. *Testing fulfillment locally with ngrok.io*

Ngrok

Ngrok allows you to expose a web server running on your local machine to the Internet. Just tell ngrok what port your web server is listening on. If you don't know what port your web server is listening on, it's probably port 80, the default for HTTP.

You can run the following command from your local fulfillment webhook code folder in the command line to expose your webhook:

```
ngrok http 80
```

When you start ngrok, it will display the public URL of your tunnel and other status and metrics information about connections made over your tunnel:

```
Tunnel Status          online
Version                2.0/2.0
Web Interface          http://127.0.0.1:4040
Forwarding             http://92832de0.ngrok.io -> localhost:80
Forwarding             https://92832de0.ngrok.io -> localhost:80

Connections       ttl     opn     rt1     rt5     p50     p90
                   0       0       0.00    0.00    0.00    0.00
```

The generated forwarding **HTTPS URL** is what you will need to type into your Webhook section in the Dialogflow Fulfillment page; see Figure 10-16.

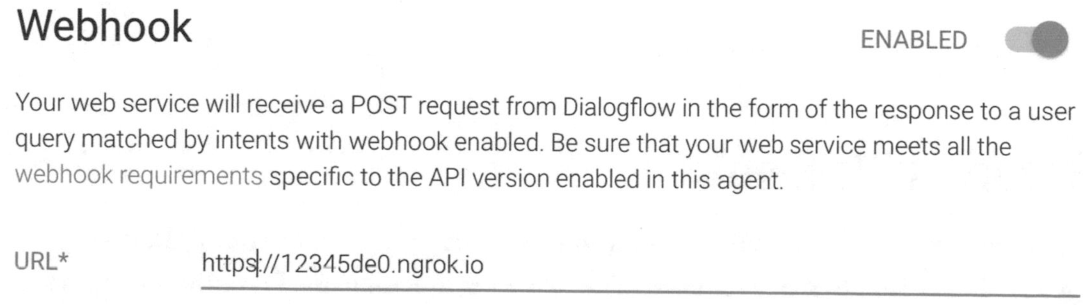

Webhook   ENABLED ⬤

Your web service will receive a POST request from Dialogflow in the form of the response to a user query matched by intents with webhook enabled. Be sure that your web service meets all the webhook requirements specific to the API version enabled in this agent.

URL*   https://12345de0.ngrok.io

Figure 10-16. Webhooks with ngrok

When you run the ngrok command from your local app code folder, it connects to the ngrok cloud service, which accepts traffic on a public address and relays that traffic through to the ngrok process running on your machine and then on to the local address you specified.

> **Tip**   On the ngrok free plan, ngrok's URLs are randomly generated and temporary. If you want to use the same URL every time, you need to upgrade to a paid plan to use the subdomain option for a stable URL with HTTP or TLS tunnels and the remote-addr option for a stable address with TCP tunnels.

Testing Your Fulfillment Without Dialogflow and ngrok

It's also possible to test your webhook code without connecting to Dialogflow and without using ngrok. This makes sense if you just want to test your local code, which can be handy while writing the code. We can do this by posting stub JSON files to your webhook (pretending that it's Dialogflow).

In the Dialogflow console, click **Fulfillments ➤ Diagnostic Info**.

Copy and paste the contents of the Fulfillment request tab.

Store this in a local file: **stub.json**.

This JSON code is unique to your agent as it includes session ids, project names, and intent and response ids unique to your agent.

Once you have the stub.json file, you can make a **Curl** POST call from your command line, which uses the stub file as a POST message:

```
curl -X POST -H "Content-Type: application/json" -d @stub.json http://
localhost:8080/fulfillment
```

This will execute your local code.

Securing Webhooks

It's possible to secure your fulfillment webhook so that only you or your Dialogflow agent is authorized to make requests. The following mechanisms for authentication are supported:

- Basic authentication with login and password

- Authentication with authentication headers

- Mutual TLS authentication

Note   Dialogflow is a conversational tool for NLP, intent matching, and parameter slot filling. It does not come with a CMS and therefore it won't have a user login system or OAuth implementation.

Basic Authentication

Basic access authentication is a method for an HTTP user agent (such as a web browser) to provide a user and password when making a request. In basic HTTP authentication, a request contains a header field with the following format: `Authorization: Basic <credentials>`, where credentials are the Base64 encoding of ID and password joined by a single colon.

It provides no confidentiality protection for the transmitted credentials. They are merely encoded with Base64 in transit but not encrypted or hashed in any way. Therefore, basic authentication is typically used in conjunction with HTTPS to provide confidentiality. Luckily, both happen out of the box with Dialogflow. Dialogflow webhooks only allow HTTPS URLs.

You can set up **Basic Auth** in the Dialogflow Fulfillment page; see Figure 10-17. Besides the URL, you will have to specify the user id and the password.

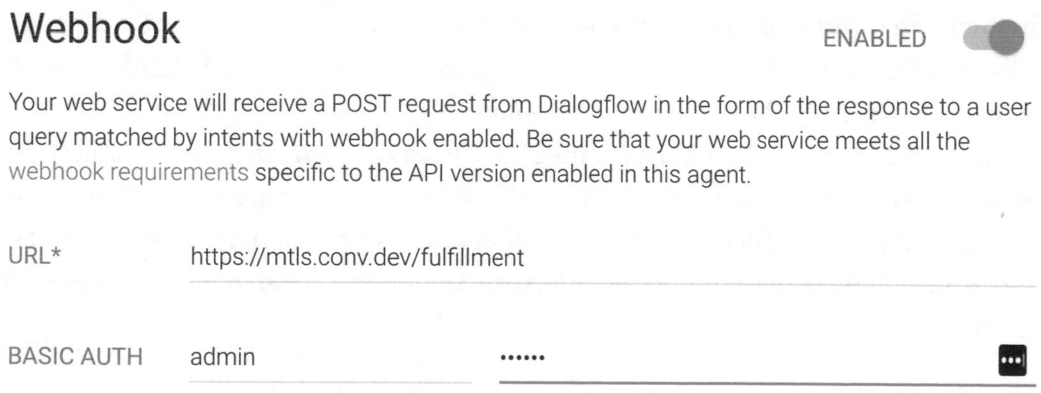

Webhook   ENABLED ●

Your web service will receive a POST request from Dialogflow in the form of the response to a user query matched by intents with webhook enabled. Be sure that your web service meets all the webhook requirements specific to the API version enabled in this agent.

URL*   https://mtls.conv.dev/fulfillment

BASIC AUTH   admin   ••••••   •••

Figure 10-17. *A secure webhook in Dialogflow*

Using the Basic Auth options in Dialogflow also requires you to handle the access controls in your fulfillment webhook. Let's assume you have built a back end with Node. js and Express. Express has a basic auth middleware plugin. The middleware will check incoming requests for a basic auth (Authorization) header, parse it, and check if the credentials are legit. If a request is not authorized, it will respond with HTTP 401 and a configurable body (default empty).

In Listing 10-18, the middleware will check incoming requests to match the credentials **admin:supersecret**, which were passed into the Dialogflow Webhook, Basic Auth fields.

Listing 10-18. Basic authentication in your webhook

```
const app = require('express')()
const basicAuth = require('express-basic-auth')

app.use(basicAuth({
    users: { 'admin': 'supersecret' }
}));
```

Authentication with Authentication Headers

HTTP provides a general framework for access control and authentication. The most common HTTP authentication is based on the "Basic Auth" schema, as you have seen in the previous section. But there are other schemes as well, such as Bearer JWT Tokens or Digest. Dialogflow allows you to specify your own custom headers, which you can use for authentication or, for example, to set character encoding.

You can set up custom **headers** on the Dialogflow Fulfillment page. Besides the URL, you will have to specify the header key and value.

Listing 10-19 shows an example of checking if a header is present in the fulfillment webhook code. A custom header with the key **x-auth** and the value **true** has been set in the Dialogflow console. This code checks if this header is present; if not, it sends a 403 HTTP error, which means that the webhook code understands the request but refuses to authorize it.

Listing 10-19. Header authentication in your webhook

```
app.use(function(req, res, next) {
   if (!req.headers['x-auth']) {
     return res.status(403).json({ error: 'No auth headers sent!'});
```

```
    }
    next();
});
```

Figure 10-18 shows how to configure the Dialogflow webhook in order to work with the code of Listing 10-19. Note the **x-auth** header.

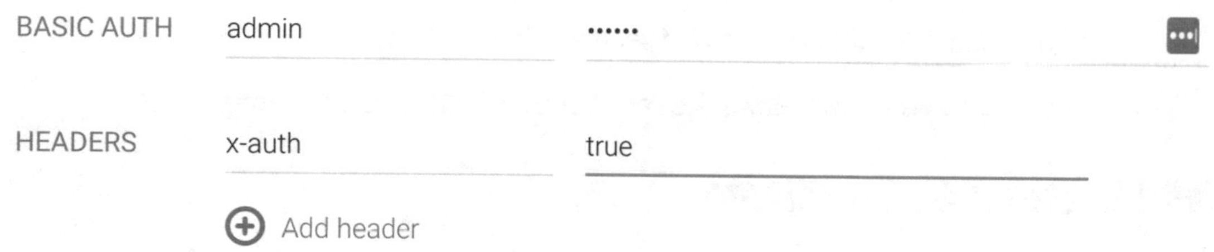

BASIC AUTH	admin	......	....
HEADERS	x-auth	true	

⊕ Add header

Figure 10-18. *A secure webhook with headers*

Tip   If you want to work with Bearer JWT tokens, you might wonder how to set the headers, since the JWT token should change all the time.

Typically, the headers look like Authorization - Token token='yourtokenhere.

To set these in the Dialogflow console won't make much sense. You would likely want to do this programmatically. With the Dialogflow SDK, it is possible to call the updateFulfillment method, which allows you to pass in a Fulfillment with a GenericWebservice.

How would you receive a new JWT token/redirect? Maybe by putting your chatbot integration behind a web login? It also means that your code implementation will need to check the JWT tokens and provide JWT tokens since Dialogflow won't do this.

Mutual TLS Authentication

The network traffic initiated by Dialogflow for webhook requests is sent on a public network. To ensure that traffic is both secure and trusted in both directions, Dialogflow optionally supports Mutual TLS authentication (mTLS). With mTLS, both the client (Dialogflow) and the server (your webhook server) present a certificate during a TLS handshake, which mutually proves identity.

You won't need to configure mTLS in the Dialogflow console, but you will have to do this on the fulfillment webhook server. Typically, you won't configure this in your Node.js app code since Node.js apps in production will always be behind a server such as Apache, NGINX, or maybe a cloud load balancer. That's the place where you will configure your server, and when a TLS handshake proves mutually, then forward the request to your Node.js app code on a different port (on HTTP).

The configuration will have the following requirements:

- Your app code will need a valid secure SSL certificate.

- You will need to download the root CA that Dialogflow is using.

Valid Secure SSL Certificate

Web pages and apps which run over HTTPS require a valid SSL certificate. There are two ways how you can get these for free, but there are some caveats:

- You can generate self-signed certificate requests with **OpenSSL**; however, the CA won't be trusted. You could add the certificate to your browser or OS certificates keychain store, but everyone using this public IP will have to take these steps. It's possible to sign your certificate by a trusted authority such as GlobalSign; this will cost money. Dialogflow mTLS won't work without a trusted CA.

- Use a tool like **Let's Encrypt**. It can generate trusted certificates with trusted CAs for free; however, you will need to connect a domain to your public IP.

Figure 10-19 shows how it looks like if your SSL certificate is secure.

Figure 10-19. *A secure website with an SSL certificate*

Root CA

Run the following two commands on your command line to download the root CA which will be used by Dialogflow. This will add GTS101.crt and GSR2.crt to the local file: **ca-crt.pem**:

```
curl https://pki.goog/gsr2/GTS101.crt | openssl x509 -inform der >>
ca-crt.pem
curl https://pki.goog/gsr2/GSR2.crt | openssl x509 -inform der >>
ca-crt.pem
```

Here's an example on how to enable mTLS for Apache2. These settings belong in the **ssl.conf**:

```
SSLVerifyClient require
SSLVerifyDepth 2
SSLCACertificateFile "ca-crt.pem"
```

And this is the access control, which will make sure that only Dialogflow.com can call the fulfillment webhook:

```
<If "%{SSL_CLIENT_S_DN_CN} != '*.dialogflow.com'">
Require all denied
</If>
```

HTTPS Authentication Setup with Apache

Instead of setting up HTTP authentication in your (Node.js) app code, you will fix this on the server side. To password-protect a directory on an Apache server, you will need a **.htaccess** and a **.htpasswd** file. The **.htaccess** file typically looks like this:

```
AuthType Basic AuthName "Access to the staging site"
AuthUserFile /path/to/.htpasswd Require valid-user
```

The **.htaccess** file references a **.htpasswd** file in which each line consists of a username and a password separated by a colon (":"). You cannot see the actual passwords as they are encrypted (md5 in this case). Note that you can name your .htpasswd file differently if you like, but keep in mind this file shouldn't be accessible to anyone. (Apache is usually configured to prevent access to .ht* files).

For example:

```
admin:$apr1$ZjTqBB3f$IF9gdYAGlMrs2fuINjHsz.
```

A Full Example for Setting Up Mutual TLS Authentication

HTTPS is the secured version of HTTP (HyperText Transfer Protocol). HTTP is the protocol used by your browser and web servers to communicate and exchange information. When that exchange of data is encrypted with SSL/TLS, then we call it HTTPS. The "S" stands for Secure.

Anytime you use a web browser to connect to a secure site (https://something), you're using Transport Layer Security (TLS). TLS is the successor to SSL, and it's an excellent standard with many features. TLS guarantees the server's identity to the client and provides a two-way encrypted channel between the server and the client.

But for a webhook application such as Dialogflow, that's not enough since your application is the server, and you want to confirm the client's identity, Dialogflow. What's the solution?

Mutual TLS to the rescue! It's an optional feature for TLS. It enables the server to authenticate the identity of the client.

Deployed Cloud Run apps (HTTPS or gRPC) and serverless cloud functions will provide a valid "server cert" trusted by root CA stores. Cloud Run and Cloud Functions don't support bring-your-own cert. Cloud Run's *.run.app* URLs provide their own valid TLS server cert.

Suppose mTLS authentication is required for your webhook. In that case, you may want to consider one of the following Google Cloud solutions: Compute Engine (VMs), Google Kubernetes Engine (Containers), or Cloud Run on Anthos (Cloud Run container on GKE with Istio).

Here's how to set up a Dialogflow fulfillment VM on Compute Engine with mTLS enabled.

Create a Node.js VM on Compute Engine

Create a Node.js VM with the following steps:

From the Cloud Console menu, select **Marketplace**.

Choose **Node.js by Google Click to deploy image (VM)** (see Figure 10-20).

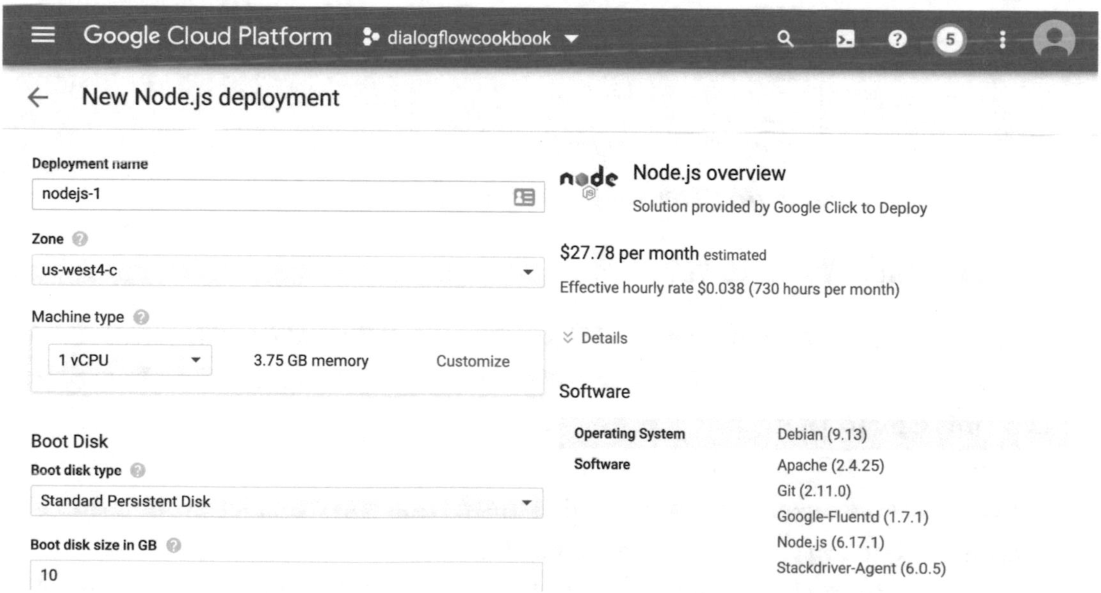

Figure 10-20. *Node.js Compute VM in Google Cloud*

Select a region. Make sure HTTP and HTTPS is checked.

From the Cloud Console menu, select **VPC Network ➤ Firewall ➤ Create a new firewall rule** (see Figure 10-21).

Targets: **All instances in network**

Source IP ranges: **0.0.0.0/0**

Specified ports: **tcp > 3000**

Click **Create**.

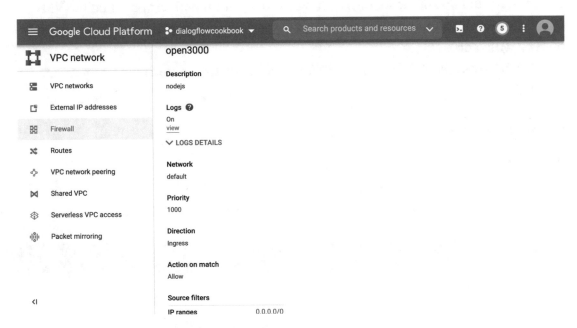

Figure 10-21. *Opening up a firewall for port 3000*

Attach a Domain Name to Your VM

From the Cloud Console menu, select **VPC Networks ➤ External IP addresses**.

You should see your new VM instance. We will now reserve a static IP address so we can bind this later to a domain.

Set the type from Ephemeral to **Static**.

This will reserve a static IP address, which means that you won't lose your current IP address after rebooting your VM. Make a note of this address.

To make this tutorial work, you will need a valid SSL certificate provided by a valid Certificate Authority. If not, Chrome and likely other applications, like Dialogflow, will block your website; once your website is blocked, Dialogflow can't reach your fulfillment URL, even when it's available on HTTPS.

We will use Certbot with Let's Encrypt, a free tool to get a free valid SSL certificate. However, you will need a domain name that you can attach to it. If you instead attach the certificate to an IP address, you could create a self-signed certificate via OpenSSL; however, you will still need a valid Certificate Authority, which you will likely need to order. So instead we will go with the domain option.

You can buy a domain via https://domains.google.com/.

I've used the following settings, within my domain registrar, mtls.conv.dev, to create the subdomain mtls:

Mtls	A	1h	<external compute IP address>

Once this is linked, we will go back to the Google Cloud console.

From the Cloud Console menu, select **Compute Engine** and **SSH** into the newly created VM.

Once you are logged in, run this command on the command line to install Certbot:

```
sudo apt-get install certbot python-certbot-apache
```

Run this command to get a certificate and have Certbot edit your Apache configuration automatically to serve it, turning on HTTPS access in a single step:

```
sudo certbot --apache
```

Restart the Apache server:

```
sudo /etc/init.d/apache2 restart
```

Now open a new browser tab, and test out your domain name. It should bring you to the default Apache setup (see Figure 10-22).

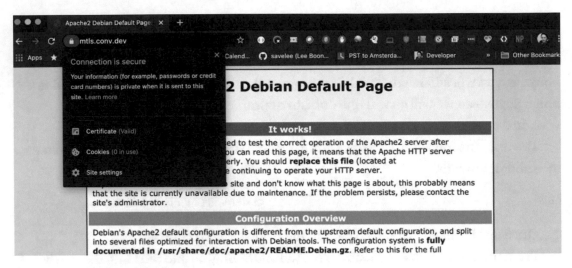

Figure 10-22.   *Running the Apache secure*

Set Up Your Node Application

With the infrastructure all set up, let's write the application code. As seen earlier in this chapter, we will create a Node.js Express implementation, just like we did before.

```
sudo mkdir /var/www/projects
sudo chown $USER /var/www/projects
cd /var/www/projects

nano index.js
```

Use the following contents of Listing 10-20:

Listing 10-20.   Setting up mTLS index.js app code

```
'use strict';
const express = require('express');
const app = express();
const bodyParser = require('body-parser');
const basicAuth = require('express-basic-auth');
const fs = require('fs');

const { WebhookClient, Card, Suggestion } =
require('dialogflow-fulfillment');
```

```
process.env.DEBUG = 'dialogflow:debug'; // enables lib debugging statements
// Dialogflow Fulfillment Code
function welcome(agent) {
    agent.add('Welcome to my agent!');
  }

function fallback(agent) {
    agent.add('I didn't understand');
    agent.add('I'm sorry, can you try again?');
}

function yourFunctionHandler(agent) {
    agent.add('Ok. Buying product:');
    console.log(agent.parameters);
    agent.add(new Card({
        title: agent.parameters.producttype,
        imageUrl: 'https://dummyimage.com/300x200/000/fff',
        text: 'This is the body text of a card.  You can even use
        line\n  breaks and emoji! 🐧',
        buttonText: 'This is a button',
        buttonUrl: 'https://console.dialogflow.com/'
        })
    );
    agent.add(new Suggestion('Quick Reply'));
    agent.add(new Suggestion('Suggestion'));
    agent.context.set({ name: 'gamestore-picked', lifespan: 2, parameters:
{ gameStore: 'DialogflowGameStore' }});
}

app.post('/fulfillment', (request, response) => {;
    const agent = new WebhookClient({ request, response });
    console.log('Dialogflow Request headers: ' + JSON.stringify(request.
    headers));
    console.log('Dialogflow Request body: ' + JSON.stringify(request.body));
    // Run the proper function handler based on the matched Dialogflow
        intent name
    let intentMap = new Map();
```

```
    intentMap.set('Default Welcome Intent', welcome);
    intentMap.set('Default Fallback Intent', fallback);
    intentMap.set('Buy product regex', yourFunctionHandler);
    agent.handleRequest(intentMap);
});

app.get('/', (req, res) => {
    res.send('OK');
});
const port = process.env.PORT || 3000;
app.listen(port, () => {
    console.log('Dialogflow Fulfillment listening on port', port);
});
```

```
nano package.json
```

Use the following contents of Listing 10-21:

Listing 10-21. Setting up mTLS package.json

```
{
  "name": "dialogflow-fulfillment",
  "description": "This is the default fulfillment for a Dialogflow agents
  using Compute with mTLS",
  "version": "0.0.1",
  "private": true,
  "license": "Apache Version 2.0",
  "author": "Lee Boonstra",
  "engines": {
    "node": "8"
  },
  "dependencies": {
    "actions-on-google": "^2.5.0",
    "body-parser": "^1.19.0",
    "dialogflow-fulfillment": "^0.6.1",
    "express": "^4.17.1",
    "express-basic-auth": "^1.2.0"
  }
}
```

```
npm install
```

We will have to enable the proxy modules:

```
sudo a2enmod proxy
sudo a2enmod proxy_http
```

Now let's modify the Apache configuration:

```
sudo nano /etc/apache2/sites-available/000-default-le-ssl.conf
```

Use the following **000-default-le-ssl.conf** this will use the following configuration for Apache. Use the following contents of Listing 10-22.

Listing 10-22. Setting up mTLS 000-default-le-ssl.conf

```
<IfModule mod_ssl.c>
<VirtualHost *:443>
        # The ServerName directive sets the request scheme, hostname and port
        # that the server uses to identify itself. This is used when creating
        # redirection URLs. In the context of virtual hosts, the ServerName
        # specifies what hostname must appear in the request's Host: header to
        # match this virtual host. For the default virtual host (this file) this
        # value is not decisive as it is used as a last resort host regardless.
        # However, you must set it for any further virtual host explicitly.
        #ServerName www.example.com

        ServerAdmin webmaster@localhost
        #DocumentRoot /var/www/projects

        # Available loglevels: trace8, ..., trace1, debug, info, notice, warn,
        # error, crit, alert, emerg.
        # It is also possible to configure the loglevel for particular
        # modules, e.g.
        LogLevel info ssl:debug

        ErrorLog /var/www/projects/error.log
        CustomLog /var/www/projects/access.log combined
```

```
    ServerName mtls.conv.dev
    SSLCertificateFile /etc/letsencrypt/live/mtls.conv.dev/fullchain.pem
    SSLCertificateKeyFile /etc/letsencrypt/live/mtls.conv.dev/privkey.pem
    Include /etc/letsencrypt/options-ssl-apache.conf

    SSLVerifyClient require
    SSLVerifyDepth 2
    SSLCACertificateFile "/var/www/projects/ca-crt.pem"

    # access control, only allow dialogflow.com to connect to fulfillment
    <If "%{SSL_CLIENT_S_DN_CN} != '*.dialogflow.com'">
        Require all denied
    </If>

    # sudo a2enmod proxy
    # sudo a2enmod proxy_http

    ProxyPass / http://localhost:3000/
    ProxyPassReverse / http://localhost:3000/

</VirtualHost>
</IfModule>
```

Set Up mTLS

First, make sure that in Dialogflow, you are pointing to your new VM from the **fulfillments** screen.

Run the following two commands to download the root CA which will be used by Dialogflow. This will add GTS101.crt and GSR2.crt to the local file, **ca-crt.pem**:

```
curl https://pki.goog/gsr2/GTS101.crt | openssl x509 -inform der >> ca-crt.pem
curl https://pki.goog/gsr2/GSR2.crt | openssl x509 -inform der >> ca-crt.pem
```

These settings in /etc/apache2/sites-available/000-default-le-ssl.conf are specific for setting up mTLS:

```
SSLVerifyClient require
SSLVerifyDepth 2
SSLCACertificateFile "/var/www/projects/ca-crt.pem"
```

And this is the access control, which will make sure that only Dialogflow.com can call the fulfillment webhook:

```
<If "%{SSL_CLIENT_S_DN_CN} != '*.dialogflow.com'">
Require all denied
</If>
```

Now you can test it. We will only let Dialogflow with a certificate CN: *.dialogflow.com go through to access the fulfillment. When the CA of Dialogflow is not the same as the CA we expect it to be, the Dialogflow fulfillment status will be UNKNOWN.

The Apache error.log shows (`tail error.log`).

[Fri Jun 26 11:45:54.732961 2020] [authz_core:error] [pid 10152:tid 139735259326208] [client 64.233.172.238:36290] AH01630: client denied by server configuration: proxy:http://localhost:3000/fulfillment

Else, it will go through. You could test it in the Dialogflow simulator. I've used intent **Buy product regex** with a user utterance: *Buy ms12345678* to display results.

(Don't believe it? Flip the != to == in the access control: 000-default-le-ssl.conf to something else than *.dialogflow.com.)

Figure 10-23 shows a screenshot of how the Dialogflow CA certificate looks like.

```
{
  subject: [Object: null prototype] {
    C: 'US',
    ST: 'California',
    L: 'Mountain View',
    O: 'Google LLC',
    CN: '*.dialogflow.com'
  },
  issuer: [Object: null prototype] {
    C: 'US',
    O: 'Google Trust Services',
    CN: 'GTS CA 1O1'
  },
  subjectaltname: 'DNS:*.dialogflow.com',
  infoAccess: [Object: null prototype] {
    'OCSP - URI': [ 'http://ocsp.pki.goog/gts1o1' ],
    'CA Issuers - URI': [ 'http://pki.goog/gsr2/GTS1O1.crt' ]
  },
  modulus: 'B91E9334CA746F302421EA922DA0DB4B410039F178D097CBDC279A0D65C5400F9FDC
6B71240001635CBFC190D64E43D2930D5915334B7C3762BA437DA64164FD57A56E65872A422E7674
51B39BA6963CA3E2936A0F27F1B68D00EAFBB72A43DC53D09F94CE4FF1912B515581EBAC8B3E8894
  bits: 2048,
  exponent: '0x10001',
  pubkey: <Buffer 30 82 01 22 30 0d 06 09 2a 86 48 86 f7 0d 01 01 01 05 00 03 82
  valid_from: 'Sep  5 21:18:39 2019 GMT',
  valid_to: 'Sep  3 21:18:39 2020 GMT',
  fingerprint: '3C:05:02:DD:7A:D9:91:B9:0C:AA:85:94:81:63:85:C6:5F:31:01:2A',
  fingerprint256: '85:01:B9:63:1D:E4:5C:A7:3D:5C:4D:85:C9:D9:EE:9B:A7:50:6D:D2:2
  ext_key_usage: [ '1.3.6.1.5.5.7.3.2' ],
  serialNumber: '35AC0EF24853B94308000000000131959',
  raw: <Buffer 30 82 05 8d 30 82 04 75 a0 03 02 01 02 02 10 35 ac 0e f2 48 53 b9
```

Figure 10-23. *The Dialogflow CA certificate*

Summary

This chapter contains information about fulfillments. You will learn the following tasks:

- You want to fetch data from a web service and write your fulfillment code in the built-in editor.

- You want to fetch data from a web service and write your fulfillment code within your own (cloud) environment, such as Cloud Run.

- You want to fetch data from a web service, but your Dialogflow agent has multilingual support, so how can you organize your webhook?

- You want to fetch data from a local data source for testing purposes with ngrok.

- You want to ensure that traffic to and from Dialogflow is secure by using authentication via basic authentication, authentication headers, and mutual TLS.

On top of this, you have seen code snippets to implement fulfillment via

- The npm dialogflow-fulfillment package

- The Actions on Google package

- Manually without using any library

The intents that I have been using for this chapter are

- Buy product regex

- Default Welcome Intent

- Default Fallback Intent

- Get_Price

- Get_Delivery_Date

- Get_Total_Number

In case you want to build this example, the source code for this book is available on GitHub via the book's product page, located at www.apress.com/978-1-4842-7013-4. Look into the **webhook-fulfillment-lib**, **webhook-aog**, **webhook-manual**, **webhook-cloudrun**, **webhook-localized**, **secure-auth**, and **secure-compute-mtls** folders.

Further Reading

- Dialogflow documentation on fulfillment in general

  ```
  https://cloud.google.com/dialogflow/es/docs/fulfillment-
  webhook
  ```

- Google Cloud documentation on using Cloud Functions

  ```
  https://cloud.google.com/functions/docs/quickstarts
  ```

- Google Cloud documentation on using Cloud Run

  ```
  https://cloud.google.com/run/docs/quickstarts
  ```

- Dialogflow documentation on the fulfillment inline editor

  `https://cloud.google.com/dialogflow/es/docs/fulfillment-inline-editor`

- Dialogflow documentation on fulfillment in general

  `https://cloud.google.com/dialogflow/es/docs/fulfillment-webhook`

- The npm package dialogflow-fulfillment which is used by the inline editor by default

  `https://www.npmjs.com/package/dialogflow-fulfillment`

- The npm package actions-on-google for when building fulfillments for the Google Assistant

  `https://www.npmjs.com/package/actions-on-google`

- Actions on Google specs

  `https://actions-on-google.github.io/actions-on-google-nodejs/2.12.0/index.html`

- Actions on Google rich messages spec

  `https://cloud.google.com/dialogflow/docs/reference/rest/v2beta1/projects.agent.intents#card`

- i18n library for working with translations

  `https://www.npmjs.com/package/i18n`

- Moment.js localized date-time library

  `https://momentjs.com/`

- Numeral.js library to format numbers and currencies

  `http://numeraljs.com/`

- ngrok npm package

  `https://www.npmjs.com/package/ngrok`

- NPM Basic Auth middleware for Express

  `https://www.npmjs.com/package/express-basic-auth`

- Dialogflow SDK methods for manually setting headers

  `https://cloud.google.com/dialogflow/docs/reference/rest/v2/projects.agent/updateFulfillment` and `https://cloud.google.com/dialogflow/docs/reference/rest/v2/Fulfillment`

- Dialogflow documentation on mTLS for fulfillments

  `https://cloud.google.com/dialogflow/docs/fulfillment-mtls`

- Google Security Primer on Encryption in Transit

  `https://cloud.google.com/security/encryption-in-transit/`

- Mutual TLS simply explained

  `https://codeburst.io/how-mutual-tls-work-aec3d91451ce`

- Google Maps has a good primer on mTLS

  `https://developers.google.com/maps/root-ca-faq`

- Setting up Certbot

  `https://certbot.eff.org/`

- Google Domains

  `https://domains.google.com/`

CHAPTER 11

Creating a Custom Integration with the Dialogflow SDK

In the previous chapter, we described webhooks; they fulfill an intent to send back dynamic code after the intent is matched. You could use Dialogflow fulfillment libraries to do this or just retrieve the results from the posted Dialogflow request. It executes your own (back-end) code. After the intent detection happens by the Dialogflow integrations, you don't need to call the detectIntent method manually.

Dialogflow also provides an SDK, and this is handy for when you want to build your own integrations instead of using the out-of-the-box integrations in Dialogflow. Examples are implementing a chatbot in your own mobile app, on your own hardware, and integrating it in your own website. This means that you will manually have to call/provide the following steps (see Figure 11-1):

- UI implementation for the integration (front end) typically includes a textarea field to display responses and an input field to enter utterances.

- Implementation back end which integrates the Dialogflow SDK for

  - Session management

  - Authentication

  - Intent detection (detectIntent)

  - Returning responses

- Rich responses in the UI of the implementation.

© Lee Boonstra 2021

L. Boonstra, *The Definitive Guide to Conversational AI with Dialogflow and Google Cloud*,
https://doi.org/10.1007/978-1-4842-7014-1_11

Figure 11-1. *The architecture of a custom integration. From a UI implementation to a back-end app that communicates with the Dialogflow SDK*

Your user talks to the UI of your integration (e.g., your website front end).

The UI passes the typed chatbot messages (or incoming audio streams) to the back-end integration. The back-end integration talks to the Dialogflow SDK.

Dialogflow returns answers to the back-end code, and the back-end code send it back to the UI so that the UI can display the chatbot responses on the screen. An additional advantage of taking this approach is that it also won't expose your service account (authentication keys) to the front end, which is what you should not want, as hackers could easily read and use your keys.

Implementing a Custom Chatbot in Your Website Front End, Setup

To implement a custom integration, for example, on a website, you will need to make sure you have the Dialogflow API enabled:

```
gcloud services enable dialogflow.googleapis.com
```

It also requires you to download the Dialogflow Integrations service account to your hard disk and assign it to the GOOGLE_APPLICATION_CREDENTIALS environment variable.

Afterward, you will need to make sure you are logged in with the command-line tools to the right project:

```
gcloud init
```

When you don't take these steps, you will get this error:

```
(node:95119) UnhandledPromiseRejectionWarning:
Error: 7 PERMISSION_DENIED: IAM permission 'dialogflow.sessions.
detectIntent' on 'projects/project-id/agent' denied.
```

Review Chapter 1 on how to configure your Dialogflow project for more information.

UI Implementation

Listing 11-1 shows an example of an HTML page that includes a Dialogflow chatbot UI. In the real world, you probably might want to use a client-side framework such as Angular, but to keep this demo simple, let's keep it nice and compact.

Listing 11-1. An example of a chatbot UI in HTML

```
<!DOCTYPE html>
<html>
<head>
    <meta charset="utf-8" />
    <title>Custom Web Chat</title>
    <link rel="stylesheet" href="https://fonts.googleapis.com/
    icon?family=Material+Icons">
    <link rel="stylesheet" href="https://code.getmdl.io/1.3.0/material.
    indigo-pink.min.css">
    <!-- //1 -->
    <script src="https://cdnjs.cloudflare.com/ajax/libs/socket.io/2.3.0/
    socket.io.js"></script>
    <!-- //2 Find the stylesheet in the Git repo of this book-->
    <link rel="stylesheet" href="style.css">
</head>

<body>
    <!-- //3-->
    <form id="chatbox" autocomplete="off">
        <h1 style="font-size: 18px;">Custom Web Chat</h1>
        <div class="chatarea" id="ca">
            <ul id="messages" class="history"></ul>
        </div>

        <div class="chatfooter">
            <!-- //4-->
            <div class="chatinput">
```

```
            <input id="queryText" class="chatinput" placeholder="Reply
            to chatbot...">
        </div>
        <button type="submit" id="submit">Send</button>
    </div>
</form>

<script>

//a) Load socket io
const socketio = io();

//b) Once socket.io made a connection with a server app,
// execute this block
const socket = socketio.on('connect', function() {
    console.log('connected');

    //c) Run this block when the server responds with a fulfillment
    socketio.on('returnResults', function (data) {
        var objDiv = document.getElementById("ca");
        console.log(data);

        //d) If there are queryResults then dynamically
        // create list items to append to the messages list.
        if(data[0].queryResult){
            var agent = document.createElement("li");
            agent.className = 'balloon agent';
            agent.innerHTML = data[0].queryResult.fulfillmentText;
            messages.appendChild(agent);
            objDiv.scrollTop = objDiv.scrollHeight;
        }
    });

    //welcome
    socketio.emit('welcome');
});
```

```
//e) Create some pointers to other HTML elements
const textarea = document.getElementById('textarea');
const textInput = document.getElementById('queryText');
const submitBtn = document.getElementById('submit');
const messages = document.getElementById('messages');

//f) On submit of a user utterance,
// create list items to append to the messages list.
submitBtn.onclick = function(e) {
    e.preventDefault();
    socketio.emit('message', textInput.value);
    var user = document.createElement("li");
    user.className = 'balloon user';
    user.innerHTML = textInput.value;
    messages.appendChild(user);
    textInput.value = "";
}
</script>
</body>
</html>
```

There are a couple of crucial points to notice when viewing this code:

1. In the header, I am loading a JavaScript file from a CDN: **socket.io.js** Socket.IO enables real-time, bidirectional, and event-based communication. It works on every platform, browser, or device, focusing equally on reliability and speed.

2. The stylesheet, **style.css**, will load some lovely styles to make the user and agent text look like text balloons.

3. In the body of the HTML document, I am creating a form element. This form element will contain a list of chatbot messages. These are user messages and Dialogflow agent messages.

4. The form also contains an input text field with a submit button; this allows the user to type questions to the chatbot.

5. Now there's some client-side JavaScript to run:

    a. First, load the Socket.IO JavaScript object.

    b. Once Socket.IO made a connection with a server app, execute this block of code.

    c. Run this block when the server responds with a fulfillment.

    d. If there are **queryResults**, then dynamically create list items to append to the messages list.

    e. Create some pointers to other HTML elements.

    f. On submit of a user utterance, create list items to append to the messages list.

Back-End Implementation

Now let's move on to the back-end code. It's a Node.js Express application. For this project, we will make use of the npm libraries in Listing 11-2.

Listing 11-2. Back-end package.json, containing all the libraries

```
{
    "name": "dialogflow-custom-integration",
    "version": "1.0.0",
    "author": "Lee Boonstra",
    "license": "Apache-2.0",
    "description": "Custom Web integration with the Dialogflow SDK",
    "engines": {
      "node": ">=10.9.0 <13.0.0",
      "yarn": ">=1.17.3 <=1.19.1"
    },
    "scripts": {
      "start": "node app.js"
    },
    "private": true,
    "dependencies": {
      "cors": "^2.8.5",
```

```
      "dialogflow": "^0.14.1",
      "dotenv": "^8.2.0",
      "express": "^4.17.1",
      "socket.io": "^2.3.0",
      "uuid": "^3.3.3"
   }
 }
```

Here's the code which will run the chatbot back-end integration.

Listing 11-3. The back-end integration code which talks to the Dialogflow SDK

```
//1) These system variables can be set from the command-line with
--PROJECT_ID, --PORT and --LANGUAGE
const projectId = process.env.npm_config_PROJECT_ID;
const port = ( process.env.npm_config_PORT || 3000 );
const languageCode = (process.env.npm_config_LANGUAGE || 'en-US');

//2) Load all the libraries needed by this app
const socketIo = require('socket.io');
const http = require('http');
const cors = require('cors');
const express = require('express');
const path = require('path');
// These are specific to Dialogflow
const uuid = require('uuid');
const df = require('dialogflow').v2beta1;

//3) Create an express app
const app = express();

//4) Setup Express, and load the static files and HTML page
app.use(cors());
app.use(express.static(__dirname + '/../ui/'));
app.get('/', function(req, res) {
    res.sendFile(path.join(__dirname + '/../ui/index.html'));
});

//5) Create the Server and listen to the PORT variable
server = http.createServer(app);
```

```
io = socketIo(server);
server.listen(port, () => {
    console.log('Running server on port %s', port);
});

//6 Socket.io listener, once the client connect to the server socket
// then execute this block.
io.on('connect', (client) => {
    console.log(`Client connected [id=${client.id}]`);
    client.emit('server_setup', `Server connected [id=${client.id}]`);

    //7) When the client sends 'message' events
    // then execute this block
    client.on('message', async function(msg) {
        //console.log(msg);

        //8) A promise to do intent matching
        const results = await detectIntent(msg);
        console.log(results);

        //9) Return the Dialogflow after intent matching to the client UI.
        client.emit('returnResults', results);
    });
});

/**
 * Setup Dialogflow Integration
 */
function setupDialogflow(){
    //10) Dialogflow will need a session Id
    sessionId = uuid.v4();

    //11) Dialogflow will need a DF Session Client
    // So each DF session is unique
    sessionClient = new df.SessionsClient();

    //12) Create a session path from the Session client,
    // which is a combination of the projectId and sessionId.
    sessionPath = sessionClient.sessionPath(projectId, sessionId);
```

```
    //13) These objects are in the Dialogflow request
    request = {
      session: sessionPath,
      queryInput: {}
    }
}

 /*
  * Dialogflow Detect Intent based on Text
  * @param text - string
  * @return response promise
  */
async function detectIntent(text){
    //14) Get the user utterance from the UI
    request.queryInput.text =  {
        languageCode: languageCode,
        text: text
    };
    console.log(request);

    //15) The Dialogflow SDK method for intent detection.
    // It returns a Promise, which will be resolved once the
    // fulfillment data comes in.
    const responses = await sessionClient.detectIntent(request);
    return responses;
}

//Run this code.
setupDialogflow();
```

1. These system variables can be set from the command line with

    ```
    --PROJECT_ID, --PORT and --LANGUAGE
    ```

2. Load all the libraries needed by this app with the last ones specific to Dialogflow.

3. Create an Express app.

4. Set up Express and load the static files and HTML page.

5. Create the Server and listen to the PORT variable.

6. Socket.IO listener, once the client connects to the server socket, then executes this block.

7. When the client sends 'message' events, then execute this block.

8. This contains a function to do the intent matching.

9. Once the results come in, return them to the client UI.

10. Dialogflow will need a unique session id:

```
sessionId = uuid.v4();
```

11. Dialogflow will need a Dialogflow Session Client to make this session unique to its user:

```
sessionClient = new df.SessionsClient();
```

12. Create a session path from the Session Client, a combination of the projectId and sessionId. Now the session will belong only to your Dialogflow agent.

```
sessionPath = sessionClient.sessionPath(projectId, sessionId);
```

13. These objects are in the Dialogflow request:

```
request = {
  session: sessionPath,
  queryInput: {
    text: {
        languageCode: languageCode
    }
  }
}
```

14. Get the user utterance from the UI.

15. This is the Dialogflow SDK method for intent detection. It returns a promise, which will be resolved once the fulfillment data comes in:

```
await sessionClient.detectIntent(request);
```

Figure 11-2 shows how it will look.

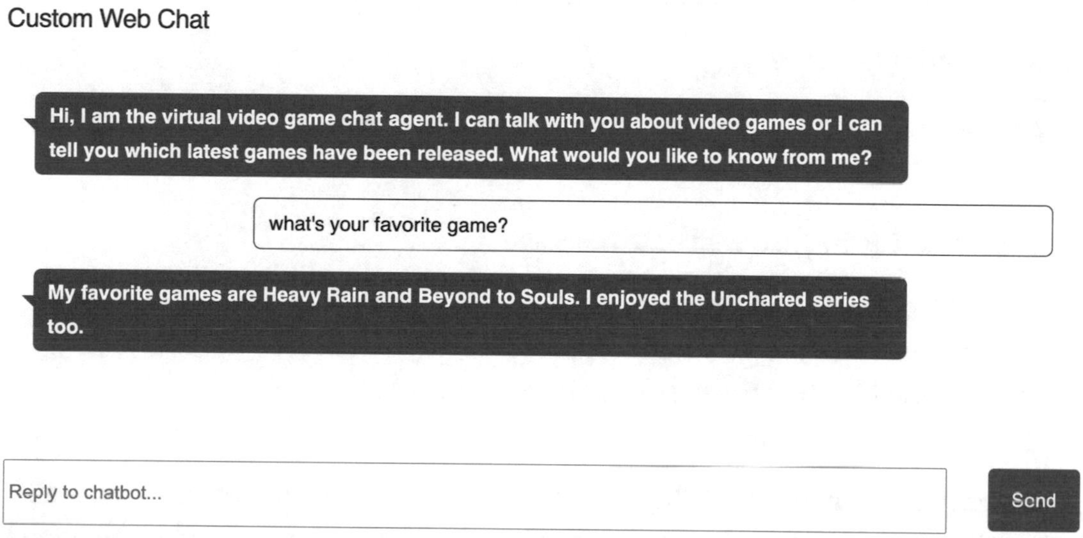

Custom Web Chat

Hi, I am the virtual video game chat agent. I can talk with you about video games or I can tell you which latest games have been released. What would you like to know from me?

what's your favorite game?

My favorite games are Heavy Rain and Beyond to Souls. I enjoyed the Uncharted series too.

Reply to chatbot...   Send

Figure 11-2. *A working custom chat integration in a web browser*

To run this example from the GitHub repo, which belongs to this book, you will need to cd into the **back-end** folder.

From there, install the required libraries:

```
npm install
```

Start the Node app:

```
npm --PROJECT_ID=[your-google-cloud-project-id] run start
```

Browse to http://localhost:3000.

Welcome Message

A common question that I get all the time from people implementing their own integrations is: how can I make sure my chatbot greets the user when opening the chat? It's not so difficult; we can fire events to Dialogflow, and we will do this as soon as Socket.IO has a proper connection with a client (which happens after the page is loaded). Note Listing 11-4.

Add to the **index.html** within the connect listener:

```
socketio.emit('welcome');
```

Then in your back-end app.js, within the connect listener, we will listen to welcome messages sent from the UI.

Listing 11-4. Listing to a welcome message

```
client.on('welcome', async function() {
    const welcomeResults = await detectIntentByEventName('welcome');
    client.emit('returnResults', welcomeResults);
});
```

The next new function in Listing 11-5 works quite similar to the detectIntent call from Listing 11-3, but instead of passing in text query input, we will use an **event name**.

Listing 11-5. Detecting an intent by event name

```
async function detectIntentByEventName(eventName){
    request.queryInput.event = {
        languageCode: languageCode,
        name: eventName
    };
    const responses = await sessionClient.detectIntent(request);
    //remove the event, so the welcome event wont be triggered again
    delete request.queryInput.event;
    return responses;
}
```

Which event name? The welcome event, as our welcome intent has that event attached to it, which you can see in Figure 11-3.

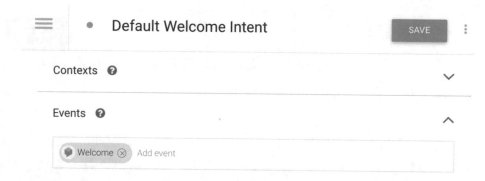

Figure 11-3. *The Welcome event in Dialogflow*

Creating Rich Responses in Your Chatbot Integration

When you want to use rich response messages in your implementation, you will have to build these manually. This makes sense, as you control the UI.

Let's build a few rich response messages in our integration.

A Hyperlink Component, a Google Map, and an Image Component

First, create a new intent with training phrases like "Do you have a web address?"

You don't need to specify a text response. Instead, you will create a new **custom payload**, which uses our custom JSON as seen in Figure 11-4:

```
{
  "web": {
    "type": "hyperlink",
    "text": "Check My Website",
    "link": "http://www.leeboonstra.com"
  }
}
```

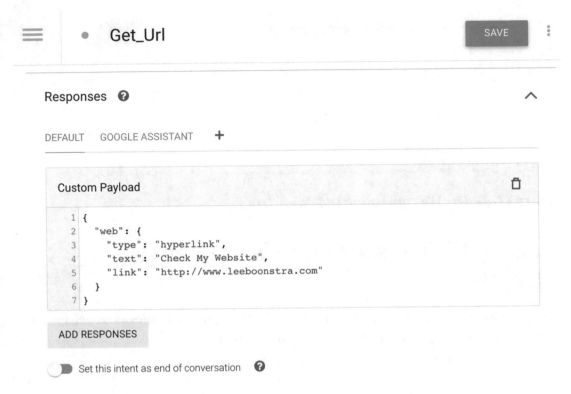

Figure 11-4. The custom payload for a custom hyperlink rich message

In your back-end integration, after running the detectIntent method, you would need to loop through the queryResult.fulfillmentMessages array. It should contain an object with the message set to the **payload**.

```
fulfillmentMessages: Array(1)
    0:
        message: "payload"
        payload:
            fields:
                platform: {stringValue: "custom-web", kind: "stringValue"}
                web: {structValue: {...}, kind: "structValue"}
                __proto__: Object
            __proto__: Object
        platform: "PLATFORM_UNSPECIFIED"
        __proto__: Object
```

```
    length: 1
    __proto__: Array(0)
fulfillmentText: ""
```

Tip   Did you notice that there is something weird with the payload object? It's not holding the same JSON object as what you have entered in the Dialogflow console.

That's because the Google gRPC API uses protocol buffers (`google.protobuf.Struct`). Protocol buffers are Google's language-neutral, platform-neutral, extensible mechanism for serializing structured data.

You would need to convert the protobuf to JSON. In my GitHub for this example, I've included a simple converter script.

Your back-end code should return the results to the UI. Your client-side JavaScript will loop through all the results and present the results on the screen with custom styling. Figure 11-5 shows how it will look.

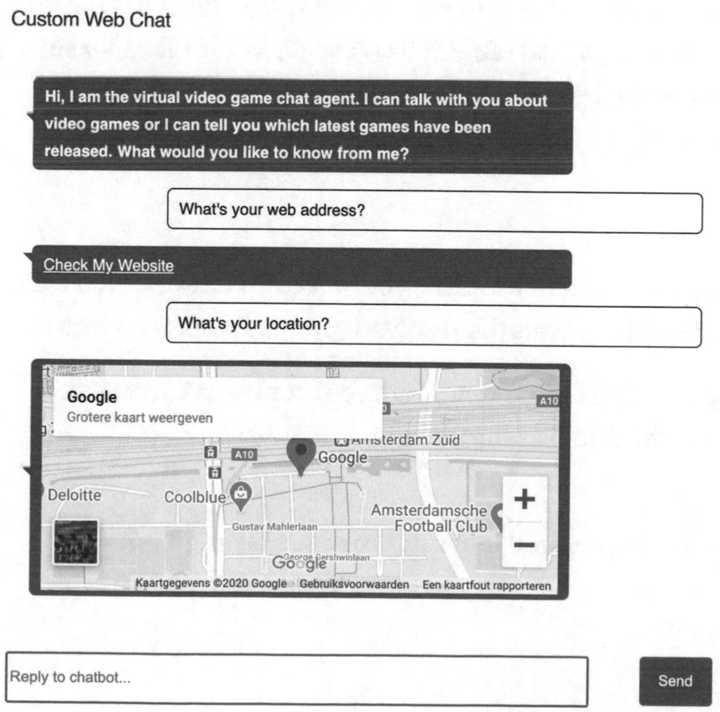

Figure 11-5. Example of a custom integration with rich messages support

Implementation

Let's look at a full implementation of rich messages for hyperlinks, Google Maps, and images. We have seen an example of a hyperlink custom payload already; Listing 11-6 shows some examples of an image and a Google Map.

Listing 11-6. A custom payload in the Dialogflow console

```
{
  "web": {
    "type": "image",
    "alt": "Lee Boonstra",
    "src": "https://www.leeboonstra.com/images/profile.jpg"
  }
}
{
  "web": {
    "link": "https://www.google.com/maps/embed?pb=!1m18!1m12!1m3!1d2437.799
    5043017927!2d4.869772751476948!3d52.33778327968087!2m3!1f0!2f0!3f0!3m2!
    1i1024!2i768!4f13.1!3m3!1m2!1s0x47c60a05af168f5b%3A0x3e5bfe6e0b2ce441!2
    sGoogle+Amsterdam!5e0!3m2!1sen!2snl!4v1520965060384",
    "type": "map"
  }
}
```

Right after the detectIntent promise, you can call a new method called **getRichContent()** which passes the resolved promise responses into it.

```
const responses = await sessionClient.detectIntent(request);
let data = getRichContent(responses);
return data;
```

The getRichContent method looks like this; see Listing 11-7.

Listing 11-7. The getRichContent method gets the object from the protobuf

```
function getRichContent(responses){
    const result = responses[0].queryResult;
    let messages = [];

    if(result.fulfillmentMessages.length > 0) {
        for (let index = 0; index < result.fulfillmentMessages.length;
        index++) {
            const msg = result.fulfillmentMessages[index];
            if (msg.payload){
                let data = structJson.structProtoToJson(msg.payload);
                messages.push(data.web);
            } else {
                messages.push(msg.text.text);
            }
        }
        return messages;
    }
}
```

It first checks if the fulfillmentMessages contains an Array that has at least one element. It's possible to have multiple fulfillment messages, for example, a text message and two rich messages, so we will have to loop through these. If the message contains a custom payload, we will need to get the data and convert the protobuf to JSON. Else, we can add the text version to the new messages array. This array will be sent to the UI. Technically, you could also create the HTML markup on this place, but it will be nicer to do this in the front end, so your front-end UI code is nicely decoupled from your back-end code.

I'm using this little converter script to work with proto buffers. I can convert from JSON to Struct or from Struct to JSON. You can find this script in the GitHub repo from this book. The last one is what we need: structProtoToJson(data.web);

Don't forget to include file in the top of your app.js back-end code:

```
const structJson = require('../back-end/structToJson');
```

Here's the code that we will use in the UI. My **index.html** will contain the following block once the data has been received by Socket.IO. Have a look into Listing 11-8.

Listing 11-8. Looping through the results to find the custom payload type and displaying it right on the screen

```
socketio.on('returnResults', function (data) {
    console.log(data);

    //d) If there are queryResults then dynamically
    // create list items to append to the messages list.

    for (let index = 0; index < data.length; index++) {
        var e = data[index];
        if (e.type == 'hyperlink'){
            var balloon = document.createElement("li");
            balloon.className = 'balloon agent';
            balloon.innerHTML = `<a href="${e.link}">${e.text}</a>`;
            console.log(`<a href="${e.link}">${e.text}</a>`);
            messages.appendChild(balloon);
        } else if (e.type == 'map') {
            var balloon = document.createElement("li");
            balloon.className = 'balloon agent';
            balloon.innerHTML = `<iframe src="${e.link}" width="400"
            height="200" />`;
            messages.appendChild(balloon);
        } else if (e.type == 'image') {
            var balloon = document.createElement("li");
            balloon.className = 'balloon agent';
            balloon.innerHTML = `<img src="${e.src}" alt="${e.alt}" />"`;
            messages.appendChild(balloon);
        } else {
            var balloon = document.createElement("li");
            balloon.className = 'balloon agent';
            balloon.innerHTML = e;
            messages.appendChild(balloon);
        }
    }
});
```

It checks the messaging types. If the type is a hyperlink, then we will create an anchor tag with the link and the link text provided by the custom payload in the Dialogflow console. If the type is an image, you will create an image tag with an image src and alt tag, provided by the custom payload in the Dialogflow console. And when it's a map, then it will use an iframe with a Google Maps URL which was provided by the custom payload in the Dialogflow console.

The possibilities are endless. If you want to create custom cards, it will probably contain some div elements, but with custom stylesheet code to make it look nice.

Using Markdown Syntax and Conditional Templates in Your Dialogflow Responses

When working with large teams, the UX designer or copywriter often maintains the Dialogflow console conversation. They want to have control over the text's styling, without using HTML markup in the text, for example, to highlight certain words or to display hyperlinks.

When you are building your own custom integration, integrating supporting markdown is actually very easy.

Just make sure your UI **index.html** includes a markdown library such as **Marked**.

```
<script src="https://cdn.jsdelivr.net/npm/marked/marked.min.js"></script>
<script>
```

Your intent responses. can now contain markdown syntax, such as seen in Figure 11-6:

```
**Lee**  is a *Conversational AI Developer Advocate* at Google. In this
role, she is focusing on *Dialogflow*, *Contact Center AI* & *Speech*
technology. Here's her  [website](https://www.leeboonstra.com)
```

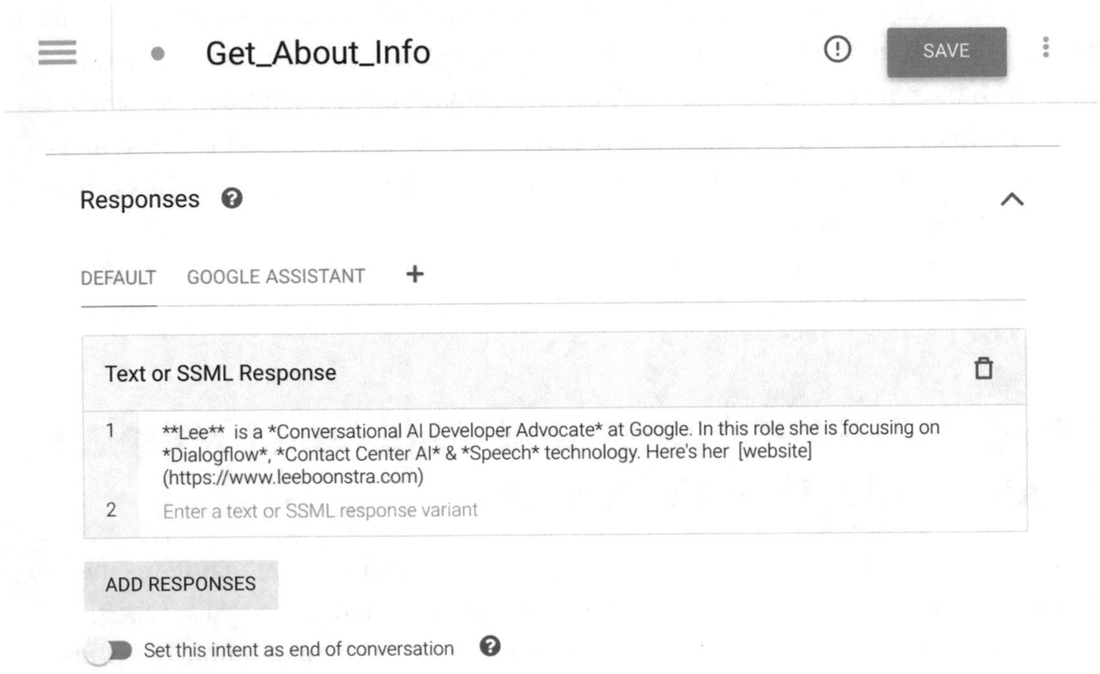

Figure 11-6. *Using markdown text in the Dialogflow response text fields*

Figure 11-7 shows how this will render to the screen.

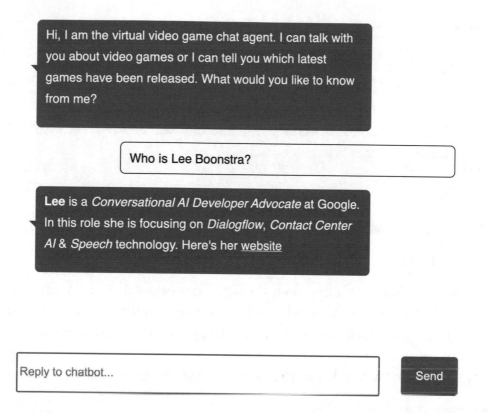

Figure 11-7. *The custom integration can handle markdown after importing the Marked library*

Branching the Conversation

Besides markdown, it is also possible to use templates and conditional branching from within the Dialogflow Console.

Think **Jinja** (for Python or Java developers), **Smarty** (PHP), or **Jade/Pug**, **Handlebars**, and **Mustache** (for JavaScript developers). Here's an example with the Pug.js library (formerly known as Jade). It works really well.

The trick here is to make use of the **custom payload** response setting and use of a templating library, so you can provide readable templates and variables that can be injected. Note Listing 11-9.

Listing 11-9. Example of branching in the Dialogflow console, as a custom payload

```
{ "custom":
    {
        "locals": {
        "username": "$username"
    },
        "pug": [ "if username\n", " | Hello $username\n", "else\n", " |
        Hello stranger" ]
    }
}
```

The training phrase which belongs to this example is

```
My name is: Lee
```

The values of the `locals` object are the parameter values that were passed in as a username. In the pug object, I wrote a multiline string template with an if-else branch. When using Pug, the line indenting is essential. Pay attention to the newline **\n** code and the | for using plain text.

My integration back-end code will need to include the pub library:

```
const pug = require('pug');
```

A custom function that can get the template from the custom payload to compile it with the passed in variables. See Listing 11-10.

Listing 11-10. The template helper function to compile for Pug

```
function templateHelper(payload) {
    var str = payload.custom.pug;
    if(Array.isArray(payload.custom.pug)) {
      str = payload.custom.pug.join("");
    };

    var fn = pug.compile(str);
    var text = fn(payload.custom.locals);
    return text;
}
```

After the intent was detected, you will only need to invoke the templateHelper method with the payload. See Listing 11-11.

Listing 11-11. Invoke the templateHelper method

```
io.on('connect', (client) => {
    console.log(`Client connected [id=${client.id}]`);
    client.emit('server_setup', `Server connected [id=${client.id}]`);

    client.on('message', async function(msg) {
        const results = await detectIntent(msg);
        var responseMsg = results[0].queryResult.fulfillmentText;

        var payload = results[0].queryResult.fulfillmentMessages[0];
        let data = structJson.structProtoToJson(payload.payload);
        console.log(data);
        if (data && data.custom){
            client.emit('returnResults', templateHelper(data));
        } else {
            client.emit('returnResults', responseMsg);
        }
    });
});
```

Once a message comes in, we will detect the intent as usual, but we will need to check if the matched intent data contains a payload, which is custom. Notice this is a protobuf, which will need to be converted to a JSON object first. The script for this can be found in the GitHub repo, which belongs to this book. Based on this custom payload, we will call the templateHelper and pass in the payload data. Else, we will just return the fulfillmentText as a response message. See the result in Figure 11-8.

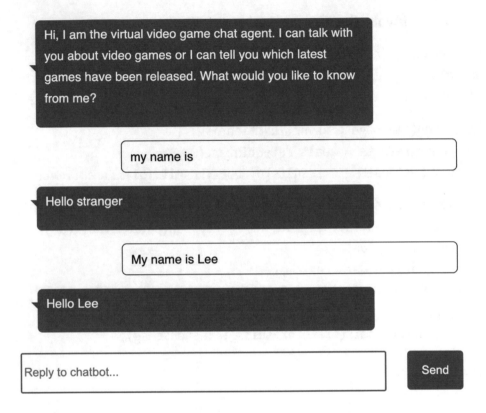

Figure 11-8. Branching of the conversation in a custom UI via the Dialogflow console

Building an Integration to Run a Dialogflow Agent in a Native Mobile Android or iOS App with Flutter

The past sections showed you how to integrate Dialogflow in your website or web application by creating a front-end UI and a back-end server. If you would make this website mobile-friendly, then it could run on a mobile device. However, maybe you are interested in integrating a Dialogflow agent in a native mobile app. This is where Google's technology, Flutter, comes in.

Flutter is an open source UI software development kit created by Google. It is used to develop applications for Android, iOS, Linux, Mac, Windows, and the Web from a single (Dart code) codebase. With Flutter, you can develop apps fast as it can hot-reload changes while saving your code. Flutter ships with a rich set of customizable widgets to create native end user experiences with native performance, as it gets compiled to native ARM machine code using Dart's native compilers. Like npm for Node.js, Dart and Flutter have their own package manager, pub.dev package management, allowing you to download prebuilt Flutter packages and integrate this in your app.

Two Techniques for Integrating Dialogflow in a Flutter Application

There are two techniques for integrating a Dialogflow agent into a Flutter app. Both solutions will come with pros and cons, and it's up to you to figure out which solution fits best for your business.

The first solution is the most obvious one: using a Dialogflow package, integrating the Dialogflow SDK directly into your (mobile app) client. The other solution would be to incorporate the Dialogflow SDK in a back-end server application and let your (mobile app) client talk to the back end over HTTP(s).

By building it directly into Flutter, you will only need to write the codebase once. As an enterprise, you will either have your Dart/Flutter experience in house, or you hire a freelancer or agency to build the app for you. With Flutter 2, you can even support desktop and web applications instead of just Android and iOS apps. However, you will need to develop a solution to serve and store Google Cloud's service accounts and API keys in a secure way.

Caution   Storing the service account in a client asset folder (or even in a secure key client keychain) can be dangerous if it's not handled well. First of all, you will need to be very careful with your service accounts. Which read and access rights will you give your components? When you give admin rights to Google Cloud's compute engine, you can imagine that attackers could hack and decompile your app. When they get access to your compute engine, they could drive you into costs by, for example, mining Bitcoins for them. Now, even when you don't give compute access rights to your Google Cloud service accounts, you still won't expose your keys. Even though for Dialogflow, it only gives you access to your chatbot within your project, it might be possible for attackers to read PII data from the chat history if your end users were sharing PII data in the chat. That can be a huge problem.

On top of that, it's not so easy to change service account keys in applications, as you don't want the app to stop working for current users. So how can you serve service accounts and keys secure in mobile clients? By, for example, building a mechanism to rotate (a second set of) keys. Like working with JSON Web Tokens (JWT), an Internet proposed standard for creating data with optional signature and optional encryption whose payload holds JSON that asserts some number of claims. The tokens are signed either using a private secret or a public/private key. Or you can run parts of your integration on a server.

Integrating the Dialogflow SDK in a back-end/server application requires you to write application code in another programming language. For enterprises, this typically means that you would have to deal with another team or agency of developers, and you will have to work together. This solution will also mean that you will need to pay for server computing costs, as you will need to host your codebase somewhere. The advantage here is that you won't expose your service accounts to the client, making this solution very safe.

Another significant advantage in taking this approach is when you want to build a chat/voice platform that needs to support various integration channels. For creating multichannel or omnichannel experiences, this is the right approach to go, as you only need to maintain the Dialogflow integration in one place, treating every integration as its own channel. If you want, you could even build it that way that you can switch between Dialogflow Essentials and Dialogflow CX agents. Let's have a look at both solutions.

Integrating the Dialogflow SDK Directly into Your Flutter App

When you search on pub.dev for Dialogflow, you will find many open source Dialogflow Flutter packages, including mine: **dialogflow_grpc**. The Dialogflow gRPC package makes use of the gRPC library for Dialogflow. Only with the gRPC library is it possible to do streaming, should you want to make use of the built-in Dialogflow Speech to Text and Text to Speech capabilities. For what's worth, the underlying gRPC API is also faster than the REST API, which is often used for integrating Dialogflow with Dart and Flutter.

For demo purposes, we will include the Google Cloud service account in an assets folder. As we know by now, for production apps, you will have to come up with a more secure strategy.

Edit the **pubspec.yaml** file with the **dialogflow_grpc** dependency. And point to your service account (e.g., assets/credentials.json), as seen in Listing 11-12.

Listing 11-12. pubspec.yaml

```
dependencies:
  dialogflow_grpc: any

# The following section is specific to Flutter.
flutter:

  uses-material-design: true
  assets:
    - assets/credentials.json
```

Import this package in your code. Load your service account, and create a DialogflowGrpc instance; see Listing 11-13.

Listing 11-13. Loading the service account

```
import 'package:dialogflow_grpc/v2beta1.dart';
import 'package:dialogflow_grpc/generated/google/cloud/dialogflow/v2beta1/
session.pb.dart';
import 'package:dialogflow_grpc/dialogflow_auth.dart';

final serviceAccount = ServiceAccount.fromString(
    '${(await rootBundle.loadString('assets/credentials.json'))}');

DialogflowGrpc dialogflow = DialogflowGrpc.viaServiceAccount(serviceAccount);
```

With the following line of code, you can detect an intent based on text input:

```
var data = await dialogflow.detectIntent(text, 'en-US');
print(data.queryResult.fulfillmentText);
```

Listing 11-14 shows you how you can detect an intent based on an audio stream. Integrating audio streaming requires working with a microphone component in your Flutter app. Typically, pub.dev will have various open source microphone components available. Keep in mind that Flutter microphone libraries are wrappers around native hardware components. Thus, the implementations might differ across devices (Android, iOS, Web, macOS, or Windows).

Listing 11-14. Streaming audio to Dialogflow

```
// 1)
var biasList = SpeechContextV2Beta1(
    phrases: [
        'Dialogflow CX',
        'Dialogflow Essentials',
        'Action Builder',
        'HIPAA'
    ],
    boost: 20.0
 );

// 2)
var config = InputConfigV2beta1(
    encoding: 'AUDIO_ENCODING_LINEAR_16',
    languageCode: 'en-US',
    sampleRateHertz: 16000,
    singleUtterance: false,
    speechContexts: [biasList]
 );

//3)
final responseStream = dialogflow.streamingDetectIntent(config,
_audioStream);
responseStream.listen((data) {
    print(data);
});
```

1. You can create a speech recognition bias list to give certain words a boost. This makes sense for the times that your speech model does not seem to understand you. (See Chapter 7 for more details on speech adaptation.)

2. This is where you annotate your audio config, and it depends on the hardware of the device you are using. For example, your phone could make use of AUDIO_ENCODING_LINEAR_16 encoding and 16000 hertz. You will also need to specify the language you

are listing for and if you want to detect the single utterance. By default (which is set to false), recognition does not cease until the client closes the stream. If true, the recognizer will detect a single spoken utterance in the input audio. Lastly, you want to specify the bias list.

3. Make the `streamingDetectIntent` call, with the specified InputConfig and the audio stream. Such an audio stream you can get from a microphone component.

The next chapter will talk in more detail about streaming audio to Dialogflow.

Figure 11-9 shows an example of a Flutter app with Flutter UI components, which integrates the Dialogflow gRPC package in your application. The Flutter gRPC package comes with a full working demo of an audio streaming app for mobile devices.

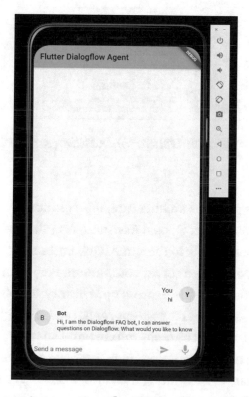

Figure 11-9. *A demo app integrating the Dialogflow gRPC package in a Flutter UI app*

A Flutter App That Communicates with a Back-End Dialogflow SDK App

When you are building a bot platform that needs to support multiple channels (or an omnichannel experience, where chat messages can travel through the various integrations), it could make more sense to build an architecture like shown in Figure 11-10.

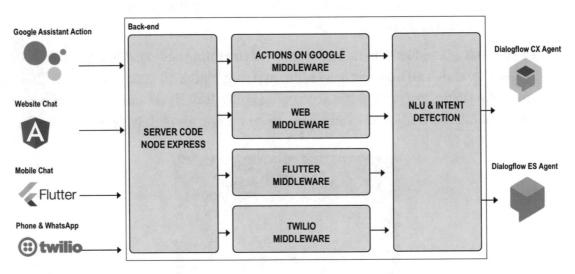

Figure 11-10. *An example architecture for building a bot platform that supports multiple channels*

As you can see in the previous architecture, this solution contains various integration channels, such as the mobile app, Google Assistant, Angular web app, phone, and WhatsApp. These channels all talk to the same back-end server.

The back-end server exists as a server component. For example, in a Node.js application, the server could use the Express npm library. The Google Assistant could POST against `https://www.example.com/app/googleassistant`; the Flutter app could POST to `https://www.example.com/app/mobile`; and so on.

The server can route all the incoming (Ajax) messages to the channel middleman. This middleware takes care of integrating the various SDKs. For example, the Google Assistant middleware will integrate with Actions on Google, the phone and WhatsApp middleware will integrate with Twilio, the Angular website and the Flutter app will create the views to return manually.

All these integration middleware layers will connect to the code that integrates with the Dialogflow SDK, as seen in this chapter's first section. The advantage is that you only need to set up Dialogflow in one place. This part talks to the Dialogflow agent. It should not contain any rich messages, UI components, or SSML texts, just plain NLU and intent detection.

When building an architecture like this, don't forget to create an analytics data pipeline architecture. Chapter 13 describes how to do this.

Summary

This chapter contains information about building your own integrations. You will learn the following tasks:

- You want to create a chatbot on your own website by using the Dialogflow SDK and WebSockets.

- You want to integrate rich responses such as cards, images, hyperlinks, or Google Maps in your custom web chat integration.

- You want to use markdown syntax in your chatbot integration and do branching.

- You want to integrate the Dialogflow SDK in a mobile app with Flutter to build native Android, iOS, Windows, MacOS, or web chat apps.

- You want to build a multichannel bot platform by building a back-end integration.

In case you want to build this example, the source code for this book is available on GitHub via the book's product page, located at `www.apress.com/978-1-4842-7013-4`. Look into the **custom-integration-web**, **custom-integration-markdown**, and **custom-integration-rich-messages** folders.

Further Reading

- Dialogflow SDK method for detecting an Intent

  `https://cloud.google.com/dialogflow/es/docs/reference/rest/v2/projects.agent.sessions/detectIntent`

- Dialogflow SDK on QueryInput looks like

    `https://cloud.google.com/dialogflow/es/docs/reference/`
    `rest/v2/QueryInput`

- A real-world approach example of a chatbot integrated into a website

    `https://github.com/savelee/kube-django-ng`

- SDK documentation on QueryResults

    `https://cloud.google.com/dialogflow/es/docs/reference/`
    `rest/v2/DetectIntentResponse#queryresult`

- More information on protocol buffers

    `https://developers.google.com/protocol-buffers`

- MarkedJS library for allowing markdown syntax in your custom web integration

    `https://github.com/markedjs/marked`

- Pug.js library for supporting conditional templates in your custom web integration

    `https://www.npmjs.com/package/pug`

- Flutter

    `https://flutter.dev`

- Dialogflow gRPC package

    `https://pub.dev/packages/dialogflow_grpc`

- Learn more about integrating gRPC and building your own Flutter package

    `https://www.leeboonstra.dev/apis/dialogflow_flutter_grpc/`

CHAPTER 12

Implementing a Dialogflow Voice Agent in Your Website or App Using the SDK

When COVID-19 started in 2019, many businesses realized that customers are not keen on touching public keyboards and touch interfaces, sources that easily spread bacteria. For example, people started to prefer contactless payments in stores and not touch self-service kiosk devices which you can find at airports, railway stations, or shops. Therefore, it's a great solution to build voice AI in your hardware devices and applications.

This chapter is not about the Google Assistant. It's about integrating your Dialogflow voice agent in a website or app. Doing so takes a couple of steps, which is divided across the sections of this chapter:

- Building the client-side app and UX, which allows you to use a microphone

- Building the back-end app which allows you to use the Google Cloud machine learning APIs for understanding the spoken voice and returning synthesized voice

- Playing generated audio streams in your (browser) app

But before we continue, let's pay attention to why you should not pick the Google Assistant for this particular use case.

© Lee Boonstra 2021
L. Boonstra, *The Definitive Guide to Conversational AI with Dialogflow and Google Cloud*,
https://doi.org/10.1007/978-1-4842-7014-1_12

Reasons for Not Picking Google Assistant

I often speak with customers, and their wish is to include the Google Assistant in their business web apps. Unless you are a manufacturer for TV setup boxes or headphones, I always answer:

"Is this really what you want? Or do you mean you want to extend your own app with a conversational AI?"

Suppose you have one or more of the following requirements. In that case, you probably want to make direct use of the Google Cloud Speech and Dialogflow APIs, instead of packing your voice AI as an action in the Google Assistant or wrapping the open source Google Assistant SDK in your own app.

Reasons for not picking the Google Assistant over building your own voice AI:

- This application shouldn't be publicly available.

- This application doesn't need to be available on the Google Assistant/Nest Home.

- You don't want to start your app with the wake words: "Hey Google, talk to <my app>."

- The application doesn't need to answer native Google Assistant questions, such as "what's the weather in Amsterdam."

- The application has specific technical requirements, such as having the microphone open longer than 30 seconds.

- The application can only use the enterprise Google Cloud terms and conditions instead of combining it with the Google Assistant's consumer terms and conditions.

Compared to the Google Assistant, by extending your apps with a conversational AI manually with the preceding tools, you no longer are part of the Google Assistant ecosystem. That ecosystem is excellent if you are building consumer or campaign apps (voice actions) that everyone can find by invoking it through the <Hey Google, talk to my app> invocation. But when you are an enterprise, that whole ecosystem might be overkill. Figure 12-1 will show you the Google Assistant ecosystem; as seen in the picture, the ecosystem contains millions of actions, which need to be invoked. If you want to extend your custom AI with voice, the Google Assistant ecosystem might be an overkill.

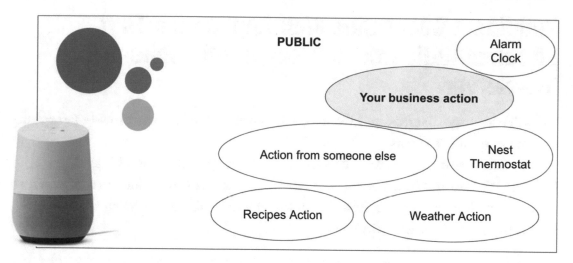

Figure 12-1. *The Google Assistant ecosystem could be an overkill*

Are you convinced that you want to extend your own (mobile) web app by integrating voice AI capabilities? This chapter explains on implementing voice streaming from a web application to Speech-to-Text, Dialogflow, and Text-to-Speech.

Figure 12-2 will show you how the architecture of this voice integration will look like.

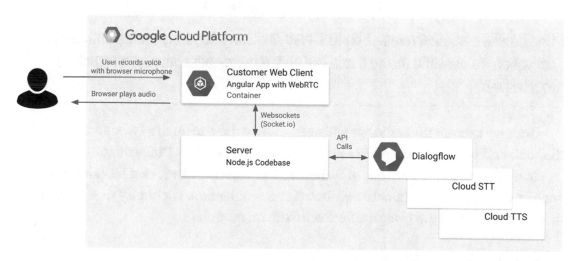

Figure 12-2. *The user will speak via a microphone in a browser web application. This front-end web application will bring the stream to a back-end server which will make calls to Dialogflow, Speech-to-Text, and Text-to-Speech*

Building a Client-Side Web Application That Streams Audio from a Browser Microphone to a Server

You will use the `getUserMedia()` WebRTC JavaScript method in your browser to capture microphone audio streams.

To make sure it works across all modern browsers, you could use a library like **RecordRTC**. RecordRTC is a WebRTC JavaScript library for audio/video as well as screen activity recording. It supports Chrome, Firefox, Opera, Android, and Microsoft Edge. Platforms: Linux, Mac, and Windows.

Note   When running your application on iOS devices, you might run into various problems. First of all, iOS doesn't support the JavaScript getUserMedia and WebRTC methods in any other mobile browser than Safari. You could show a pop-up warning when it's opened on an iOS browser other than mobile Safari.

To use the getUserMedia() WebRTC method, you will need to allow the permissions pop-up, which only shows up once running from HTTPS.

One crucial limitation remains on iOS: Web Audio is effectively muted until user activation. To play and record audio in iOS, it requires user interaction (such as touch start).

Once we capture the audio, we will need to send the stream to a back-end server. So the back-end server can integrate with the Google APIs such as Dialogflow.

To do this, you can make use of WebSockets or a library like Socket.IO. Socket.IO enables real-time bidirectional event-based communication. For binary stream transfers through Socket.IO, I am using the Socket.io-Stream module.

Build the Front End

First, your client-side app/HTML page will at least need a button (or two) to stop and start the browser microphone. Note Listing 12-1. You could also show a text area field for demo purposes, which later can show the returned text results.

Listing 12-1. The HTML elements needed for building a custom voice AI

```
<div>
    <button id="start-recording" disabled>Start Recording</button>
    <button id="stop-recording" disabled>Stop Recording</button>
</div>
<textarea id="results"></textarea>
```

Make sure you will load the RecordRTC and Socket.IO libraries on your page.

Then you will need a piece of JavaScript that can take care of the microphone recording and stream the audio object to a back-end server.

Listing 12-2. Handling the microphone recording and streaming the audio object to a back-end server app

```
//1)
const startRecording = document.getElementById('start-recording');
const stopRecording = document.getElementById('stop-recording');
let recordAudio;

//2)
const socketio = io();
const socket = socketio.on('connect', function() {
    startRecording.disabled = false;
});

//3)
startRecording.onclick = function() {
    startRecording.disabled = true;

    //4)
    navigator.getUserMedia({
        audio: true
    }, function(stream) {

        //5)
        recordAudio = RecordRTC(stream, {
            type: 'audio',
```

```
        //6)
            mimeType: 'audio/webm',
            sampleRate: 44100,
            // used by StereoAudioRecorder
            // the range 22050 to 96000.
            // let us force 16khz recording:
            desiredSampRate: 16000,

            // MediaStreamRecorder, StereoAudioRecorder, WebAssembly
            Recorder
            // CanvasRecorder, GifRecorder, WhammyRecorder
            recorderType: StereoAudioRecorder,
            // Dialogflow / STT requires mono audio
            numberOfAudioChannels: 1
    });

    recordAudio.startRecording();
    stopRecording.disabled = false;
}, function(error) {
    console.error(JSON.stringify(error));
});
};
```

1. First, I will create some pointers to the start and stop buttons.

2. Next, I am instantiating Socket.IO, and I am opening a connection.

3. I've created two event listeners for starting and stopping the recording. The start button onclick event will disable the start button, so you can't press the button twice and therefore record audio twice.

4. `navigator.getUserMedia()` is an important part of the code. It's part of a set of WebRTC APIs which provides the means to access the user's local camera/microphone stream. In our case, we only use the microphone (*audio: true*). This gives us access to the stream.

5. Now, I am making use of the library **RecordRTC**. I could have chosen to write this part of the code by myself. But RecordRTC solves a lot of complicated stuff, such as converting buffers (from Float32 to Int16), cross-browser support, and so on.

6. RecordRTC takes two arguments. The first argument is the `MediaStream` from the `getUserMedia()` call. The second argument is a configuration object with settings to optimize the stream. There are a couple of necessary settings that I am making, which should be in line with your settings, later in the server-side code (documentation for `InputAudioConfig` in Dialogflow or `RecognitionConfig` in STT):

    - The mime-type is set to **audio/webm**—which would be a right setting when using **AUDIO_ENCODING_LINEAR_16** or **LINEAR16** as an AudioEncoding config in Dialogflow or STT.

    - The `sampleRate` is the input sampling frequency in hertz. I am resampling it to 16000Hz (`desiredSampleRate`), so the size of the messages over the network will be smaller and match the sample hertz setting in my Dialogflow or STT calls.

    - Also, Dialogflow and STT require mono sound, which means I should set the `numberOfAudioChannels` to 1. `RecorderType` `StereoAudioRecorder` allows me to change the number of audio channels from 2 to 1.

Short Utterance vs. Streaming

There are typically two approaches on how to integrate voice in your application:

1. **Short utterances/detect intent**: This means your end user presses a record button and speaks, and when they press stop, we collect the audio stream to return results. In your code, this means that once the client web app collects the full audio recording, it sends it to the server to do a call to Dialogflow or the Speech-to-Text API.

2. **Streaming of long utterances/detect intents in a stream**: This means your end user presses the record button, speaks, and will see the results on the fly. When detecting intents, it could mean that it will detect better matches once you have talked more. In your code, this means the client starts making a bidirectional stream and streams chunks to the server to make a call with event listeners on incoming data, and thus it's real time. When there is an intent match, we can either show the results on screen by presenting the text, or we can synthesize (read out) the results by streaming an audio buffer back to the client, which will be played via the WebRTC AudioBufferSourceNode (or audio player).

Record Single Utterances

Short utterances means your end-user presses a record button and speaks, and when they press stop, we collect the audio stream to return results. In your code, this means that once the client web app collects the full audio recording, it sends it to the server to do a call to Dialogflow or the Speech-to-Text API. For this use case, the magic will be in the stop button onclick event listener.

Listing 12-3. Recording single utterances in the front end

```
// 1)
stopRecording.onclick = function() {
    // recording stopped
    startRecording.disabled = false;
    stopRecording.disabled = true;

    // stop audio recorder
    recordAudio.stopRecording(function() {
        // after stopping the audio, get the audio data
        recordAudio.getDataURL(function(audioDataURL) {

            //2)
            var files = {
                audio: {
                    type: recordAudio.getBlob().type || 'audio/wav',
```

```
                    dataURL: audioDataURL
                }
            };
            // submit the audio file to the server
            socketio.emit('message', files);
        });
    });
};

// 3)
// when the server found results send
// it back to the client
const resultpreview = document.getElementById('results');
socketio.on('results', function (data) {
    console.log(data);
    // show the results on the screen
    if(data[0].queryResult){
        resultpreview.innerHTML += "" + data[0].queryResult.
        fulfillmentText;
    }
});
```

1. When you click stop, it will first reset the buttons, then stop the
   recording. And while stopping the recording, it will request the
   audioDataURL, which is part of the RecordRTC API, in a callback
   function. This will return a string dataURL, with a Base64 string that
   contains your audio stream. This long string looks like this:

   data:audio/wav;base64,UklGRiRgAgBXQVZFZm1OIBAAAAABAAEARKwAA

2. We can create an object from it, which also sets the audio type,
   and then we are sending it to the server with Socket.IO: *socketio.*
   emit('message', files);. We will set a name. Once the server
   makes a connection to this socket, it will look for the 'message'
   event name to respond on. And it will receive the files object.

3. The last part of this script will run once the server makes a call to Dialogflow/Speech API and makes a WebSockets callback to the server to return the results. In this example, I am just printing the results in a textarea box. For Dialogflow, the `fulfillmentText` is part of the `queryResult`.

Record Audio Streams

Recording streams means your end user presses the record button, speaks, and will see the results on the fly. When detecting intents with Dialogflow, it could mean that it will detect better matches once you have talked more or collected multiple results. In your code, this means the client starts making a bidirectional stream and streams chunks to the server to make a call with event listeners on incoming data, and thus it's real time.

You might choose this approach because the audio you are expecting is long. Or, in the case of Dialogflow, you might want to show intermediate results on the screen, in real time, while speaking. In this case, you don't need the stopRecording callback function, which sends the base64 URL string to the server. Instead, it will send the stream to the server in real time!

Listing 12-4. Recording full audio streams in the front end

```
// 1)
 timeSlice: 4000,

 // 2)
 // as soon as the stream is available
 ondataavailable: function(blob) {

    // 3
    // making use of socket.io-stream for bi-directional
    // streaming, create a stream
    var stream = ss.createStream();
    // stream directly to server
    // it will be temp. stored locally
    ss(socket).emit('stream', stream, {
        name: 'stream.wav',
        size: blob.size
    });
```

```
    // pipe the audio blob to the read stream
    ss.createBlobReadStream(blob).pipe(stream);
}

// 4 ...
```

The magic, in this case, is in the RecordRTC object and the `ondataavailable` event listener:

1. First, you will need to set a **timeSlice**—the timeSlice sets intervals for creating audio chunks. In the case of Dialogflow, you likely might not want to detect the intents each second (as you might not be finished speaking a sentence) and instead build in a timer. timeSlice is set to milliseconds, so I am using *4000* (4 seconds).

2. Then there is the **ondataavailable** event listener, which gets triggered once there is data and will contain chunks of blobs (audio buffers), in my case, every 4 seconds.

3. Here's where **socketio-stream** comes in. I use bidirectional streams (I'm sending a stream with chunks every 4 seconds, but I also might want to receive results from the server in between). So I am creating the stream, which will be temporarily stored on my local drive, with *ss(socket).emit()*. I am streaming it to the server, and while I do so, I am piping the audio buffer into the stream. The purpose of stream.pipe() is to limit data buffering to acceptable levels such that sources and destinations of differing speeds will not overwhelm the available memory.

In case you want to see an end-to-end example, please look into the Airport Self Service Kiosk demo; you can find the link in the "Further Reading" section.

Note   I've seen solutions online where the microphone is directly streamed to Dialogflow, without a server in between. The REST calls were made directly in the web client with JavaScript. I would consider this as an anti-pattern. You will likely expose your service account/private key in your client-side code. Anyone handy with Chrome Dev tools could steal your key and make (paid) API calls via your account. A better approach is to let a server handle the Google Cloud authentication. This way, the service account won't be exposed to the public.

Building a Web Server That Receives a Browser Microphone Stream to Detect Intents

Here are the steps for creating a Node.js Express application that integrates the Dialogflow SDK. As described in the previous section, you will need a working front-end application to get AudioBuffers live from an HTML5 microphone.

Typically, the server-side code will exist of the following parts:

- Importing all the required libraries

- Loading the environment vars

- Setting up the Express server with Socket.IO listeners

- Google Cloud API calls: Dialogflow Audio DetectIntent and DetectStream calls

This section will use a Node.js server that will serve the static content (such as the HTML page) and connect to the Dialogflow SDK. You could use any other programming language as well. All Google Cloud services have various client SDKs (such as Node.js, Java, Python, Go, etc.) and REST and gRPC libraries.

The Dialogflow agent I am connecting to should contain some example intents, entities, or FAQ knowledge bases.

Optionally, you could also include Google Cloud Speech-to-Text StreamingRecognize and Google Cloud Text-to-Speech synthesize calls. This could be handy if you want to alter the incoming speech before sending it to Dialogflow, for example, to translate incoming speech calls, Text-to-Speech synthesize calls (for speaking out the results). Figure 12-3 is an architectural picture of the overall solution.

To see this example up and running, look in the "Further Reading" section, and use the links to the SelfServiceKiosk demo.

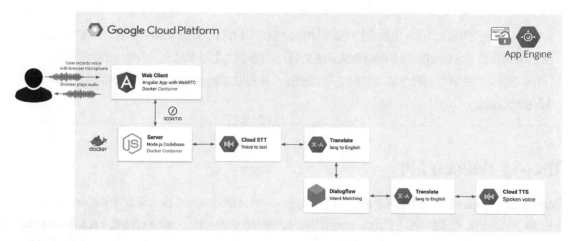

Figure 12-3. *An example architecture for building your own voice AI, with popular Cloud AI tools, such as Speech-to-Text AI, Translate API, Dialogflow, and Text-to-Speech API*

Dialogflow vs. Text-to-Speech API vs. Speech-to-Text API

Although many of us will use Dialogflow with text input, for web or social media chatbots, it is also possible to do intent matching with your voice as audio input. It can even return spoken text (TTS) as an audio result.

Dialogflow speech detection and output will overlap with Google Cloud Speech-to-Text API (STT) and Google Cloud Text-to-Speech (TTS). The API calls look similar, and that is because Dialogflow is making use of Google Cloud Speech-to-Text under the hood.

However, those services are different, and they have been used in separate use cases. For example, Dialogflow is used in conversations when you are expecting answers/ results, while Google Cloud Text-to-Speech is often used for transcribing purposes. (Think of generating subtitles or taking notes.)

Speech-to-Text API

Google Cloud **Speech-to-Text (STT)** transcribes spoken words to written text. This is great for when you want to generate subtitles in a video, generate text transcripts from meetings, and so on. You could also combine it with Dialogflow chatbots (detect intent from text transcripts) to synthesize the chatbot answers. However, STT doesn't do intent detection as Dialogflow does. STT is very powerful, as the API call response will return the written transcript with the highest confidence score, and it will return an array with alternative transcript options.

Note   The Speech-to-Text `StreamingDetectIntent` incoming audio streams are billed in 15 seconds intervals. After 15 seconds, the speech recognizer will time out if there is silence. Ideally, if there is a silence, it should not wait the whole 15 seconds.

Text-to-Speech API

With Google Cloud **Text-to-Speech (TTS)**, you can send a text or SSML (text with voice markup) input, and it will return audio bytes, which you can use to create an mp3 file or directly stream to an audio player (in your browser).

By now, you have seen how to build a web application that streams audio from a microphone on your local device through your browser to a back-end application, and fetches results from Dialogflow, and displays it in the user interface. It would be even nicer when the browser could play the audio streams. This is what the next chapter is all about!

Build the Back End

Since my example application uses Node.js and npm, I will need to download external Node libraries. The npm package which is essential for this chapter is called **dialogflow**. And it will be used to interact with Dialogflow and do intent matching (on speech).

For demo purposes, I won't discuss how to set up a Node.js application with an Express server. But as a reference, you can look into my **simple server code**, which has been used for the simple **client-side examples**, and you can also look into the code of the **Airport Self Service Kiosk** end-to-end example. The links can be found in the "Further Reading" section of this chapter.

When you browse through these code listings, you will be able to see the Express server. They all communicate via Socket.IO like Listing 12-5.

Listing 12-5. Using Socket.IO for sending audio streams from the front end to the back end

```
//1
io.on('connect', (client) => {
    //2
    client.on('message', async function(data) {
        const dataURL = data.audio.dataURL.split(',').pop();
        let fileBuffer = Buffer.from(dataURL, 'base64');

        //3 ...
    });

    // 4
    ss(client).on('stream', function(stream, data) {
        const filename = path.basename(data.name);
        stream.pipe(fs.createWriteStream(filename));

        //5 ...
    });
});
```

1. With Socket.IO instantiated, I can listen to the **connect emit**. As soon as a Socket.IO client connects to the server, this code will execute.

2. When connected to a socket, and the 'message' event was fired by the client, execute this code. It will retrieve the data which was set when stopping the WebRTC recorder. To recall from my previous chapter, I have created an object with a child object, which contains the mime-type (**audio/webm**) and the **audioDataURL**, which is the Base64 string containing the audio recording. Let's take that Base64 string and convert it to a Node.js file Buffer.

3. With that **fileBuffer**, I could call my custom Dialogflow DetectIntent implementation, which will be explained later in this chapter.

```
const results = await detectIntent(fileBuffer);
client.emit('results', results);
```

315

It will be an asynchronous call and return a promise with the results. These results will be sent to the client-side app. The client could listen to the socket emit like this:

```
socketio.on('results', function (data) {
    console.log(data);
});
```

4. Here's an example of a second event fired by the client, in this case, a streaming event. Now, I will retrieve the data when the WebRTC recorder streams chunks of audio data in the **ondataavailable** listener. Note that the client socket is wrapped with **socket.io-stream** for streaming binary data transfers.

   I am retrieving the audio chunks, plus additional data, such as the stream name (a string). This can be used to store a temporary audio file on the server, in which I can pipe the incoming audio stream. It's used as a holder to activate my custom Dialogflow implementation.

5. Like the DetectIntentStreaming implementation, explained later in this chapter:

```
detectIntentStream(stream, function(results){
    client.emit('results', results);
});
```

In this call, I pass in the stream and a callback function to execute once the results are in. These results will be sent to the client-side app.

The client could listen to the socket emit like this:

```
socketio.on('results', function (data) {
    console.log(data);
});
```

API Calls to Dialogflow

I will use the Dialogflow Node.js client SDK to manually detect the intent, based on finished audio buffers and incoming audio streams.

```
const df = require('dialogflow');
```

Let's first prepare the client and the request. Later, I can modify the request by adding the audio input:

Listing 12-6. Prepare the speech request

```
// 1)
sessionId = uuid.v4();
// 2)
sessionClient = new df.SessionsClient();
sessionPath = sessionClient.sessionPath(projectId, sessionId);
// 3)
request = {
  session: sessionPath,
  queryInput: {
    // 4)
    audioConfig: {
      sampleRateHertz: sampleRateHertz,
      encoding: encoding,
      languageCode: languageCode
    },
    singleUtterance: singleUtterance
  }
}
```

1. Dialogflow will need a session ID. Let's use UUID to generate a random https://www.ietf.org/rfc/rfc4122.txt RFC4122 id, in a format like '1b9d6bcd-bbfd-4b2d-9b5d-ab8dfbbd4bed'.

2. Afterward, let's create a Dialogflow session path. The session path can be created from a Dialogflow Session Client object. It needs a session ID to make Dialogflow session unique. And it needs the Google Cloud project id, which points to a Google Cloud project with a working Dialogflow agent.

3. Let's already set up a request object, which will be used for each Dialogflow API call. In case this request is used when streaming audio, this request will be used as the initial request. This means it first connects to the SDK without the audio stream, but prepares the API with audio configurations it can use. Afterward, the chunks of audio will stream in. It needs to have a sessionPath (which now will point to a client session and a particular Dialogflow agent). Even without the audio input, I can already set up the **queryInput**.

4. Since this application works with speech, I will need to set the **audioConfig** object. The audioConfig object requires a sample rate hertz (this number has to be the same as the **desiredSampleRateHertz** from your client-side code). It requires a **languageCode** that contains the spoken text's language, and it should be a language set in Dialogflow. It will need to have an encoding, which also needs to be the same as the encoding used in the client. In my Self Service Kiosk code demos, I am using the configurations from the **.env** file.

Now let's have a look into both calls, **DetectIntent** and **StreamingDetectIntent**.

DetectIntent

After Dialogflow detected the intent, the back-end app receives the intent match results after all audio has been sent and processed. I'm creating an asynchronous function, which takes the AudioBuffer and adds it to the request. Next, I'm calling detectIntent, by passing in the request. It returns a promise, which will be chainable.

Listing 12-7. Using Socket.IO for sending audio streams from the front end to the back end

```
async function detectIntent(audio){
    request.inputAudio = audio;
    const responses = await sessionClient.detectIntent(request);
    return responses;
};
```

This will return a **DetectIntentResponse**. It contains a **queryResult**. In case you passed in the DetectIntentRequest an output audio config, you will be able to retrieve audio data bytes generated based on the values of the default platform text responses found in the queryResult.fulfillmentMessages field. If multiple default text responses exist, they will be concatenated when generating audio. If no default platform text responses exist, the generated audio content will be empty.

StreamingDetectIntent

The **StreamingDetectIntent** performs bidirectional streaming intent detection: receive results while sending audio. This method is only available via the gRPC API (not REST).

Listing 12-8. Detecting the intent based on an audio stream

```
// 1)
async function detectIntentStream(audio, cb) {
    // 2)
    const stream = sessionClient.streamingDetectIntent()
      .on('data', function(data){
        // 3)
        if (data.recognitionResult) {
          console.log(
            `Intermediate transcript:
            ${data.recognitionResult.transcript}`
          );
        } else {
            console.log(`Detected intent:`);
            cb(data);
        }
      })
      // 4)
      .on('error', (e) => {
        console.log(e);
      })
      .on('end', () => {
        console.log('on end');
      });

    // 5)
    stream.write(request);
```

```
    // 6)
    await pump(
      audio,
      // 7)
      new Transform({
        objectMode: true,
        transform: (obj, _, next) => {
          next(null, { inputAudio: obj, outputAudioConfig: {
            audioEncoding: `OUTPUT_AUDIO_ENCODING_LINEAR_16`
          } });
        }
      }),
      stream
    );
};
```

1. I'm creating an asynchronous function, which takes the AudioBuffer and adds it to the request, and the name of the callback function will execute with the results once the API fetches the results.

2. Execute the **streamingDetectIntent()** call.

3. There's an on('data') event listener, which executes once audio chunks are streamed in. You could create some conditional logic here; if there's a data.recognitionResult in the response, then the intermediate transcript is recognized. Otherwise, likely the intent has been detected (or a fallback intent was triggered, in case there wasn't a match). I'm returning the results by executing the callback function.

4. You could also listen to **error** events when something went wrong with the request. Or you could listen to **end** events when streaming to Dialogflow stopped.

5. How this works is that we will let the Dialogflow API know that there will be a **streamingDetectIntent** call with all the **queryInput** and **audioConfigs** that can be retrieved from the requests. Afterward, all the other messages that will come in will contain the audio stream via inputAudio.

6. Let's use a small node module called **pump**, which pipes the streams together and destroys all of them if one closes.

7. Here, I will transform the stream, so the request will now also contain **inputAudio** with the audioBuffer streaming in.

This will return a **StreamingIntentResponse**. It contains a **queryResult**.

In case you passed in the **StreamingDetectIntentRequest** and output audio config, you will be able to retrieve audio data bytes generated based on the values of the default platform text responses found in the queryResult.fulfillmentMessages field. If multiple default text responses exist, they will be concatenated when generating audio. If no default platform text responses exist, the generated audio content will be empty.

Retrieving Audio Results from Dialogflow and Playing It in Your Browser

When you make a Text to Speech call, either with the Google Cloud Text-to-Speech API or using the built-in speech return from Dialogflow, it will return audio byte data. Both Cloud TTS and Dialogflow can be called from server-side code. To stream and play this in a browser, you could make use of WebSockets. Once the AudioBuffer (ArrayBuffer in the browser's JavaScript code) is returned to the client, it can be played by using WebRTC methods.

Figure 12-4 is an example of a browser flow by using Dialogflow. In this example, a user speaks in the microphone (similar to the preceding examples), but Dialogflow returns an AudioBuffer as the result.

Figure 12-4. The user streams their voice from the client app to the server application connected to Dialogflow. Once Dialogflow matches the intent, the result audio stream will be sent back to the client app, to be played in the browser

Now, it's time to focus on the last part, ensuring we are getting an audio buffer as a detected result from Dialogflow, streaming it back to the client via Socket.IO and making sure it will autoplay.

Dialogflow can also return AudioBuffers once it detects the intent. You would only need to specify an outputAudioConfig in the Dialogflow **DetectIntentRequest**, to also get an AudioBuffer as part of the response:

```
outputAudioConfig: {
    audioEncoding: `OUTPUT_AUDIO_ENCODING_LINEAR_16`,
},
```

The response for a detect intent request is a **DetectIntentResponse** type. Normally, when you detect intents with text contents, it populates the **fulfillmentMessages** field in the **queryResult**. But when you provide spoken audio as contents, the DetectIntentResponse. outputAudio field is populated with audio based on the values of default platform text responses found in the DetectIntentResponse.queryResult.fulfillmentMessages field.

If multiple default text responses exist, they will be concatenated when generating audio. If no default platform text responses exist, the generated audio content will be empty.

Client-Side Code to Play the Audio

In your client-side app, you will need to make sure you are loading socket.io and socket.io-stream again. Socket.IO is a real-time, bidirectional event-based communication library. One of the transports that it uses is WebSockets, but it also provides other transports (XHR/JSONP), not just as a fallback but also for situations where WebSockets aren't supported/required/wanted.

You could load this from the CDN.

Listing 12-9. Loading Socket.IO from the CDN

```
<script src="https://cdnjs.cloudflare.com/ajax/libs/socket.io/2.3.0/socket.
io.js"></script>
<script src="https://cdnjs.cloudflare.com/ajax/libs/socket.io-stream/0.9.1/
socket.io-stream.js"></script>
```

Once the client is connected to the server, I can start listening to an event that was fired from the server. In my case, this is the *'results'* event. It will run once the data from the server side is retrieved in the browser. This will call my custom **playOutput** method, which I will show later.

Listing 12-10. Once the results are sent back to the client, play the audio

```
const socketio = io();
const socket = socketio.on('connect', function() {});
   socketio.on('results', function (data) {
   console.log(data);
   playOutput(data);
});
```

Listing 12-11, shows the code for playing the output in your browser from your device speakers.

Listing 12-11. How to play the audio stream in a browser

```
// 1)
 function playOutput(arrayBuffer){
    lct audioContext = new AudioConLext();
    let outputSource;
    try {
        if(arrayBuffer.byteLength > 0){
            // 2)
            audioContext.decodeAudioData(arrayBuffer,
            function(buffer){
                // 3)
                audioContext.resume();
                outputSource = audioContext.createBufferSource();
                outputSource.connect(audioContext.destination);
                outputSource.buffer = buffer;
                outputSource.start(0);
            },
```

```
            function(){
                console.log(arguments);
            });
        }
    } catch(e) {
        console.log(e);
    }
}
```

1. Here's the **playOutput** function, which takes the **arrayBuffer**
   that I retrieved from the back-end code. Here, I can create a new
   AudioContext object. The AudioContext interface represents an
   audio-processing graph built from audio modules linked together,
   represented by an **AudioNode**. An audio context controls both the
   creation of audio nodes it contains and the execution of the audio
   processing or decoding.

2. Now, let's create an audio source for Web Audio API from an
   ArrayBuffer. The decoded AudioBuffer is resampled to the
   AudioContext's sampling rate, then passed to a callback.

3. A user agent could block autoplay, hence why I run
   audioContext.resume as a trick first. Afterward, create a new
   AudioBufferSourceNode to connect to the audioContext
   destination, which is, in our case, the device speakers. The buffer
   property of the AudioBufferSourceNode interface provides the
   ability to play back audio using an AudioBuffer as the source of
   the sound data. Finally, let's play the audio.

Caution   Be aware of using Dialogflow detectIntent on streaming audio. When
you use simple detectIntent calls without streaming, you stop the microphone,
and you will play the TTS audio buffer. However, when you do streaming, you keep
your microphone open. You don't want to end up in an endless loop, where the
speech synthesizer records new streams based on the TTS response through your
microphone. :-)

The AudioBufferSourceNode has an onended event handler, which will run once the AudioBufferSourceNode stopped playing the audio. In case you want to solve the preceding problem, you could set a boolean flag, isPlaying, which should block the recorder from sending the stream to the back end when it's set to true.

Congratulations! By reading this chapter, you now know how to build an end-to-end solution for streaming audio from a microphone to a server and stream and play the audio results back in the browser!

Summary

This chapter contains information about building your own custom voice AI in your website or app vs. using a virtual assistant, such as the Google Assistant.

It addresses the following tasks:

- You want to create a voice AI in your own website or app by streaming audio from a browser microphone to a web server.

- You want to integrate a voice AI in your own web server and detect intents on an audio stream received from the browser microphone.

- You want to incorporate a voice AI in your own website and play the audio results in your browser.

The full working example which belongs to the sections in the book can be found here:

https://github.com/dialogflow/selfservicekiosk-audio-streaming

You can run the demo and play with it via this URL:

http://selfservicedesk.appspot.com/

Further Reading

- RecordRTC library

  https://github.com/muaz-khan/RecordRTC

- Socket.IO library

  https://www.npmjs.com/package/socket.io

- Socket.io-Stream module

  https://www.npmjs.com/package/socket.io-stream

- My blog post on how to build a SelfServiceKiosk

  https://medium.com/google-cloud/building-your-own-
  conversational-voice-ai-with-dialogflow-speech-to-text-
  in-web-apps-part-i-b92770bd8b47

- SelfServiceKiosk demo codebase

  https://github.com/dialogflow/selfservicekiosk-audio-
  streaming/blob/master/client/src/app/microphone/
  microphone.component.ts

- My blog post on how to build a SelfServiceKiosk

  https://medium.com/google-cloud/building-your-own-
  conversational-voice-ai-with-dialogflow-speech-to-text-
  in-web-apps-part-i-b92770bd8b47

- Self Service Kiosk demo codebase

  https://github.com/dialogflow/selfservicekiosk-audio-
  streaming/blob/master/client/src/app/microphone/
  microphone.component.ts

- Example of the package.json file, which could be used for this chapter

  https://github.com/dialogflow/selfservicekiosk-audio-
  streaming/blob/master/examples/package.json

- Play around and test with the Service Kiosk demo

  http://selfservicedesk.appspot.com/

- Dialogflow npm package

  `https://www.npmjs.com/package/dialogflow`

- SimpleServer example

  `https://github.com/dialogflow/selfservicekiosk-audio-streaming/blob/master/examples/simpleserver.js`

- Client-side examples

  `https://github.com/dialogflow/selfservicekiosk-audio-streaming/tree/master/examples`

- Documentation on AudioConfig

  `https://cloud.google.com/dialogflow/es/docs/reference/rpc/google.cloud.dialogflow.v2#google.cloud.dialogflow.v2.InputAudioConfig`

- Documentation on DetectIntentResponse

  `https://cloud.google.com/dialogflow/es/docs/reference/rpc/google.cloud.dialogflow.v2#google.cloud.dialogflow.v2.DetectIntentResponse`

- Documentation on StreamingDetectResponse

  `https://cloud.google.com/speech-to-text/docs/reference/rpc/google.cloud.speech.v1#google.cloud.speech.v1.StreamingRecognizeResponse`

- Documentation on DetectIntentRequest in Dialogflow

  `https://cloud.google.com/dialogflow/es/docs/reference/rpc/google.cloud.dialogflow.v2#detectintentrequest`

- Guide to detect intents with audio

  `https://cloud.google.com/dialogflow/es/docs/how/detect-intent-tts`

- Documentation on AudioBufferSourceNode

  `https://developer.mozilla.org/en-US/docs/Web/API/AudioBufferSourceNode`

## CHAPTER 13

Collecting and Monitoring Conversational Analytics

I think we have all experienced it before. You are talking to a virtual assistant or typing into a chatbot, and the virtual agent doesn't understand what you mean. It asks you to repeat yourself, it returns a fallback, or worse it gives you the wrong answer! That's a lousy customer experience. When this happens too much, you risk the chance that your visitors are not coming back; "that bot doesn't work." As a matter of fact, often the chat or voice bot did work, but it was taught to answer different types of questions.

Of course, with good conversation UX design, you could have steered your dialogues to a successful outcome. For example, when you start the virtual agent, it shouldn't just show you a welcome greeting. It should also tell you what it can do for you. So likely, your visitors will ask the right types of questions.

You are building a chatbot or virtual assistant. How will it benefit your visitors? What problem will it solve? As a brand or business, you'll likely have this data. Is this your first attempt at building a virtual agent? Then look into your data from other channels so that you can understand your customers better. Do you have a contact center and do you have audio recordings? Do you monitor social media? Incoming email? What's the most common question people ask? What topic is popular? What are people complaining about?

When building voice and chatbots, it's essential to go into production as fast as possible but capture analytics. Too often, I hear customers saying: "Chatbot insights that's on our road map for version two. We want to perfect the conversations first." It shouldn't be that way. Bot analytics isn't a "nice to have" feature to display in a dashboard; they are essential for improving your customer experience.

© Lee Boonstra 2021
L. Boonstra, *The Definitive Guide to Conversational AI with Dialogflow and Google Cloud*,
https://doi.org/10.1007/978-1-4842-7014-1_13

Don't spend a year perfecting conversations, while you can learn the most from your existing (live) traffic. Even if you go live with only a few main topics and directly monitor the incoming questions, you can grow your chatbot over time and make it much smarter. You can implement other essential topics based on the number of occurrences. This way, you can learn how your customers think of your brand and how you can better your virtual agent over time.

Many businesses are already familiar with capturing analytics. They rely on web analytics data, such as click rates, page views, and session lengths, to gain customer behavior insights, typically gathered with tools such as Google Analytics. This is why conversational analytics is much more powerful than web analytics. No longer will the emphasis be on how users react to what is presented to them, but rather what "intent" they convey through natural language. In fact, the market predicts that conversational analytics will grow from \$4.2 billion in 2019 to \$15.7 billion in 2024!

There are four types of metrics you might want to monitor or capture.

Conversation-Related Metrics

Conversation-related metrics will give you answers on questions like what has been said by your end users, when, and where (on what platform). For this, you would need a way to store all your conversations. A data warehouse like BigQuery is a great way to collect all your chat transcripts.

A data warehouse is a system used for reporting and data analysis. Think about a database, but much more extensive, where you can connect many sources to. You can store all structured data you like in your data warehouse. Think about website data, website logs, login data, advertising data, and your Dialogflow chatbot conversations. The more data you have, the better you can understand your customers.

Customer Rating Metrics

Many businesses use NPS, CES, and CSAT ratings as research methods to find out their customers' loyalty by asking simple questions. You can implement this in your agent.

Chat Session and Funnel Metrics

You can use Dialogflow or Chatbase to get the flow of the session, which will show you a chat funnel. It visually summarizes the conversational paths your end users have taken when engaging with your agent.

Bot Model Health Metrics

When working with Dialogflow, it will use machine learning to understand the user utterances and match this to an intent (intent classification). With bot model metrics, it will be possible to calculate the quality of the underlying machine learning model of your agent.

Capturing Conversation-Related Metrics to Store in BigQuery

Tools like Dialogflow have their own built-in Analytics. You can browse through simple analytics by providing a date-time. However, you might want to build your own custom repository in a data warehouse to collect a powerful analytics system. An example of a data warehouse is BigQuery. Maybe you are already using it for your Ads data.

BigQuery

BigQuery is a fully managed, serverless data warehouse that enables scalable analysis over petabytes of data. It is a serverless Software as a Service (SaaS) that supports querying using ANSI SQL.

Using BigQuery analytics over the built-in Dialogflow Analytics has a couple of advantages, which matter a lot to enterprises that have to deal with compliances (such as the GDPR). When you store your chatbot conversations in BigQuery, you can

- Choose where the data is located

- Choose how long the data is being stored

- Create a backup of your conversational data

- Remove sensitive PII data from your dataset before storage (e.g., according to the GDPR, you can't store PII data)

- Create many more data points (e.g., chat translations, user sentiment)

- Combine your chatbot conversations with other valuable data

---

Note   In case you are choosing this solution because of compliance reasons, you will likely also want to turn off your data logging in the Dialogflow settings panel.

This would also mean that you will not see any data on analytics and history tabs in the Dialogflow console.

Why is it a benefit to combine your chatbot analytics with other data? Because you can create omnichannel experiences and insights with this. Imagine a user visiting your banking website. The user was logged in, and the user is browsing through banking web pages about mortgages. A week later, the user returns to the website and starts a chat with the banking chatbot. (It could even be a voice agent via a phone call.) The user explains that he has fraudulent transactions, and the chatbot offers to block those. Before the conversation is over, the chatbot provides a mortgage deal. Since the chat data plus the website advertising data has been stored in the same data warehouse, it was easy to make this link.

Capture Points

Let's look in a few capture points, which will make it helpful to gather insights from bot conversations. We can use these metrics to query our datasets on.

Session Id

A **session id** is handy for finding all transcripts of a certain session, to read the **full conversation transcript** and to figure out the total of unique users.

Bot building tools like Dialogflow will maintain a session path per chat session. This chat session path is bound to your agent account (so no one else can snoop in), and it's unique as it contains a uuid.

```
const sessionId = uuid.v4();
```

```
const sessionClient = new df.SessionsClient();
const sessionPath = sessionClient.sessionPath(projectId, sessionId);
```

When you use BigQuery, you should collect every incoming user utterance with its session id. Once you know a particular session id, you can retrieve the full chat transcript with every other data field that was stored. The SQL query for retrieving the session would look like this:

```
SELECT * FROM `chat_msg_table` WHERE SESSION_ID = 'projects/myagent/agent/
sessions/db33b345-663c-4867-8021-fecd50c5e8b1' ORDER BY DATETIME
```

Return everything from the chat messages table where the session id equals some string, and it will be ordered on the date and time, so the first message of the session will be displayed first.

Date/Timestamp

You will need a **date/timestamp** for finding all transcripts based on a certain time and to calculate the full **session length**.

You can set your own date/timestamp before storing the object in BigQuery. Make sure it takes the format the way how your data warehouse expects it:

```
const timestamp = new Date().getTime()/1000;
```

Each date and timestamp should be stored together with a session id and its other metrics into BigQuery. With that, you can easily run a SQL query which will return everything from the chat messages table where the datetime is between August 1 and August 10, ordered descending by datetime, so the newest comes first:

```
SELECT * FROM `chat_msg_table` WHERE DATETIME > '2020-08-01 10:00:00' AND
POSTED < '2020-08-10 00:00:00' ORDER BY DATETIME DESC
```

Sentiment Score

You can use a sentiment score for finding all transcripts based on a particular sentiment. For example, you might be interested in the most "negative" chat transcripts of the week to figure out why your customers are upset.

Tools like Dialogflow can have sentiment enabled for certain languages. However, when you want to use the sentiment analysis of unsupported languages such as "Dutch," you will have to translate your user utterances first.

This is something you could do with the following tools:

- Cloud Translate

- Cloud Natural Language

```
const sentiment_score: queryTextSentiment.score;
const sentiment_magnitude: queryTextSentiment.magnitude;
```

The **score** of a document's sentiment indicates the overall emotion of a document. The **magnitude** of a document's sentiment indicates how much emotional content is present within the document, and this value is often proportional to the length of the document.

Each sentiment score should be stored together with a session id and its other metrics in the data warehouse. With that, you can easily run a SQL query which will return everything from the chat messages table where the sentiment score is negative (below 0), and it will be ordered on the sentiment score, ascending from worst to best:

```
SELECT * FROM `chat_msg_table` WHERE SENTIMENT_SCORE < 0 ORDER BY
SENTIMENT_SCORE ASC
```

Tip How should you work with sarcasm? As a matter of fact, sarcasm is even for a human sometimes hard to understand. However, we do have tools in Google Cloud to build a model with a custom sentiment. Think about a user utterance like

"Yay! The game Beyond Good and Evil is delayed again! Great work!"

The built-in sentiment of Google Cloud will probably detect that this is very positive because of the words "Yay!" and Great Work!". Maybe it will be even a 90% (0.9) sentiment score. However, we want to classify this as very negative because we are talking here about delayed games, which isn't fun, so we would expect a negative sentiment score. It's good to know that you can train your own sentiment models with AutoML Natural Language in Google Cloud. It has a feature: sentiment analysis. The model inspects a document and identifies the prevailing emotional opinion within it, especially to determine a writer's attitude as positive, negative, or neutral.

Language and Keyword

You can use a dialogue **language** for finding all transcripts for a certain language. For example, you might be interested in finding a transcript based on its language. Maybe you want to combine this with a certain **keyword**.

In Dialogflow, you can retrieve the `languageCode` in the `queryResult` from a `detectIntentResponse`:

```
queryResult.languageCode
```

You don't need to store separate keywords; you can retrieve this from the user utterance. Later in this section, we will discuss topic mining. With this technique, you can store keywords in a separate BigQuery column.

Each language metric should be stored together with a session id, the user utterance, and other metrics in the data warehouse. With that, you can easily run a SQL query which will return everything from the chat messages table where the language code equals "NL," and the word you are looking for is "fraud."

```
SELECT * FROM `chat_msg_table` WHERE LANGUAGE = "en-us" AND USER_UTTERANCE
LIKE '%my keyword%'
```

Platform

You can use a **platform** setting for finding all the transcripts for a certain platform. For example, you might be interested in finding the latest conversations on the Google Assistant.

You will have to set the platform metric yourself based on the implementation you are using. Certain implementations can have their own settings, such as the Google Assistant that has configs per device surface: Surface Capabilities.

When you build your own web interface with a chat integrated, you will need to set the platform name yourself.

```
const platform = 'web';
```

Each platform metric should be stored together with a session id and its other metrics into BigQuery. With that, you can easily run a SQL query which will return everything from the chat messages table where the platform equals to "web":

```
SELECT * FROM `chat_msg_table` WHERE PLATFORM = "web"
```

Intent Detection

When Dialogflow detects your intent, it can contain various valuable information, which you would like to store in your data warehouse as well. For example, this will help you to figure out in a transcript if the bot returned a wrong answer.

The following data points you might want to store: **detected intent name**, **confidence threshold** (the confidence level Dialogflow based its intent match on), if it's a **fallback**, and if it's the **end of the interaction** (to detect if it's the end of the flow).

In Dialogflow, you can retrieve the detected intent name in the queryResult.intent from a detectIntentResponse:

```
queryResult.intent.displayName
```

In Dialogflow, you can retrieve a boolean value if it's a fallback in the queryResult. intent from a detectIntentResponse:

```
queryResult.intent.isFallback
```

In Dialogflow, you can retrieve a boolean value if it's the end of the interaction in the queryResult.intent from a detectIntentResponse:

```
queryResult.intent.endInteraction
```

In Dialogflow, you can retrieve the confidence threshold in the queryResult from a detectIntentResponse:

```
queryResult.intentDetectionConfidence
```

Solutions

In this section, I will present three popular solutions for collecting metrics.

Building a Platform for Capturing Conversation-Related Metrics and Redacting Sensitive Information

To build a solution for capturing conversation-related metrics, you will need to make use of the following Google Cloud services:

- Dialogflow Essentials (pay-as-you-go tier)

- BigQuery

- Pub/Sub (messaging channel)

- DLP API (to redact the information before storing the data)

- Cloud Functions (code which will be triggered on events)

Let's have a look into an architecture as shown in Figure 13-1.

When a customer writes text into the chatbot or talks to a voice agent, the Dialogflow agent matches the answer (with the detectIntent method). This includes the information such as the user utterance, the Dialogflow response, the matched intent, and so on, but more critical also the session id. In real time, we can push the data to a messaging channel (Pub/Sub), so other software pieces can register and listen to incoming data (via an event-based Cloud Function).

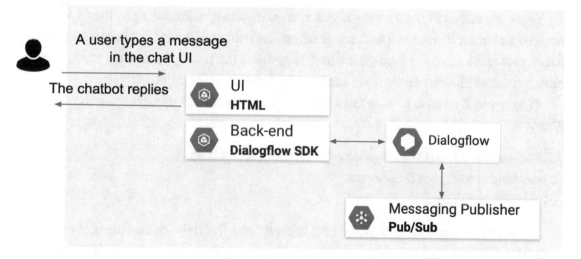

Figure 13-1. *Using an architecture with Pub/Sub to create a data pipeline (part 1)*

The cloud function has a subscription on the Pub/Sub channel. Note Figure 13-2; every time a message comes in, the message will be passed to the DLP API to remove sensitive information before storing the data in BigQuery.

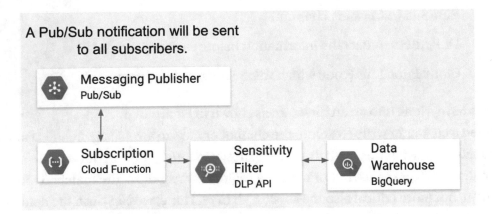

Figure 13-2. Using an architecture with Pub/Sub to create a data pipeline (part 2)

Once it's stored in BigQuery, you can run queries to get, for example, the top 10 user utterances that returned in a fallback or where the user sentiment was negative. You could also run a query to figure out which intent was the most popular. Or, in case you have a session id, you can query to retrieve the full chat transcript.

First, we will need to enable the following APIs. We can do this from the command line:

```
gcloud services enable bigquery-json.googleapis.com \
  cloudfunctions.googleapis.com \
  dlp.googleapis.com
```

Afterward, we will need to make sure that we have the right permissions. We will run a script that can create datasets and tables in BigQuery; we will need to modify the user permissions in the **IAM & Admin** panel. Go to the **IAM** page.

Find the Dialogflow Service Account, which is used by Dialogflow. (You can find the service account (email address) on the **Dialogflow ➤ Settings ➤ General page**.) On the IAM page, edit the service account which Dialogflow is using (see Figure 13-3).

Give your service account the following permissions:

- BigQuery Data Owner

- BigQuery Job User

- Pub/Sub Admin

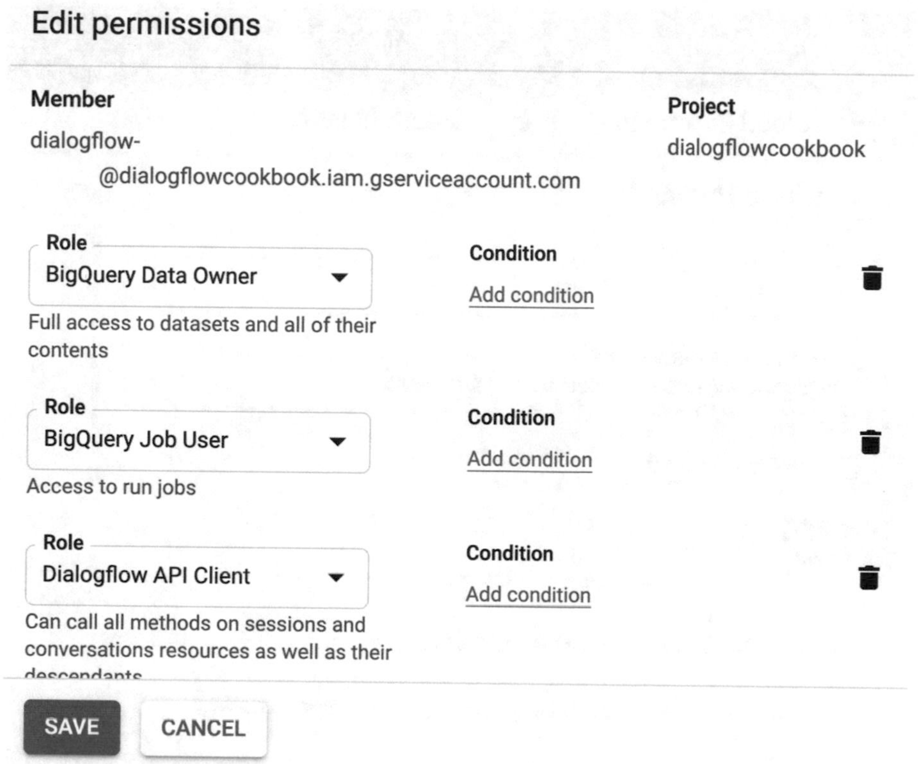

Edit permissions

Member	Project
dialogflow-	dialogflowcookbook
@dialogflowcookbook.iam.gserviceaccount.com	

Role
BigQuery Data Owner ▼

Full access to datasets and all of their contents

Condition
Add condition

Role
BigQuery Job User ▼

Access to run jobs

Condition
Add condition

Role
Dialogflow API Client ▼

Can call all methods on sessions and conversations resources as well as their descendants

Condition
Add condition

SAVE   CANCEL

Figure 13-3. *Assigning the correct roles to your IAM account*

Then, we will need to create the Cloud Function, which will listen to the messaging channel. Click **Cloud Functions ➤ Create Function**.

Specify the following settings; instead of *[project_id]*, use your own Google Cloud project id, as seen in Figure 13-4.

- Name: **chatanalytics**

- Memory allocated: **256MB**

- Trigger: **Cloud Pub/Sub**

- Pub/Sub topic: **projects/[project_id]/topics/chatbotanalytics**

- Function to execute: **subscribe**

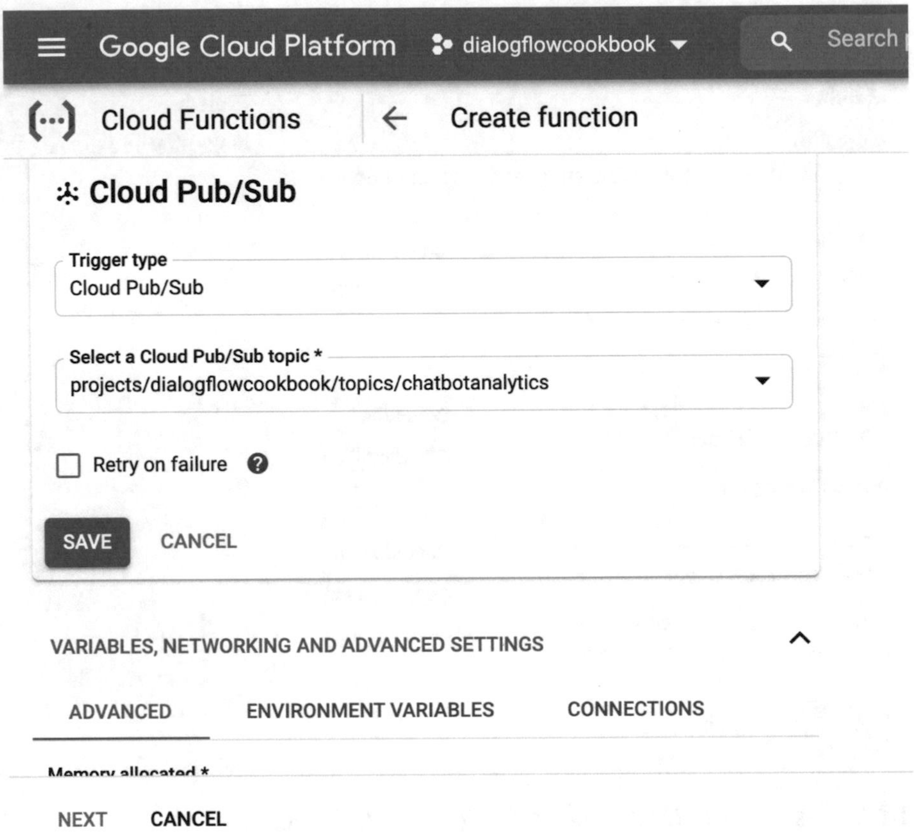

Figure 13-4. *Preparing the Cloud Function in the data pipeline*

Click the environment variables tab to add the following environment variable (see Figure 13-5):

- Environment variables: **GCLOUD_PROJECT - [project_id]**

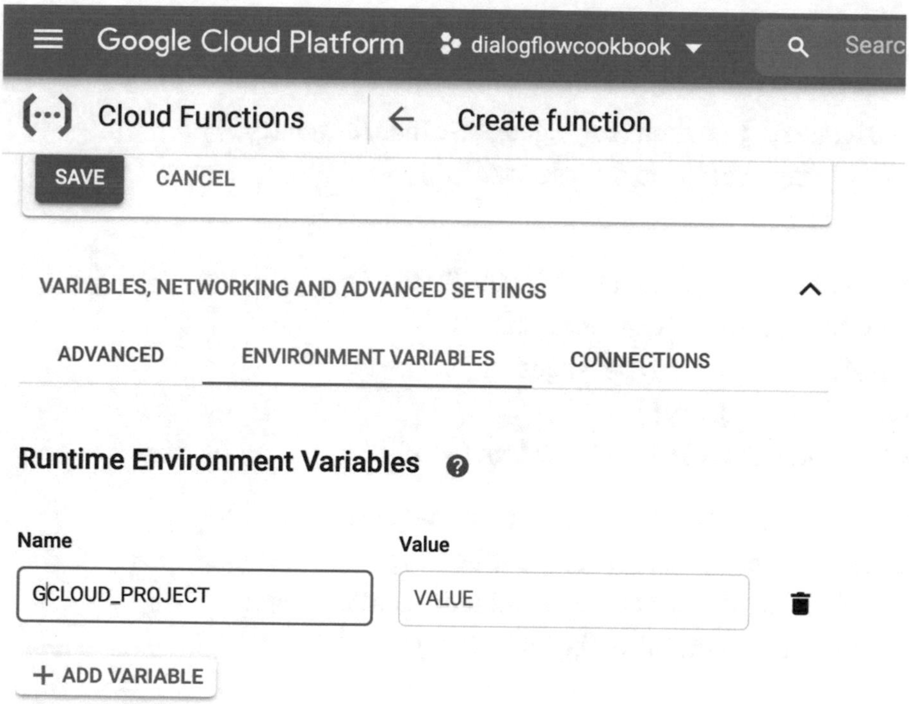

Figure 13-5. *Set the environment variables in the Cloud Function*

Listing 13-1 shows the contents for the **package.json** to import BigQuery and the DLP libraries.

Listing 13-1. *package.json*

```
{
    "name": "chatanalytics",
    "version": "1.0.2",
    "dependencies": {
      "@google-cloud/bigquery": "^5.0.0",
      "@google-cloud/dlp": "^1.2.0"
    }
}
```

The Cloud Function **index.js** code will look like Listing 13-2.

Listing 13-2. *index.js*

```
//1)
const { BigQuery } = require('@google-cloud/bigquery');
const DLP = require('@google-cloud/dlp');

//2)
const projectId = process.env.GCLOUD_PROJECT;
const bqDataSetName = 'chatanalytics'
const bqTableName = 'chatmessages';
const bq = new BigQuery();
const dlp = new DLP.DlpServiceClient();

// Make use of a dataset called: chatanalytics
const dataset = bq.dataset(bqDataSetName);
// Make use of a BigQuery table called: chatmessages
const table = dataset.table(bqTableName);

//3)
var detectPIIData = async function(text, callback) {
  // The minimum likelihood required before returning a match
  const minLikelihood = 'LIKELIHOOD_UNSPECIFIED';

  //4)
  // The infoTypes of information to match
  const infoTypes = [
    {name: 'PERSON_NAME'},
    {name: 'FIRST_NAME'},
    {name: 'LAST_NAME'},
    {name: 'MALE_NAME'},
    {name: 'FEMALE_NAME'},
    {name: 'IBAN_CODE'},
    {name: 'IP_ADDRESS'},
    {name: 'LOCATION'},
    {name: 'SWIFT_CODE'},
    {name: 'PASSPORT'},
    {name: 'PHONE_NUMBER'},
    {name: 'NETHERLANDS_BSN_NUMBER'},
```

```javascript
    {name: 'NETHERLANDS_PASSPORT'}
];

// Construct transformation config, which replaces sensitive info with
    its info type.
// E.g., "Her email is xxx@example.com" => "Her email is [EMAIL_ADDRESS]"
const replaceWithInfoTypeTransformation = {
  primitiveTransformation: {
    replaceWithInfoTypeConfig: {},
  },
};

// Construct redaction request
const request = {
  parent: dlp.projectPath(projectId),
  item: {
    value: text,
  },
  deidentifyConfig: {
    infoTypeTransformations: {
      transformations: [replaceWithInfoTypeTransformation],
    },
  },
  inspectConfig: {
    minLikelihood: minLikelihood,
    infoTypes: infoTypes,
  },
};

// Run string redaction
try {
  //5)
  const [response] = await dlp.deidentifyContent(request);
  const resultString = response.item.value;
  console.log(`REDACTED TEXT: ${resultString}`);
  if (resultString) {
    callback(resultString);
```

```
    } else {
      callback(text);
    }
  } catch (err) {
    console.log(`Error in deidentifyContent: ${err.message || err}`);
    callback(text);
  }
}

  //6)
  //Insert rows in BigQuery
  var insertInBq = function(row){

    console.log(row);

    table.insert(row, function(err, apiResponse){
      if (!err) {
        console.log("[BIGQUERY] - Saved.");
      } else {
        console.error(err);
      }
    });
  };

  //7)
  exports.subscribe = (data, context) => {
    const pubSubMessage = data;
    const buffer = Buffer.from(pubSubMessage.data, 'base64').toString();
    var buf = JSON.parse(buffer);

    var bqRow = {
      BOT_NAME: buf.botName,
      POSTED: (buf.posted/1000),
      INTENT_RESPONSE: buf.intentResponse.toString(),
      INTENT_NAME: buf.intentName,
      IS_FALLBACK: buf.isFallback,
      IS_END_INTERACTION: buf.isEndInteraction,
      CONFIDENCE: buf.confidence,
```

```
    PLATFORM: buf.platform,
    SESSION: buf.session,
    SCORE: buf.score,
    MAGNITUDE: buf.magnitude
  };

  //8)
  detectPIIData(buf.text, function(formattedText) {
    bqRow['TEXT'] = formattedText;
    insertInBq(bqRow);
  });
};
```

This piece of code does the following:

1) Imports the BigQuery and DLP library.

2) Sets constants to point to the dataset, table name.

3) The `detectPIIData` method sets the infotypes to look for, such as the passport number, phone numbers, or person names.

4) The list with info types to look for.

5) The actual DLP request `dlp.deidentifyContent(request)` to start redacting.

6) The `insertInBQ()` method runs the BigQuery method, `table.insert()`, which will start a job in the background to insert a row in the data warehouse.

7) `exports.subscribe = (data, context) => {}` is the Pub/Sub subscription method, which listens for incoming messages. It gets the data out of a buffer and prepares an object which can be inserted into BigQuery.

8) The last part is calling the `detectPIIData` function and chains the callback to the `insertInBQ` method.

As we can recall from the architecture as seen in Figure 13-1, we will need a back-end script that integrates with the Dialogflow SDK. In Listing 13-3, you will see the full back-end script: **app.js**.

Listing 13-3. *app*.js

```
//1)
const analytics = require('../back-end/analytics');
const structJson = require('../back-end/structToJson');

const projectId = process.env.npm_config_PROJECT_ID;
const port = ( process.env.npm_config_PORT || 3000 );
const languageCode = (process.env.npm_config_LANGUAGE || 'en-US');

const socketIo = require('socket.io');
const http = require('http');
const cors = require('cors');
const express = require('express');
const path = require('path');
const uuid = require('uuid');
const df = require('dialogflow').v2beta1;

//2)
const sessionId = uuid.v4();

const app = express();

app.use(cors());
app.use(express.static(__dirname + '/../ui/'));
app.get('/', function(req, res) {
    res.sendFile(path.join(__dirname + '/../ui/index.html'));
});

server = http.createServer(app);
io = socketIo(server);
server.listen(port, () => {
    console.log('Running server on port %s', port);
});

io.on('connect', (client) => {
```

```
console.log(`Client connected [id=${client.id}]`);
client.emit('server_setup', `Server connected [id=${client.id}]`);

client.on('welcome', async function() {
    const welcomeResults = await detectIntentByEventName('welcome');
    client.emit('returnResults', welcomeResults);
});

//3)
client.on('message', async function(msg) {
    const results = await detectIntent(msg);
    const result = results[0].queryResult;

    const timestamp = new Date().getTime();
    const platform = "web";
    const botName = "agent";

    var messages = [];
    if(result.fulfillmentMessages.length > 0) {
        for (let index = 0; index < result.fulfillmentMessages.length;
        index++) {
            const msg = result.fulfillmentMessages[index];
            if (msg.payload){
                let data = structJson.structProtoToJson(msg.payload);
                messages.push(data.web);
            } else {
                messages.push(msg.text.text);
            }
        }
    }

    var obj = {
        text: result['queryText'],
        posted: timestamp,
        platform: platform,
        botName: botName,
        intentResponse: messages,
        language: result['languageCode'],
```

```
            platforms: result['intent'].defaultResponsePlatforms,
            intentName: result['intent'].displayName,
            isFallback: result['intent'].isFallback,
            isEndInteraction: result['intent'].endInteraction,
            confidence: result['intentDetectionConfidence'],
            session: sessionPath,
            score: result['sentimentAnalysisResult'].queryTextSentiment.score,
            magnitude: result['sentimentAnalysisResult'].queryTextSentiment.
            magnitude
        };

        console.log(obj);

        try {
            //console.log(obj);
            console.log(analytics);
            analytics.pushToChannel(obj);
        } catch (error) {
            console.log(error)
        }

        client.emit('returnResults', results);
    });
});

/**
 * Setup Dialogflow Integration
 */
function setupDialogflow(){
    sessionClient = new df.SessionsClient();
    sessionPath = sessionClient.sessionPath(projectId, sessionId);
    request = {
      session: sessionPath,
      queryInput: {}
    }
}
```

```javascript
/*
 * Dialogflow Detect Intent based on Text
 * @param text - string
 * @return response promise
 */
async function detectIntent(text){
    request.queryInput.text =  {
        languageCode: languageCode,
        text: text
    };
    console.log(request);

    const responses = await sessionClient.detectIntent(request);

    return responses;
}

/*
 * Dialogflow Detect Intent based on an Event
 * @param eventName - string
 * @return response promise
 */
async function detectIntentByEventName(eventName){
    request.queryInput.event = {
        languageCode: languageCode,
        name: eventName
    };
    const responses = await sessionClient.detectIntent(request);
    //remove the event, so the welcome event wont be triggered again
    delete request.queryInput.event;
    return responses;
}

//Run this code.
setupDialogflow();
```

Let me explain what Listing 13-3 does. First, it includes the analytics script (which we will dive into later) and a converter script to convert from a protobuf to JSON.

```
//1)
const analytics = require('../back-end/analytics');
const structJson = require('../back-end/structToJson');
```

The sessionId should be a global constant variable and will get a generated unique identifier from an npm package called uuid:

```
//2)
const sessionId = uuid.v4();
```

The magic starts at comment //3, the `client.on('message', async function(msg) { }` listener.

This part will loop through all the Dialogflow results and add them to a new object, making it easier for the cloud function to gather the data. Then it calls the analytics script by passing in the object:

```
analytics.pushToChannel(obj);
```

The analytics script that we used can be found in Listing 13-4. This script will write objects to BigQuery.

Listing 13-4. analytics.js

```
//1)
const { BigQuery } = require('@google-cloud/bigquery');
const { PubSub } = require('@google-cloud/pubsub');

//2)
const pubsub = new PubSub({
    projectId: process.env.npm_config_PROJECT_ID
});

const bigquery = new BigQuery({
    projectId: process.env.npm_config_PROJECT_ID
});

//3)
const id = process.env.npm_config_PROJECT_ID;
```

```
const dataLocation = 'US';
const datasetChatMessages = 'chatanalytics';
const tableChatMessages = 'chatmessages';
const topicChatbotMessages = 'chatbotanalytics';

//4)
// tslint:disable-next-line:no-suspicious-comment
const schemaChatMessages = `BOT_NAME,TEXT,POSTED:TIMESTAMP,SCORE:FLOAT,
MAGNITUDE:FLOAT,INTENT_RESPONSE,INTENT_NAME,CONFIDENCE:FLOAT,
IS_FALLBACK:BOOLEAN,IS_END_INTERACTION:BOOLEAN,PLATFORM,SESSION`;

//5)
/**
 * Analytics class to store chatbot analytics in BigQuery.
 */
class Analytics {

    //6)
    constructor() {
        this.setupBigQuery(datasetChatMessages,
            tableChatMessages, dataLocation, schemaChatMessages);

        this.setupPubSub(topicChatbotMessages);
    }

    //7)
    /**
     * If dataset doesn't exist, create one.
     * If table doesn't exist, create one.
     * @param {string} bqDataSetName BQ Dataset name
     * @param {string} bqTableName BQ Table name
     * @param {string} bqLocation BQ Data Location
     * @param {string} schema BQ table schema
     */
    setupBigQuery(bqDataSetName, bqTableName, bqLocation, schema) {
        const dataset = bigquery.dataset(bqDataSetName);
        const table = dataset.table(bqTableName);
```

```
dataset.exists(function(err, exists) {
    if (err) console.error('ERROR', err);
    if (!exists) {
            dataset.create({
            id: bqDataSetName,
            location: bqLocation
        }).then(function() {
            console.log("dataset created");
            // If the table doesn't exist, let's create it.
            // Note the schema that we will pass in.
            table.exists(function(err, exists) {
                if (!exists) {
                    table.create({
                        id: bqTableName,
                        schema: schema
                    }).then(function() {
                        console.log("table created");
                    });
                } else {
                    console.error('ERROR', err);
                }
            });
        });
    }
});

table.exists(function(err, exists) {
    if (err) console.error('ERROR', err);
    if (!exists) {
        table.create({
            id: bqTableName,
            schema: schema
        }).then(function() {
            console.log("table created");
        });
    }
```

```
    });
}

//8)
/**
 * If topic is not created yet, please create.
 * @param {string} topicName PubSub Topic Name
 */
setupPubSub(topicName) {
    const topic = pubsub.topic(`projects/${id}/topics/${topicName}`);
    topic.exists((err, exists) => {
        if (err) console.error('ERROR', err);
        if (!exists) {
            pubsub.createTopic(topicName).then(results => {
                console.log(results);
                console.log(`Topic ${topicName} created.`);
            })
            .catch(err => {
                console.error('ERROR:', err);
            });
        }
    });
}

//9)
/**
 * Execute Query in BigQuery
 * @param {string} sql SQL Query
 * @return {Promise<bigQueryRow>}
 */
queryBQ(sql) {
    return new Promise(function(resolve, reject) {
        if (sql) {
            bigquery.query(sql).then(function(data) {
                resolve(data);
            });
```

```
            } else {
                reject("ERROR: Missing SQL");
            }
        });
    }

    //10)
    /**
     * Push to PubSub Channel
     * @param {object} json JSON Object
     * @return {Promise<any>}
     */
    async pushToChannel(json) {
        const topic = pubsub.topic(`projects/${id}/topics/${topicChatbotMessages}`);
        let dataBuffer = Buffer.from(JSON.stringify(json), 'utf-8');
        try {
            const messageId = await topic.publish(dataBuffer);
            console.log(`Message ${messageId} published to topic:
            ${topicChatbotMessages}`);
        } catch(error) {
            console.log(error)
        }
    }
}

module.exports = analytics = new Analytics();
```

1) First, include the BigQuery and Pub/Sub libraries.

2) Instantiate the PubSub and BigQuery objects.

3) Set the constants. These names should be the same as what's been set in **cloudfunctions/index.js**.

4) Create the BigQuery SQL schema to store all the data.

5) Here starts the custom Analytics class.

6) In the constructor, we will set up BigQuery and PubSub for when you start this script for the first time.

7) `setupBigQuery` will create a dataset if it doesn't exist, and it will create a table if it doesn't exist. It will take the predefined SQL schema.

8) `setupPubSub` will create a Pub/Sub topic; the cloud function will take a subscription on this topic. Every time Pub/Sub has a subscription (an incoming chat message in our case), then the cloud function will run.

9) The method `queryBQ(SQL)` will execute a BigQuery query. You might want to use this in case you are building your own dashboards, showing, for example, the top 10 most negative chatbot messages. This demo is not using a custom dashboard. It runs the queries directly in the BigQuery console. Such a dashboard can be built in a web app or use Google Data Studio for this.

10) The method `pushToChannel()` takes the Dialogflow results object to push it to the PubSub subscription. We have called this method in the app.js file.

To test if we collected all the data the correct way, we can test this ourselves in BigQuery, before creating a UI dashboard in our website.

Go to BigQuery: `https://console.cloud.google.com/bigquery`.

Click (underneath the resources) **project ➤ chatanalytics ➤ chatmessages**.

Click **Preview**, and from one of the preview rows, copy a session id, which you can later use in the SQL query.

Use this Query to query a transcript, and replace [project_id] with your Google Cloud project id and [session_id] with a session id that's stored in your BigQuery table. Note Figure 13-6.

```
SELECT * FROM `[project_id].chatanalytics.chatmessages` WHERE
SESSION='[session_id]' ORDER BY POSTED LIMIT
```

You can run the examples in my GitHub repository to play around with this.

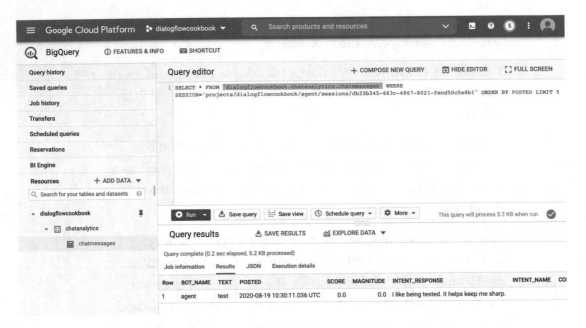

Figure 13-6. *Capturing the data in BigQuery*

Detecting User Sentiment

You might want to detect the sentiment to figure out if your users have a good or bad experience with your agent.

To build a solution for detecting sentiment, you will need the following Google Cloud services:

- Dialogflow (pay-as-you-go tier)

- (Optional) Cloud Translation API

- (Optional) Cloud Natural Language API

Sentiment analysis inspects user input and determines a user's attitude as positive, negative, or neutral. When making a detect intent request, you can specify that sentiment analysis be performed, and the response will contain sentiment analysis values.

When a very negative sentiment is returned, it might be an idea to hand off unsatisfied users to live agents.

Note   This feature is currently only available to users of the Dialogflow Essentials pay-as-you-go edition.

Sentiment Analysis is only supported for these languages:

- Chinese (Simplified and Traditional)

- English

- French

- German

- Italian

- Japanese

- Korean

- Portuguese

- Spanish

Under the hood, the Natural Language API is used by Dialogflow to perform this analysis. To enable sentiment analysis for all queries:

1. Click the **settings** button next to the agent name.

2. Select the **Advanced** tab (see Figure 13-7).

3. Toggle **Enable sentiment analysis** for the current query on.

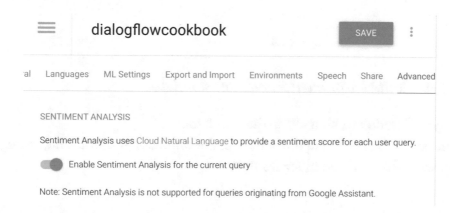

Figure 13-7. *Enabling sentiment analysis in Dialogflow*

You can interact with the agent and receive sentiment analysis results via the Dialogflow simulator.

Type "Thank you for helping me."

See the sentiment section at the bottom of the simulator. It should show a positive sentiment score, 0.9, as seen in Figure 13-8.

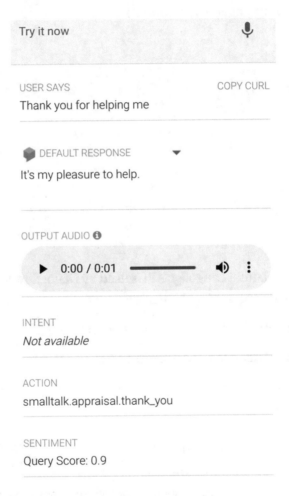

Figure 13-8. *Positive sentiment score in the simulator*

Next, type "It didn't work at all." in the simulator.

See the sentiment section at the bottom of the simulator. It should show a negative sentiment score, –0.8, as seen in Figure 13-9.

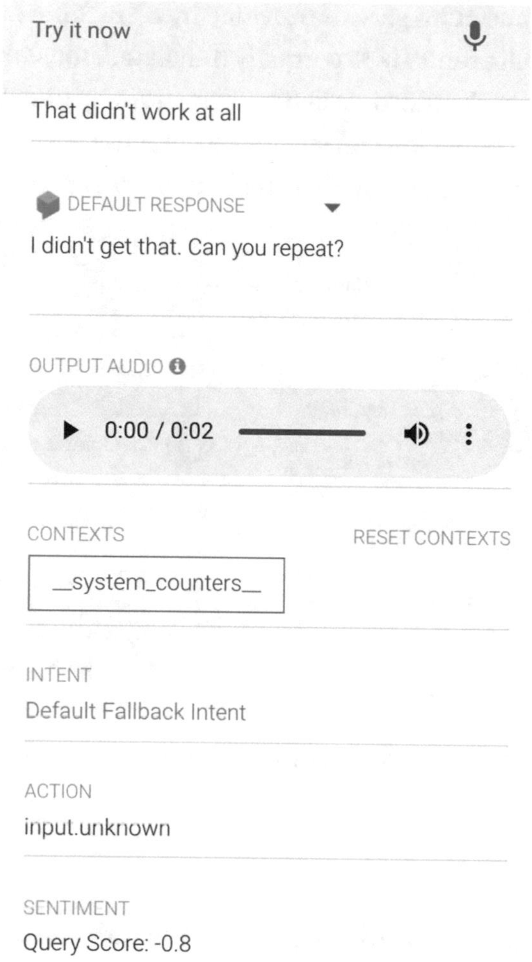

Try it now   🎤

That didn't work at all

🔷 DEFAULT RESPONSE   ▼

I didn't get that. Can you repeat?

OUTPUT AUDIO ℹ️

▶ 0:00 / 0:02 ━━━━━━━ 🔊 ⋮

CONTEXTS   RESET CONTEXTS

__system_counters__

INTENT
Default Fallback Intent

ACTION
input.unknown

SENTIMENT
Query Score: -0.8

Figure 13-9. *Negative sentiment score in the simulator*

In case you want to have sentiment analysis for your chatbots, but Dialogflow doesn't support the sentiment for this particular language (in fact, that language is not supported by the Google Cloud Natural Language API), then you can build a custom solution by calling the Translate API in parallel to detect the sentiment manually with the Google Cloud NLP API. This approach can also be handy for use cases of chatbots that need to support many more languages than what's supported in Dialogflow or for logging user conversations in various languages.

Although using a translation service provided by a Machine Learning API could return translations which aren't 100% correctly translated, for sentiment analysis, this approach often works fine. Yeah, you will have some loss by translating your message to another language, but often you can still figure out if the message was positive or negative. Figure 13-10 shows how such an architecture could look like.

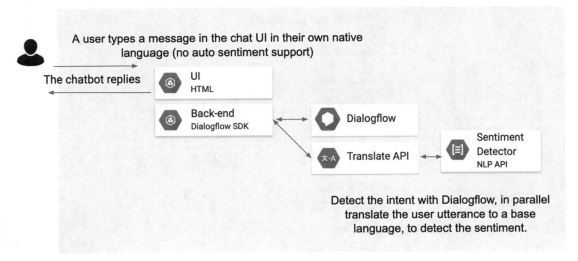

Figure 13-10. *An architecture for custom sentiment detection*

Topic Mining

Another popular solution is **topic mining**. The idea is that you will collect from every conversation the general keywords/topics. For example, is the user talking about "purchasing video games," "walkthroughs," or "release data"? Once it's stored in a separate column in BigQuery, you could query for all the latest conversations with a positive sentiment that are about "purchasing video games."

To build a solution for topic mining, you will need the following Google Cloud services:

- BigQuery

- AutoML Natural Language

Google Cloud has a tool that can be used for topic mining. It's called AutoML Natural Language. The way it works is to train your own custom NLP model by uploading lots of data that's labeled (e.g., "purchase video games," "walkthroughs," "release data," or "other").

The tool will train itself and return a machine learning model, which can be invoked through an API. Once this API is ready, you can request the topics and store this with the conversation together in BigQuery.

Collecting Customer Rating Metrics

The previous section could answer all your questions on what did my customers say, when, and where. This section is all about what your customers **think**, collecting ratings and options. Typically, you would ask your end users this in a survey. Instead of emailing your customers after the connection with your brand, you could ask these types of questions directly in your chat session. That way, you will likely receive more answers (though the answers might be more extreme).

Caution   Be aware that responses sometimes can be a bit skewed. Often, when you are collecting feedback on how well the (virtual) agent has been helping you, people can also be upset about the solution. For example, when someone interacts with your customer service about a discount campaign that just ended the day before, he might rate the experience with your chat (bot) poorly. That doesn't say anything about how well the chatbot performed. Besides this, people who are upset will likely give a more extreme rating, whereas people who were happy with the service might not even respond to the survey. This is why collecting sentiment scores with Machine Learning tools could be more effective than rating metrics.

Here are three metrics you could include.

Net Promoter Score (NPS)

The **Net Promoter Score** is a management score to calculate customer loyalty. It's calculated based on responses to a single question: *How likely is it that you would recommend our company/product/service to a friend or colleague?* Before you end your flow/session in Dialogflow, you can create this follow-up question. The scoring for this answer is most often based on a 0 to 10 scale. You could store this in BigQuery.

Those who respond with a score of 9 to 10 are called **Promoters** and are considered likely to exhibit value-creating behaviors, such as buying more, remaining customers for longer, and making more positive referrals to other potential customers. Those who respond with a score of 0 to 6 are labeled **Detractors**, and they are believed to be less likely to exhibit the value-creating behaviors. Responses of 7 and 8 are labeled **Passives**, and their behavior falls between Promoters and Detractors. NPS is calculated like this:

NPS = % promoters – % detractors

The outcome is not a percentage but just a score. For example, 10% – 60% = –50 NPS. It depends on the industry to understand if the score is above or below the average.

Caution   In the contact center, a survey is sent across after the call has ended. The survey includes questions about the overall experience of the customer. If NPS goes up after a virtual agent has been introduced, it is still very hard to quantify it as it is a cumulative effect of a lot of initiatives that were implemented within the contact center.

Customer Satisfaction (CSAT)

Customer Satisfaction Score (CSAT) is a basic measurement of a **customer's happiness** with a brand's product and services. It's usually based on a short survey that customers fill out, typically after a conversation or ticket is resolved, before ending your Dialogflow session. This survey can take many different forms, but at its core asks the customer to rate their experience on a scale ranging from good/great to bad.

For example, you might ask, "How would you rate your experience with us?" followed by a scale from 1 to 5, where 1 is very bad, and 5 is very good. CSAT is calculated like this:

CSAT = number of positive responses that voted 4 or 5 / total responses × 100%

CSAT differs from NPS as CSAT measures customer satisfaction with a product or service, whereas NPS measures customer loyalty to the organization.

Customer Effort Score (CES)

Customer Effort Score (CES) is a customer service metric that measures user experience with a product or service. Customers rank their experience on a seven-point scale ranging from "Very Difficult" to "Very Easy."

For example, before you end your flow/session in Dialogflow, you can create this follow-up question: "On a scale 1–7, where 1 is very difficult, and 7 is very easy, how much effort did it cost you to purchase this video game?" You could store the value in BigQuery.

CES is calculated like this:

CES = total of users that voted: 5, 6, or 7 / total of all users *100%

There's no definitive industry standard for customer effort score. However, customer effort score is recorded on a numeric scale, so a higher score would represent a better user experience. For a standard seven-point scale, responses of five or higher would be considered good scores.

Monitoring Chat Session and Funnel Metrics with Dialogflow, Chatbase, or Actions on Google

A **funnel** is the set of steps an end user needs to go through before reaching the conversion. Think about the funnel of a webshop. There are a few steps a visitor has to go through before they can purchase a product. They have to visit the webshop, view all products, add a product to the cart, and so on. When speaking about chatbots, a chat funnel can be the steps/turn-taking turns before you end the flow or full chat session.

Sessions represent each time a user interacts with your agent. Both complete and incomplete (where users just stopped responding) conversations are logged and count toward session-related metrics.

A **Session Flow** is a visualization that maps the most common user journeys through your bot.

Metrics to Monitor

Here are some metrics specific to the chat funnel and session flow that you might want to monitor.

Total Usage

How many people used your virtual agent?

Percentage of Users That Matches the Intent

Imagine you are an insurance company, and you have a virtual assistant for voice or a chatbot on your website. The main feature of this chatbot is providing help for filling in a declaration form. It can answer other general questions about the insurance company too.

You might be interested to see how many people interacted with your virtual agent and how many of those entered the "declaration" session flow and hit the right intents.

Completion Rate

Consider the preceding insurance use case. Your users entered the "declaration" session flow. You might be interested in figuring out if they completed the full flow. A **Completion Rate** is a percentage of end users completing the full flow, with all its follow-up questions.

Drop-Off Rate/Drop-Off Place

When your end users did not complete the flow, then you are interested in figuring out where they dropped out (**drop-off place**) and a percentage of end user users that dropped out (**drop-off rate**). This could give you some information on your virtual agent. Are you answering questions wrong, or does the virtual agent not accept incoming questions correctly? This needs some investigation!

Channel-Specific Metrics to Monitor

The following metrics are specific to the channels you are integrating with. For example, when you bring your chatbot to the Google Assistant, the Google Assistant operating system knows exactly how often you opened the action and what you did before opening the action. For a website, this type of information could, for example, be retrieved from the Google Search Console when people interact with your chatbot after first searching for your page in the Google search engine.

User Retention

Retention is the act of getting your members to use your product so that it becomes habitual. That's why we call them **users** at this stage. If you retain them, then they are literally using your product often.

User retention information can be found in Google Analytics, Google Search Console, or the Actions on Google console.

Note   When you want to experiment with voice and develop a Google Assistant action for your brand, think of user retention. You can imagine a voice action that handles an insurance claim won't be used as often compared to a Google Assistant action for a retailer, which can add groceries to a shopping cart. You would use the grocery store action much more often.

Endpoint Health

For example, when you integrate with a web service or database to fetch information and the server returns an error or is very slow in returning the information, this might crash your virtual agent or at least give a not-so-lovely user experience.

Endpoint health information can be found in your website logs; when your chatbot is deployed in Google Cloud, you can find it in Cloud Logging (previously known as Stackdriver); when your agent runs on the Google Assistant, you can find it in the Actions on Google console.

Discovery

How did your users found your agent and how did they get there?

Specific to the Google Assistant, you might be interested in figuring out how your users discovered your Action and how they invoked it. When users say a phrase related to your Action, Google will sometimes recommend that the user try your Action, even if the user did not explicitly specify your Action's invocation name.

For chatbots on websites, the information you are interested in is which websites link to yours. And which search queries did your users use. This information can be found in Google Analytics or the Google Search Console.

Dialogflow Built-in Analytics

Dialogflow can give you the metrics from the Analytics tab out of the box.

Click **Legacy ➤ Explore**.

This page shows insights on usage and NLU data.

Sessions (Figure 13-11) represent each time a user interacts with your agent. Both complete and incomplete (where users just stopped responding) conversations are logged and count toward session-related metrics.

This will show you the last total of sessions. You can filter for "yesterday," "last 7 days," or "last 30 days."

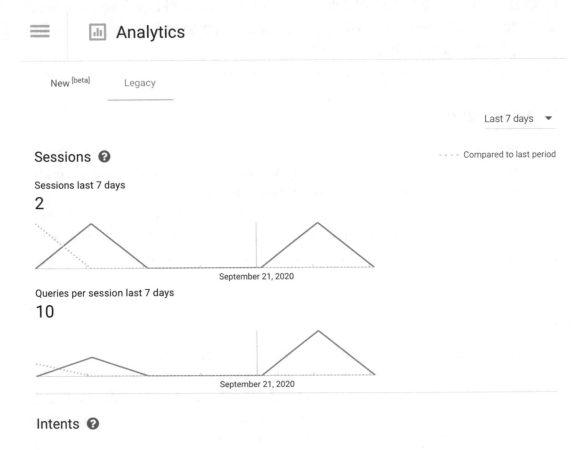

Figure 13-11. *Built-in Dialogflow analytics*

The **intents overview** will show you an overview of the most used intents. It will display the intent name, the number of sessions in which the intent was matched, a count of the total times the intent was used from all sessions, and an exit percentage, which will show you a percentage of the sessions where the user left the conversation while being in a specific intent (taken from the total number of sessions where the same intent was matched).

When you scroll down, you will see the session flow (Figure 13-12). You can click each intent to unfold the intents, which would follow up.

You can hover with your cursor over the intent names (blue boxes) to see the following information:

- The intent name

- The percentage of all users that matched the intent

- The number of requests the intent was matched to

- The drop-off rate while being on this intent

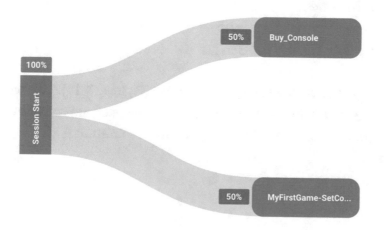

Figure 13-12. *Built-in Dialogflow analytics, session flow*

The **History** page (Figure 13-13) shows a simplified version of the conversations your agent has engaged in. You can click an event or user utterance to see a chronological transcript log.

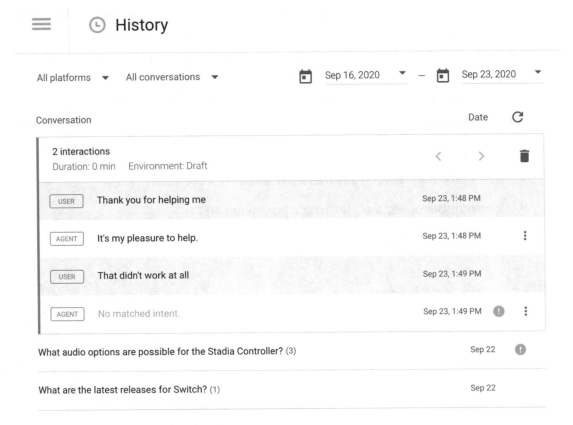

Figure 13-13. *Dialogflow History transcripts*

You can click the options menu of an agent response (Figure 13-14). This will allow you to go to **Cloud Logging** for advanced logging in the Google Cloud console or directly browse to the intent (this is handy for when you need to fix something). Or you can see the Raw API response.

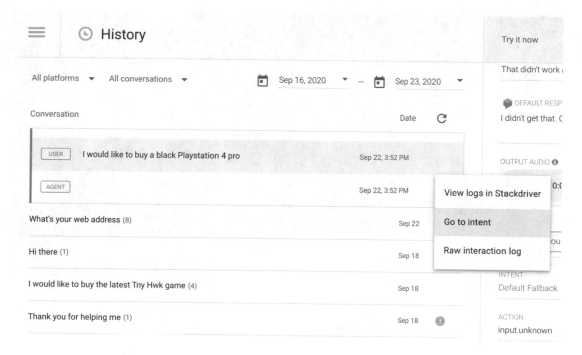

Figure 13-14. *Dialogflow History transcript, go to intent*

Note   Only default responses are shown on the History page. Other responses, like rich messages or Actions on Google Simple Responses, aren't visible. Have a look at the previous screenshot. What's your URL triggered a custom payload and therefore isn't visible in the log.

If you want to capture these things as well, you will have to manually build a logging solution, for example, with BigQuery.

Monitoring Metrics with Chatbase

Alternatively, you can also monitor the session and funnel from the Google tool: **Chatbase** (Figure 13-15); it will give you a bit more detailed overview, and besides filters for "yesterday," "last 7 days," or "last 30 days," it can also filter on "today" or the "quarter to date."

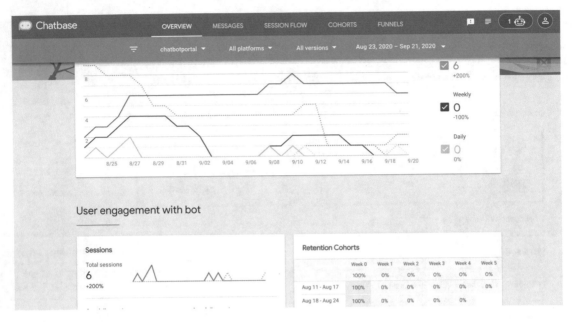

Figure 13-15. *Analytics in Chatbase*

As a matter of fact, Dialogflow uses Chatbase under the hood.

The **Retention Cohorts** block will show you the user retention over time.

Use the **Session Flow** tab to see the Session Flow (Figure 13-16); just like in Dialogflow, you can drill down to see each intent with

- The intent name

- The percentage of all users that matched the intent

- The number of requests the intent was matched to

- The drop-off rate while being on this intent

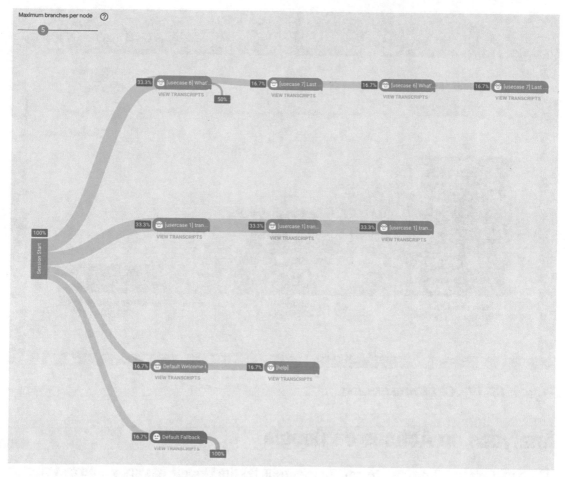

Figure 13-16.   *Session flow in Chatbase*

Chatbase has a funnel reporting tool, which offers a way to track customer success by creating your own custom workflows for up to six follow-up intents. Click the **Funnels** tab (Figure 13-17). You can create a new funnel to record and assign intents to turn-taking steps. Once you have created a funnel, you get a better visualization of the funnel, the drop-off rate, and also a **completion rate**.

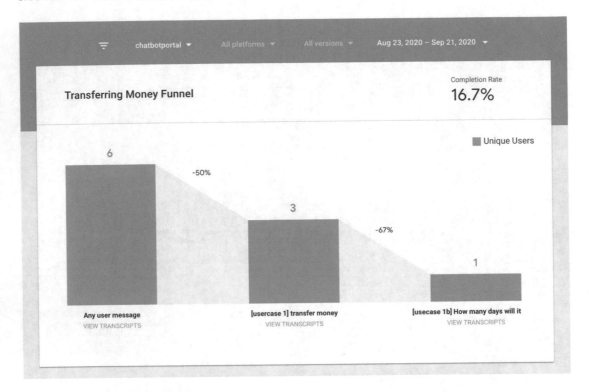

Figure 13-17.   *Chatbase funnels*

Analytics on Actions on Google

When you are building a voice bot, for example, for the Google Assistant, you can also monitor some metrics. Log in to your Actions on Google console.

A nice extra is that you can even export these metrics to BigQuery so you can capture these for a more extended period of time.

Click **Analytics ➤ Usage**.

The **Usage** page (Figure 13-18) displays three graphs, which pertain to the usage data of your Action over time.

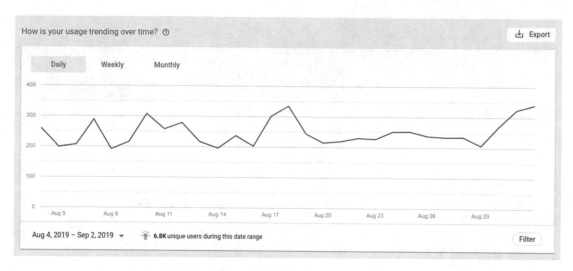

Figure 13-18. *Actions on Google usage*

And it can also show you the **user retention** (Figure 13-19).

	All users ⓘ	Week 0	Week 1	Week 2	Week 3	Week 4
Sep 01 - Sep 07, 2019	1,300	100%	1.4%	0.7%	0.0%	0.0%
Sep 08 - Sep 14, 2019	1,180	100%	1.7%	0.0%	0.0%	
Sep 15 - Sep 21, 2019	630	100%	1.6%	1.6%		
Sep 22 - Sep 28, 2019	130	100%	7.7%			
Sep 29 - Oct 05, 2019	160	100%				

How well do you retain your users? ⓘ   Export

Last 5 weeks   Filter

Figure 13-19. *Actions on Google user retention*

A nice extra which Actions on Google can show you (because it also knows the insights of your Google Assistant integration) is **health information** (Figure 13-20).

Figure 13-20. *Actions on Google health information*

- **Errors**: The number of **errors** your Action's cloud endpoint returned on a given day. If you have a large number of errors, you may want to look at your logs to identify what is causing your endpoint to crash or behave unexpectedly.

- **Actions latency**: The latency of your Action's endpoint. If latency is very high or regularly spikes, your users may be experiencing delays while interacting with your Action.

- **Experienced latency by user**: The latency felt by a user on each request to your Action. This metric illustrates what users experience when interacting with your Action.

Click **Analytics ➤ Discovery**.

The discovery page displays a table of which phrases led to Google recommending your Action (Figure 13-21).

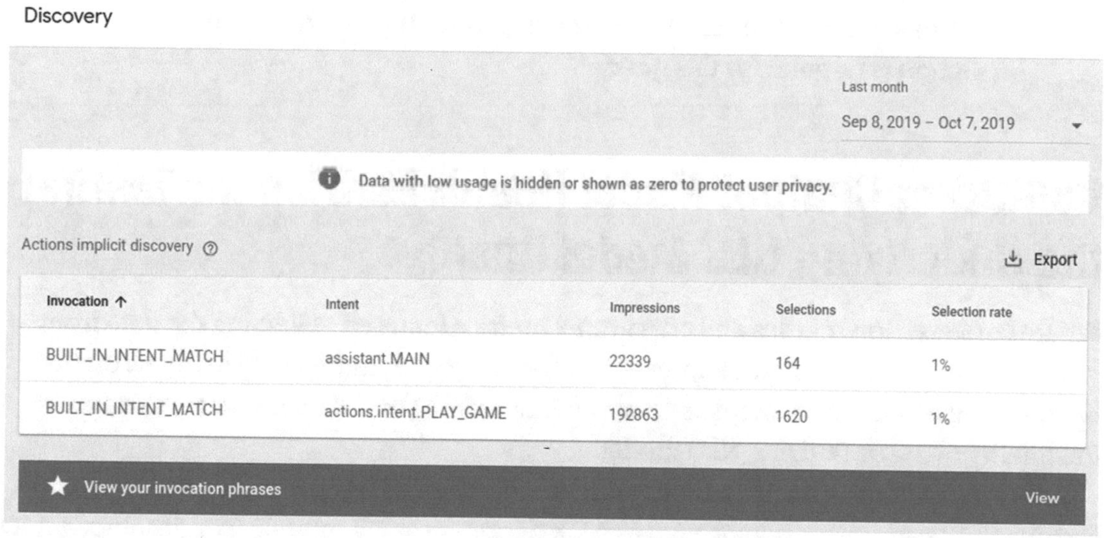

Discovery

Figure 13-21. *Actions on Google analytics discovery*

The columns in the discovery table are as follows:

- **Invocation**: The user query that led to Google recommending your Action. Aside from the actual user queries, this list includes the following values:

- BUILT_IN_INTENT: This listing indicates your Action was invoked through a built-in intent.

- AUTO_MATCHED_BY_GOOGLE: This listing indicates when implicit invocation was used.

- ACTION_LINK: This listing indicates when your Action was invoked through an Action link.

- **Intent**: The intent the user's query matched.

- **Impression**: The number of times this phrase led to Google recommending your Action.

- **Selection**: The number of times a user invoked your Action after Google recommended it. This number cannot exceed the number of impressions this phrase has.

- **Selection rate**: The percentage of impressions that led to a selection. A low percent rate indicates that many users opt to use other Actions for this particular query, whereas a high rate suggests that your Action is popular for this query.

Capturing Chatbot Model Health Metrics for Testing the Underlying NLU Model Quality

Where conversation metrics and chat funnel metrics focus on collecting the data from your end user to monitor and improve the experience, bot model metrics focus on the bot building process and might use test validation data (based on live data) to improve the quality of the underlying NLU model.

Modern chatbot/virtual assistant builder tools like Dialogflow make use of machine learning. For each virtual agent, you, as a UX designer (agent modeler) or developer, may define many intents. An **intent** categorizes a user's intention. Your combined intents can handle a complete conversation. This will train an underlying machine learning model.

When an end user writes or says something in a chatbot or virtual assistant, we call this a **user expression** or **utterance**. Dialogflow matches the expression to the best-matched intent in your bot builder based on built-in NLU (Natural Language Understanding) and the training phrases (examples) where the underlying machine learning model was trained on. Matching an intent is also known as **intent classification** or **intent matching**.

Once you have built your virtual agent, the most important question arises: how good is your machine learning model that your virtual agent uses under the hood?

There are a bunch of metrics you can use to test the quality of your virtual agent.

Typically, when working with test data, UX designers or content writers would create a validation dataset. They use this to train the Dialogflow agent model by entering it as user phrases. To create test datasets that aren't biased, use logs from chats/contact centers/virtual assistants and separate them from the intent training phrases used to train the model on. When user data contains sensitive PII data, you should anonymize or mask it.

As you have seen, these are great metrics to test your underlying machine learning model with. Once you store all these variables in a data warehouse, you can easily create dashboards to preview these insights. Developers could create unit tests that pass in the validation data as user utterances and test it against the bot builder API (in Dialogflow, this will be the detectIntent() method). The detected intent and the confidence score can be evaluated with your validation dataset.

True Positive—A Correctly Matched Intent

A true positive is an outcome where the chatbot correctly detects the right (positive) intent. For example, when your virtual agent has an intent called "Salary Intent" and it was trained with a training phrase:

"Did my salary come in?"

And the user utterance is

"Have I received my salary?"

Dialogflow should detect the following Intent: "Salary Intent."

I could write a unit test similar to how you would write unit tests in software engineering. I could create test data on the previous scenario with a user utterance: "My salary, when will I receive it?"

I expect it to be the Salary Intent. You can use the Dialogflow API, and Dialogflow would detect the Salary Intent too. So this is a true positive. The match was correct.

You could store this in BigQuery, so you can rerun the scenario each time when you make changes to your agent against the Dialogflow API. Data fields which you would need to collect are "User Utterance," "Expected Intent Name," "Detected Intent Name," and the "Result," which is TP.

True Negative—An Unsupported Request

A **true negative** is an outcome where the chatbot correctly mapped the user utterance to a fallback. Unsupported request errors occur when users ask questions that your bot wasn't designed for to answer. But instead of returning a wrong answer or a system error, it returns a friendly fallback message.

For example, when your virtual agent has an intent called "Global fallback," which gets active every time an intent could not be matched.

I could create test data on the preceding scenario with a user utterance: "Can I buy casino tokens?"

This is a banking chatbot, not a Casino chatbot. I expect it to be the "Global fallback" intent, and Dialogflow returned the "Global fallback" intent.

So this is a true negative. It behaves exactly how it was designed.

You could store a test case like the previous one in your data warehouse, so you can rerun the scenario each time when you make changes to your agent against the Dialogflow API. Data fields which you would need to collect are "User Utterance," "Expected Intent Name," "Detected Intent Name," and the "Result," which is TN.

False Positive—A Misunderstood Request

A **false positive** is an outcome where the chatbot matches the wrong intent. It should have been a different intent or, in case it didn't exist, a fallback intent, but it misunderstood the user utterance so the result is wrong. Misunderstood request errors occur when your bot cannot determine the correct user intent. This error can be caused by your bot not considering the question's context or answering a slightly different question than the one being asked.

For example, when your virtual agent has an intent called "Block credit card," and it was trained with a training phrase:

"I want to block my credit card."

Your virtual agent has another intent called "Renew credit card," and it was trained with the training phrase:

"I want to renew my credit card."

I could create test data on the preceding scenario with a user utterance: "My account is blocked, can I get a new credit card?"

I expect it to be the "Renew credit card" intent; however, Dialogflow detected the "Block credit card" intent. So this is a false positive. There was a match, but it's the wrong one!

You could store a test case like the previous one in BigQuery, so you can rerun the scenario each time when you make changes to your agent against the Dialogflow API. Data fields which you would need to collect are "User Utterance," "Expected Intent Name," "Detected Intent Name," and the "Result," which is FP.

False Negative—A Missed Request

A **false negative** is an outcome where the intent exists, but the chatbot didn't detect it, and therefore a fallback was triggered. Missed request errors occur when your bot already has a certain intent built but fails to recognize alternative phrasing or terminology.

For example, when your virtual agent has an intent called "Block credit card," and it was trained with a training phrase:

"I want to block my credit card."

I could create test data on the preceding scenario with a user utterance: "Stop the credit card right now."

I expect it to be the "Block credit card" intent; however, the virtual agent detected a fallback intent. So this is a false negative. The intent is there, but it couldn't match it.

You could store a test case like the previous one in BigQuery, so you can rerun the scenario each time when you make changes to your agent against the Dialogflow API. Data fields which you would need to collect are "User Utterance," "Expected Intent Name," "Detected Intent Name," and the "Result," which is FN.

True Positive Rate

True Positive Rate (TPR or **recall)** is a sensitivity ratio to determine if intents are too narrowly defined and missed requests. When it's above 0.5, it can be considered good.

$$TPR = total\ TPs\ /\ (total\ TPs + total\ FNs)$$

False Positive Rate

False Positive Rate (FPS or **Fallout)** is a false alarm ratio. The false positive rate is calculated as the ratio between the number of negative events where the chatbot matched the wrong intent (false positives) and the total number of actual negative events (regardless of classification).

$$\text{FPR} = \text{total FPs} / (\text{total FPs} + \text{total TNs})$$

You could store a test case like the previous one in BigQuery, so you can rerun the scenario each time when you make changes to your agent. You would need to request the total TP, FP, FN, and TN from your data warehouse. And you would store the **TPR** and **FPR** so you will be able to retrieve this later in your reports.

ROC Curve

An **ROC (Receiver Operating Characteristic) Curve** is a graphical representation which tells us how good the model is for distinguishing the given intents in terms of the detected probability. Using this info, you can decide how you want to set the confidence thresholds of your Dialogflow agent to define the classification score required for an intent match.

You'll need to calculate the **True Positive Rate** and **False Positive Rate** in order to plot this in the graph. You would do this based on various Dialogflow ML Settings thresholds.

For instance, we have set in Dialogflow the confidence threshold to 0.80, which maps the user utterances into two options match or no intent match. We assume that any probability greater than or equal to 0.80 would be an intent match, else a fallback.

The ROC Curve plots two parameters:

- True Positive Rate (recall/sensitivity ratio)

- False Positive Rate (fallout/false alarm ratio)

The blue diagonal line in Figure 13-22 reflects random guessing of 0.5 area under the curve. This means the virtual agents have half of the expected intents correct. In general, the goal is to maximize sensitivity and false alarm. In other words, the steeper the ROC (yellow) line, the better.

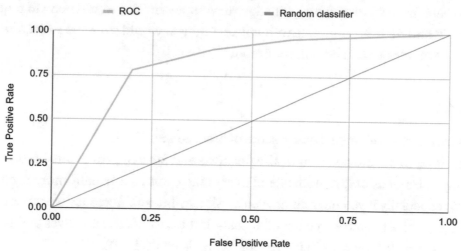

Figure 13-22. *ROC Curve*

Accuracy

Accuracy is a ratio of correctly predicted observations to the total observations—the ratio of all the correct handled intents. You can calculate it the following way:

> **total correct = total TPs + total TNs**

> **total incorrect = total FPs + total Fns**

> **accuracy = correct / correct + incorrect**

You could store a test case like the previous one in your data warehouse, so you can rerun the scenario each time when you make changes to your agent. You would need to request the total TP, TN, FP, and FN from BigQuery. And you would store the **accuracy** so you will be able to retrieve this later in your reports.

Precision

Precision is a ratio of positive prediction values to determine if there are problems with false positives/**misunderstood requests**. The higher the precision, the lower the FP rate.

> **precision = total TPs / (total TPs + total FPs)**

You could store a test case like the previous one in BigQuery, so you can rerun the scenario each time when you make changes to your agent. You would need to request the total TP and FP from your data warehouse. And you would store the **precision** so you will be able to retrieve this later in your reports.

F1 Score

The **f1 score** is the weighted average score of precision and TPR.

Therefore, this score takes both false positives and false negatives into account. Intuitively, it is not as easy to understand as accuracy, but F1 is usually more useful than accuracy, especially if you have an uneven class distribution. Accuracy works best if false positives and false negatives have similar costs. If the cost of false positives and false negatives is very different, it's better to look at precision and TPR.

$$\textbf{F1 Score} = \textbf{2*(TPR * Precision) / (TPR + Precision)}$$

You could store a test case like the previous one in BigQuery, so you can rerun the scenario each time when you make changes to your agent. You would need to request the total recall and precision from your data warehouse. And you would store the **f1 score** so you will be able to retrieve this later in your reports.

Confusion Matrix

In the field of machine learning, a **confusion matrix**, also known as an error matrix, is a specific table layout that allows visualization of the performance of an algorithm (in our case, the underlying machine learning model for the virtual agent). Each row of the matrix represents the expected intents, while each column represents the actual matched intent by the Dialogflow API.

The name stems from the fact that it makes it easy to see if the agent is confusing two classes (commonly mislabeling one as another).

When you have lots of test cases, you could render all the scores in one big matrix.

As you can see in Figure 13-23, each intent contains the sum of all the TPs. This should give you a diagonal (orange) line from the top to the bottom. The red squares are the sum of all the FPs; for example, in the following matrix, you can see that there's a test case (user utterance) which is expected to be matched to the intent, *get_price*, but that got matched to the *collect_current_playing_game* intent.

	buy_product	default_fallback	default_global_welcome	collect_current_playing_game	collect_fav_multiplayer_game	get_delivery_date	get_price	get_release_dates	precision	recall	F1 score
buy_product	11	0	1	0	0	0	0	0	0.85	0.92	0.88
default_fallback	0	9	0	1	0	1	0	0	0.9	0.82	0.86
default_global_welcome	1	0	13	0	0	1	0	0	0.81	0.87	0.84
collect_current_playing_game	0	0	1	9	0	0	0	0	0.9	0.92	0.92
collect_fav_multiplayer_game	0	0	0	0	12	0	0	0	1	1	1
get_delivery_date	0	1	0	0	0	13	0	0	0.9	0.91	0.95
get_price	0	0	0	1	0	0	10	0	0.83	0.9	0.9
get_release_dates	0	0	0	0	0	0	0	13	1	1	1

Figure 13-23. *Confusion matrix in action*

Summary

This chapter contains information about collecting and monitoring agent insights and analytics. It is divided into the following categories:

- Conversation-related metrics

    What did your users say, when, and where? You can capture conversation-related metrics and store them in a data warehouse like BigQuery.

- Customer rating metrics

    What did your users think of your brand? How can you collect ratings with Dialogflow?

- Chat session and funnel metrics

    The paths that your users took to engage with your agent. How to monitor chat sessions and funnel metrics with Dialogflow and Chatbase.

- Bot model health metrics

  How to capture chatbot model health metrics for testing the underlying machine learning model quality in order to tweak the Dialogflow machine learning threshold.

In case you want to build this example, the source code for this book is available on GitHub via the book's product page, located at `www.apress.com/978-1-4842-7013-4`. Look into the **advanced-agent-insights** folder.

Further Reading

- Dialogflow documentation on History

  `https://cloud.google.com/dialogflow/es/docs/history`

- Dialogflow documentation on Analytics

  `https://cloud.google.com/dialogflow/es/docs/analytics`

- Dialogflow documentation on training agents

  `https://cloud.google.com/dialogflow/es/docs/training`

- Google Cloud documentation on BigQuery

  `https://cloud.google.com/bigquery/docs`

- Google Cloud documentation on Pub/Sub

  `https://cloud.google.com/pubsub/docs/`

- Google Cloud documentation on Cloud Functions

  `https://cloud.google.com/functions/docs/`

- Languages that support built-in sentiment analysis

  `https://cloud.google.com/dialogflow/es/docs/reference/language`

- A real-world approach example of a chatbot integrated into a website

  `https://github.com/savelee/kube-django-ng`

- Dialogflow documentation on sentiment analysis in Dialogflow

  `https://cloud.google.com/dialogflow/es/docs/how/sentiment`

- AutoML Natural Language

  `https://cloud.google.com/automl?hl=en`

- Google Cloud documentation on AutoML Sentiment Analysis

  `https://cloud.google.com/natural-language/automl/docs/features`

- A code example on how to build human hand-off

  `https://github.com/dialogflow/agent-human-handoff-nodejs`

- queryResult.languageCode

  `https://cloud.google.com/dialogflow/es/docs/reference/rpc/google.cloud.dialogflow.v2beta1#google.cloud.dialogflow.v2beta1.QueryResult`

- queryResult.intent.displayName

  `https://cloud.google.com/dialogflow/es/docs/reference/rpc/google.cloud.dialogflow.v2beta1#google.cloud.dialogflow.v2beta1.Intent`

- queryResult.intent.isFallback

  `https://cloud.google.com/dialogflow/es/docs/reference/rpc/google.cloud.dialogflow.v2beta1#google.cloud.dialogflow.v2beta1.Intent`

- queryResult.intent.endInteraction

  `https://cloud.google.com/dialogflow/es/docs/reference/rpc/google.cloud.dialogflow.v2beta1#google.cloud.dialogflow.v2beta1.Intent`

- queryResult.intentDetectionConfidence

  `https://cloud.google.com/dialogflow/es/docs/reference/rpc/google.cloud.dialogflow.v2beta1#google.cloud.dialogflow.v2beta1.QueryResult`

- Google Data Studio for building interactive dashboards

  `https://datastudio.google.com/c/u/0/navigation/reporting`

- Google Analytics

  `https://analytics.google.com`

- Google Search Console

  `https://search.google.com`

An Introduction to Dialogflow CX

Dialogflow had a name change at the end of 2020; it's now called Dialogflow Essentials (Dialogflow ES) to make room for another Google Cloud Conversational AI tool: Dialogflow Customer Experience (Dialogflow CX). Dialogflow CX is an alternative development suite for building conversational UIs and will exist next Dialogflow ES. Google will continue to support Dialogflow ES since it has a huge user base.

By the time of writing this book, Dialogflow CX is a fresh new product. Although this book contains lots of information on how to use Dialogflow ES, I do want to end this book with some additional information on Dialogflow CX. By having the knowledge of Dialogflow ES and by reading this appendix, you will know enough to start building your chat and voice bots with Dialogflow CX. This appendix will give you an in-depth introduction, explains why there is another conversational AI tool to choose from, and how this product differs from Dialogflow ES. I will explain new concepts such as *Pages*, *Flows*, and *State Handlers* and will explain when to use which product. First, let's understand why Google developed Dialogflow CX.

How the Industry Is Changing Its Conversation Complexity

In Dialogflow ES, the main concept is intent classification. Once an intent is matched, it can return a static response, gather parameters (entity extraction), or trigger webhook code (fulfillment), for example, to fetch data from a database. See Chapter 3 which discusses this in more detail. Dialogflow ES also works with a concept called context. Just like a human, Dialogflow ES can remember the context in a second and third turn-taking turn. This is how it can keep track of previous user utterances.

L. Boonstra, *The Definitive Guide to Conversational AI with Dialogflow and Google Cloud*, https://doi.org/10.1007/978-1-4842-7014-1

Large enterprises have been using Dialogflow ES over the past years. Here's an observation I see at Google while working with customers. At the beginning (2016), most conversational UIs were simple chatbots (voice assistant bots, FAQ bots, etc.), for web or voice bots, like the Google Assistant. It typically uses one or two turn-taking turns. For example, "Hey Google, what's currently playing on ABC?"—"*The Bachelor* started at 8 p.m., an episode you have never seen before!"

As we all know, building conversational UIs is an ongoing process. When you capture the right chatbot insights, you will see what your customers are asking for (see Chapter 13). When you continue to build conversations on top of an existing agent, that bot becomes more complex over the years.

So **conversation complexity** is one observation. The other perception I made is that businesses want to be where their customers are. And thus, their chatbots will need to connect to more channels to create omnichannel experiences. Instead of building a single chatbot, companies now want to develop complete conversational platforms fed by a data lake and automate processes with robotic processes (RPA). Think of complex use cases such as replacing your customer care or HR department with robots. Having overloaded call centers and employees burned out by undervalued monotonous tasks, automation through chatbots and virtual (voice) agents can trim huge business costs. Through conversational AI in contact centers, businesses can reduce call time and on-hold time and offer 24/7 availability while improving our processes by capturing analytics.

Where Dialogflow CX Fits In

Dialogflow ES has been praised for its simplicity. You can build a chatbot or voice bot quickly. These are chat and voice applications, where a short utterance matches one intent, with a few turn-taking turns, for example, a retail chat or voice app where you can say "Put milk on my shopping list."

Now imagine you are building a voice robot for the telephony helpdesk of a grocery store. This time, customers are not speaking a few sentences; instead, they speak with whole stories: "Yesterday, right at opening time, I bought milk at So-And-So Store together with my 6-month-old baby, and when I came home, and I wanted to put the milk in the refrigerator, I noticed that the date is past the expiration date. I opened the carton and noticed the odd smell, but the taste was fine." Suddenly, it becomes much more tricky to match the intent. For a human, it can become challenging to understand the intention; for an AI, this is difficult too! Because are we talking about *buying milk*, *bad products*, or *requesting a refund*?

The conversation is long-running; the dialogue is large and can have many turn-taking turns, where we need to remember the context—branched off in hundreds of possible outcomes. And look, I am not even mentioning the technical complexity of dealing with multiple speakers, interruptions, background noises, and so on.

Creating a virtual (voice) agent for a contact center or creating an automated bot platform is far more complicated where it reaches the borders of Dialogflow ES. Sure, when you have a large team of developers, they can tailor-make a solution on top of Dialogflow ES, as users have been doing so in the past. But that means that you have to develop and maintain additional code rather than focusing on designing conversations. This is where Dialogflow CX fits in.

Dialogflow CX Features

Dialogflow CX empowers teams to accelerate creating enterprise-level conversational experiences through a visual bot builder (see Figure A-1), reusable conversations, and the ability to address multi-turn conversations.

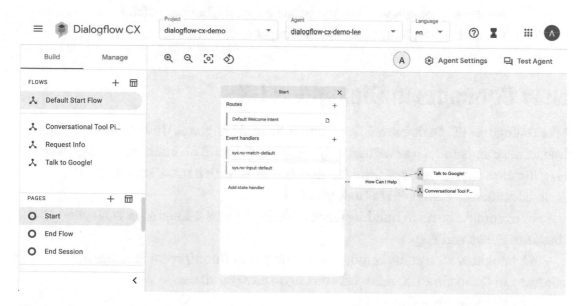

Figure A-1. *The Dialogflow CX interface and visual bot builder*

Dialogflow CX allows you to quickly create agents with

- Large and complex flows. Think of giant agent implementations with hundreds or thousands of intents.

- More than three turn-taking turns (keeping context) and conversations that branch off from each other in various outcomes.

- Repeatable dialogue parts in the flow (think of a login feature, saying yes/no to questions, etc.).

- Understanding the intent and context of long utterances.

- Working with teams collaborating on large implementations.

- Native contact center features such as DTMF, one-click telephony partner integration, barge-in, live agent hand-off.

- Agents where additional languages and regionalization (e.g., GDPR) are important.

- Flows with various outcomes and repeatable parts, for example, filing taxes. Usually, this requires you to fill out lots of forms, where questions jump to each other. If you would build a chatbot for this use case, Dialogflow CX would be great for this, because of the reusable flows, intents, and branching of answers.

New Concepts in Dialogflow CX

Like Dialogflow ES, Dialogflow CX contains a Natural Language Understanding module that understands spoken or written text, and it works based on intent matching/intent classification. However, there are a few new concepts, which make Dialogflow CX seriously different compared to Dialogflow ES.

For example, the main building block in Dialogflow ES is intents. In Dialogflow CX, these are **Flows** and **Pages**.

In Dialogflow ES, a conversation was controlled by intent/event matches and contexts. In Dialogflow CX, this works through **State Handlers**.

Let's dive into what's new.

Flows

Complex dialogs often involve multiple conversation topics. For example, a retail chatbot that sells video games could have separated flows for browsing through video game release calendar, adding to a shopping cart, and payments (see Figure A-2). As you read in Chapter 9 about mega agents to orchestrate bots, Flows are a little similar to mega agents. You can configure flows nicely in the visual bot builder.

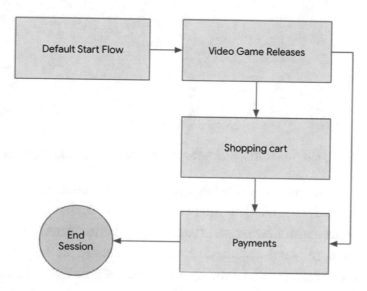

Figure A-2. *A diagram of a conversational flow*

Flows allow teams to work on individual conversation paths. A good approach would be to simplify the flow. When your flows are small, you can easily see them on a screen. So it's more modular. See Figure A-3 to know how it looks like.

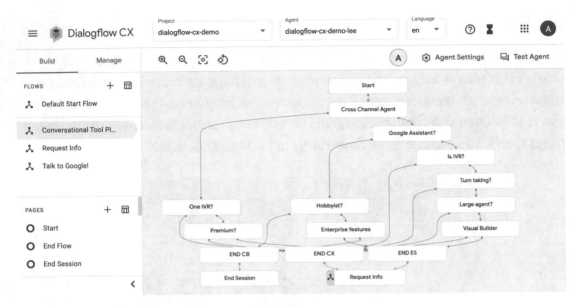

Figure A-3. *Setting up flows in Dialogflow CX with the visual builder*

In Chapter 3, we discussed the Dialogflow ES concepts, including the Machine Learning threshold, which is used for intent classification. Matches above this threshold can be considered as a match, whereas others would be considered a fallback. In Dialogflow ES, you could set the Machine Learning threshold on the agent level, whereas in Dialogflow CX you can set this on the Flow level (see Figure A-4). This is very handy when building large agents, as you don't want flows to break each other's parts.

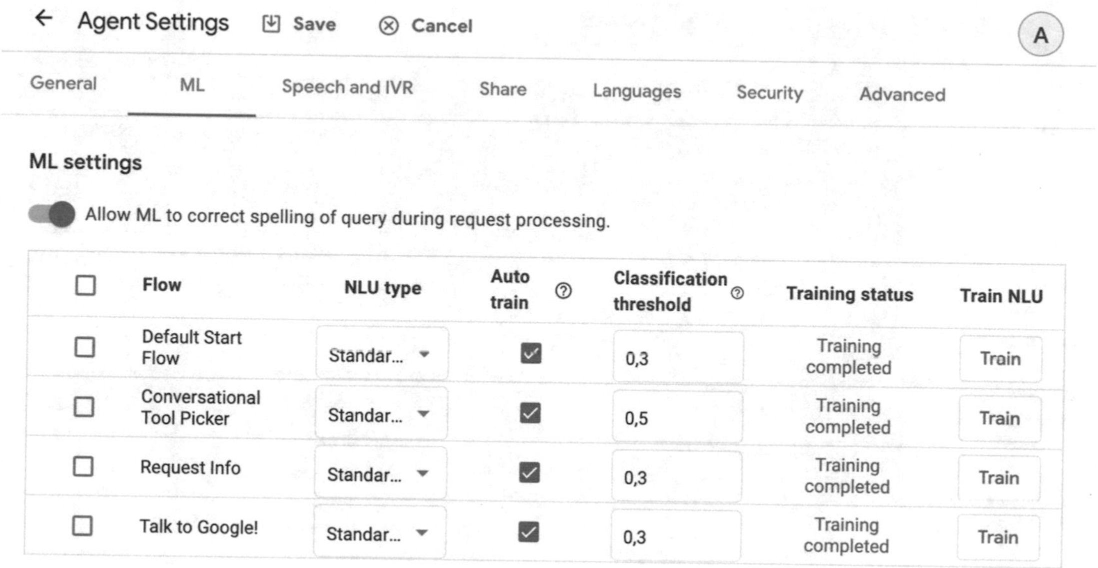

Figure A-4. *ML threshold on the Flow level can be found in the Settings screen*

A state handler could end a flow (so it will jump back to a next or previous flow), or you can end the full agent session. We will dive into state handlers in a minute.

Pages

A Dialogflow CX conversation (a session) can be described and visualized as a state machine. Think of a state machine as a vending machine. It has the states: Off, Waiting for Coins, Select Candy, Give Candy. Pages are the states for a Dialogflow CX session!

For each flow, you define many pages, where your combined pages can handle a complete conversation on the topics the flow is designed for. At any given moment, exactly one page is the **current page**, the current page is considered active, and also the flow associated with that page is considered active. See Figure A-5.

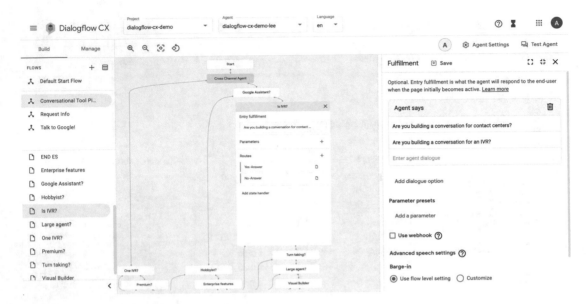

Figure A-5. *Pages in Dialogflow CX*

Every flow has a special start page. When a flow initially becomes active, the start page becomes the current page. For each conversational turn, the current page will either stay the same or transition to another page.

This concept will allow you to create larger agents with many pages and multiple turn-taking turns.

Pages contain **fulfillments** (entry dialogues and webhooks), **parameters**, and **state handlers** (like intent routes, conditions, or events).

State Handlers

A conversation in Dialogflow ES could be controlled by setting contexts, events, and intents. This worked well for simple agents, but it could become problematic when you would build large agents, as keeping context in Dialogflow ES didn't allow you to have a lot of turn-taking turns, and intents are not reusable (since everything like context, events, parameters, and fulfillment is tied to an intent).

In Dialogflow CX, conversation control happens through **State Handlers**, which allows you to create various transition routes to transition to another Dialogflow CX page, including making it conditional (for branching of conversations). In order for a handler to be evaluated, it must be in scope. Handler scope is an important and powerful tool that helps you control the conversation. By controlling the scope of a handler, you can control a conversation through the following ways:

- **Intent routes**: When an intent can be matched

- **Condition routes**: When a condition should be checked

- **Event handlers**: When a certain event can be handled

- **Page transitions**: When a page transition occurs

- **Static fulfillment**: When a static fulfillment response is provided

- **Dynamic fulfillment**: When a fulfillment webhook is called for dynamic responses

Contact Center Features

With just one click, you can turn your agent into a telephony experience, by integrating it with an IVR system of choice. Dialogflow CX provides features for barge-in (to interrupt a flow), live agent hand-off (to escalate a conversation to a human call center employee), dual-tone multi-frequency (DTMF, to allow you to use the number pad on your phone, e.g., to provide numerical options), and built-in telephony integrations.

Customer-Managed Encryption Keys (CMEKs)

By default, Google Cloud automatically encrypts data using encryption keys managed by Google. If you have specific compliance or regulatory requirements related to the keys that protect your data, you can use customer-managed encryption keys (CMEKs). All Dialogflow CX agent **data-at-rest** (when data is housed on a computer/storage in any form) and **data-in-use** (when data is active, like updated, processed, erased, accessed, or read by a system) can be protected with CMEKs.

By the time of writing, when CMEK is enabled, the features Versions, Conversation History, and Speech Adaptation Data will be disabled.

Where Both Products Differ

With both products, Dialogflow ES and Dialogflow CX, you can likely build the same chat and voice bots for your end users, although certain functionalities are improved or work slightly differently in Dialogflow CX.

Many features work similar in Dialogflow CX; think about Agent Validation, Sentiment Analysis, and Auto Speech Adaptation. Let's go through the concepts we know from Dialogflow ES and see how these differ in Dialogflow CX.

Agents

A Dialogflow CX agent is a virtual agent that handles conversations with your end users. Similar to Dialogflow ES agents, a Dialogflow CX agent can be compared with a human call center agent. You train them both to handle expected conversation scenarios, and your training does not need to be overly explicit. However, agents in Dialogflow CX might work different or are slightly different configured:

- In Dialogflow ES, you can only create one Dialogflow agent per Google Cloud project. In Dialogflow CX, you can create multiple agents per project.

- When you set up an agent in Dialogflow CX, you will have to tie it to a location explicitly. You can also create a Dialogflow ES agent in different regions, but in CX there are more regions to choose from, and there is more feature parity across Dialogflow CX features in the different regions. When you are building chatbots for financial services and you will need to be GDPR compliant, you might want to choose Dialogflow CX.

NLU

Dialogflow CX has advanced their NLU. Even though Dialogflow ES is popular because of the outstanding NLU results, there's a notable quality improvement by basing the NLU on the BERT language model.

Analytics

Like Dialogflow ES, the Dialogflow CX Console provides an analytics panel that shows various agent request and response data statistics. The main difference is that you can drill down for Speech to Text and Text to Speech interactions; see Figure A-6.

Figure A-6. *Analytics in Dialogflow CX*

Entities

Entity types are used to control how data from end user input is extracted. Dialogflow CX entities are very similar to Dialogflow ES entities. However, Dialogflow CX also has session entities. Session entities can extend or replace custom entity types and only exist during the session that they were created for. All session data, including session entities, is stored by Dialogflow for 20 minutes.

Intents

An intent categorizes an end user's intention for one conversation turn. Intents have been dramatically simplified in Dialogflow CX. See Figure A-7.

Figure A-7. *Dialogflow CX simplifies intents and therefore they are reusable*

- It's no longer a building block for conversational control. Dialogflow CX only uses intents to match what the users are saying.

- In Dialogflow ES, you had to tie everything to an intent (parameters, events, fulfillment, etc.). Intents in Dialogflow CX only contain training phrases and therefore are reusable. It no longer controls the conversation.

- In Dialogflow CX, intents can be part of a state handler to route the next active page or fulfillment.

Fulfillment and Webhooks

For an agent's conversational turn, the agent must respond to the end user with an answer to a question, a query for information, or session termination. Maybe the agent response should be dynamic by retrieving information from a back-end service (like a database or web service).

- In Dialogflow ES, fulfillments are webhooks. In Dialogflow CX, fulfillments can be static entry dialogues (and these can contain conditional logic), parameter presets to override parameter values, and can also mean dynamic webhooks.

- Dialogflow CX webhooks are similar to Dialogflow ES webhooks, except that request and response fields have been changed to support CX features. This means when you work with the Dialogflow APIs, you will likely need to rename response properties or drill deeper into objects.

APIs

Dialogflow CX also has out-of-the-box integrations, which can be enabled with a flip of a switch. However, by the time of writing, the main focus currently is on telephony integrations. Should you want integrations for popular social media platforms and so on, you can build the integration manually with the REST, gRPC, or client-side APIs for Dialogflow CX.

The client-side libraries work similarly to the libraries for Dialogflow ES, with the caveat that there are minor changes in setting up the agent (as you will also need to specify the **agent id** and **agent location**), and the request and response objects will slightly differ to support the new Dialogflow CX features.

Error Handling

Error handling in Dialogflow CX has been improved:

- In Dialogflow ES, when the end user said something that was unexpected, Dialogflow would match this to simple fallback intents; in Dialogflow CX, within active page only intents, conditions or events can be matched. You can really clearly guide the conversation. Each page has special error messages which are page specific.

- In Dialogflow ES, webhook errors were quiet to the agent. In Dialogflow CX, they are explicit and within the agent, as they fire events, so you don't need to interact with the webhook.

When to Use Dialogflow CX vs. Dialogflow ES?

When you are a freelancer, startup, or small business, when you are building a single chat or voice bot, for example, for the Google Assistant or building an FAQ bot, Dialogflow Essentials might be a better choice for you. This tool is often chosen for its simplicity.

When you are an enterprise customer building a large and complex chatbot platform or contact center customer experience when data regionalization is crucial for you (e.g., because of GDPR) or your conversation requires lots of turn-taking turns and dialogue branches, Dialogflow CX is the tool to use. This tool addresses the need for businesses to build more complex chat and contact center voice bots.

Summary

Dialogflow CX is a separate product that will coexist with Dialogflow Essentials. Developers and businesses can choose which bot building suite is the right tool for them.

This appendix on Dialogflow CX shared the following:

- Why Google Cloud created Dialogflow CX and where it fits in.

- The new concepts that are introduced in Dialogflow CX, such as Flows, Pages, State Handlers, contact center features, and customer-managed encryption keys.

- The differences between both products for agents, NLU, analytics, entities, intents, fulfillments, APIs, and error handling.

- We ended this appendix with a conclusion on when to use Dialogflow CX over Dialogflow ES and vice versa.

Further Reading

- Dialogflow CX basics explained

  https://cloud.google.com/dialogflow/cx/docs/basics

- Dialogflow CX regionalization

  https://cloud.google.com/dialogflow/cx/docs/concept/region

- What's Dialogflow CX—Video by Priyanka Vergadia, Developer Advocate at Google Cloud

  https://www.youtube.com/watch?v=6_Gilug2QYw

- More information on Flows

  https://cloud.google.com/dialogflow/cx/docs/concept/flow

- More information on Pages

  https://cloud.google.com/dialogflow/cx/docs/concept/page

- More information on State Handlers

  https://cloud.google.com/dialogflow/cx/docs/concept/handler

- Node.js client-side library for integrating Dialogflow CX

  https://www.npmjs.com/package/@google-cloud/dialogflow-cx

- CMEK

  https://cloud.google.com/dialogflow/cx/docs/concept/cmek

Index

Printed in the United States
by Baker & Taylor Publisher Services